Praise for DRIVEN BY ETERNITY

"DRIVEN BY ETERNITY bravely tackles one of the great 'mysteries' of human existence . . . eternity. With the clarity and thoroughness that characterizes all of John Bevere's work, here he examines the Bible's wisdom on the subject, inspiring his readers to live eternity-focused lives that extend beyond themselves."
—Brian Houston, pastor, Hillsong Church, Australia

"Wow! Powerful, riveting, humbling. I couldn't put it down. I want everyone to read it. Please make time for it."
—Bill McCartney, Promise Keepers

"John Bevere has done it again! The ideas in this book need to be studied, contemplated, and prayed through by every Christian. This is a book to be read with your Bible open, your mind alert, and your heart eager to find truth."
—Ted Haggard, senior pastor, New Life Church, Colorado Springs, CO

JOHN BEVERE is passionate to see individuals deepen their intimacy with God and capture an eternal perspective. An international bestselling author with award-winning teaching materials, as well as a speaker at conferences and churches, John cohosts *The Messenger* TV program, airing in 216 nations. John has a doctorate in ministry. He and his wife, Lisa, also a bestselling author, founded Messenger International in 1990, which currently has offices in Colorado, Australia, and the United Kingdom. They live in Colorado Springs with their four sons.

DRIVEN
by
ETERNITY

Making Your Life Count Today and Forever

JOHN BEVERE

NEW YORK BOSTON NASHVILLE

Unless otherwise noted, Scripture references are from the *Holy Bible,* New King
James Version.
Scripture reference marked AMP are from the *Amplified Bible,* © 1954, 1958, 1962,
1964, 1965, 1987 by The Lockman Foundation. Used by permission.
Scripture quotations marked MES are taken from *The Message: The Bible in
Contemporary Language,* © 2002. Used by permission of Navpress.
Scripture quotations marked NASB are taken from the *New American Standard
Bible,* © 1960,1962,1963,1968,1971,1972,1973,1975,1977,1995 by The Lockman
Foundation. Used by permission.
Scripture quotations marked NCV are taken from the *Holy Bible,* New Century
Version, © 1991. Used by permission.
Scripture quotations marked NIV are taken from the *Holy Bible,* New
International Version, © 1973, 1978, 1984 by International Bible Society. Used by
permission of Zondervan Publishing House.
Scripture quotations marked NLT are taken from the *Holy Bible,* New Living
Translation, © 1996. Used by permission of Tyndale House Publishers, Inc.,
Wheaton, Illinois 60189. All rights reserved.
Scripture quotations marked TEV are taken from the *Holy Bible,* Today's English
Version, © 1966, 1971, 1976 by American Bible Society. Used by permission.
Scripture quotations marked TLB are taken from *The Living Bible,* © 1971 by
Tyndale House Publishers, Inc., Wheaton, Illinois 60189. All rights reserved.

FaithWords
Hachette Book Group USA
237 Park Avenue
New York, NY 10017

Visit our Web site at www.faithwords.com.

Printed in the United States of America

Originally published in hardcover by FaithWords

First International Trade Edition: April 2006
10 9 8 7

FaithWords is a division of Hachette Book Group USA, Inc.
The FaithWords name and logo is a trademark of Hachette Book Group USA, Inc.

ISBN 978-0-446-69807-8 (pbk.)

*Cover Design by John La Porta / Eastco Multi Media Solutions
Cover Art by Stefan Klein / istockphoto*

I dedicate this book . . .

to all who labor tirelessly to build lives for eternity.
Be encouraged in your quest.
His coming is certain and His reward is with Him.

"And this is eternal life,
that they may know You, the only true God,
and Jesus Christ whom You have sent."
John 17:3-4

CONTENTS

INTRODUCTION

⁓

What is it about the word *eternity* that catches our attention; in fact, has the potential to influence an entire nation? Such is the story of Arthur Stace, an Australian born into a life of hopelessness at the turn of the century. His life was that of a bum filled with petty crime and alcoholism between the First World War and the Great Depression. All this changed when he met Jesus on August 6, 1930, and soon afterward heard his pastor cry, "I wish I could shout *eternity* through all the streets of Sydney!" He felt driven to make this cry a reality.

Arthur would rise early each morning, pray for an hour, and leave his home between 5:00 and 5:30 A.M., to go wherever he felt God led him. For hours he would write one word, *eternity,* approximately every hundred feet on the sidewalks of Sydney. For more than twenty years his work was a mystery. Who was writing this single word that caused countless thousands to pause and ponder its meaning, both immediate and long range? Had this mystery man captured the impact and portion of this single word's power? It wasn't until 1956 that the puzzle was solved.

Two years after Arthur's death in 1967, Sydney poet Douglas Stewart published these words and immortalized the word of this graffiti preacher:

That shy mysterious poet Arthur Stace
Whose work was just one single mighty word
Walked in the utmost depths of time and space
And there his word was spoken and he heard
ETERNITY, ETERNITY, it banged him like a bell
Dulcet from heaven sounding, sombre from hell.

A one-word sermon touched a nation. His message was secured for generations by architect Ridley Smith, who put it in copperplate in the Sydney Square. It was later viewed by over 4 billion souls worldwide as they watched by television the Opening Ceremony of the Sydney Olympics, and again when it was emblazoned in fireworks on the Sydney Harbor Bridge on the Eve of the new millennium.

Eternity arrests the attention of all mankind. No race, tribe, or gender can resist its draw. We were created with eternity in our hearts and sense the immanent unknown extension of our existence. Therefore, it's wise to delve deeper into what our Creator says concerning eternity; after all, His word states, "From eternity to eternity I am God. No one can oppose what I do" (Isa. 43:13, TLB). It is the very reason you've picked up this book. I believe your choice was wise.

Let's pray together before beginning. I've prayed this aloud in my study in anticipation of you praying with me:

Dear God of Eternity, Creator of all, and Lord of the Universe, I come to You in the name of Jesus Christ, Your Son. I ask in agreement with Your servant John Bevere that this day You would anoint my eyes to see; my ears to hear; and give me a heart to perceive and understand what You are saying to me through this message. I acknowledge my need for the Holy Spirit's help to know Your will and ways for my life. It is my desire to please You all the days of my life as well as throughout all eternity. Show me not only Your ways, but Your heart, that I may know You, for this is eternal life to know You intimately as my Heavenly Father. Thank You for Your amazing faithfulness, grace, and mercy.

Let's begin knowing the Holy Spirit will give you insight and understanding that you couldn't have obtained on your own. How exciting!

DRIVEN *by* ETERNITY

Chapter 1

THE ETERNAL

—

Teach us to make the most of our time . . . and make our efforts
successful. Yes, make our efforts successful!
<small>PSALM 90:12, 17, NLT</small>

The desire of most people is to live a life that counts. This is a
right and godly aspiration. It was Moses' request in the above
prayer. He began by asking for wisdom to make the most of time.
Many things lost in life can be restored; however, time misused
can never be recovered. Once the sun goes down, the day is forever gone.

His prayer concludes with, "Make our efforts successful." The
exact phrase is repeated. Why repeated? Moses didn't have a
problem with grammar or memory. Rather, this represents a lit-
erary style found in Hebrew writing. The repetition is a form of
emphasis. In English when we want to emphasize the importance
of a word or phrase, we have several methods. We can make it
bold, italicize it, underscore it, use all capitals, or add an exclama-
tion point for emphasis. These are all ways of calling the reader's
attention to something that is very important. However, the Hebrew writers would write a word or phrase twice to bring emphasis, and they weren't known to overstate—they were always

careful with their words. The fact that this was repeated twice in Scripture shows it is not only God's will for us to succeed, but He is passionate about it. He is the one who has placed emphasis on it.

We were created to be successful. God wants our life to be significant! It was God's desire first, not ours. He makes this known throughout Scripture. Let me just list two, "The Lord your God will make you *successful* in everything you do" (Deut. 30:9, NLT, emphasis mine). Notice the word *everything*, not *some things*! Again we read: "This Book of the Law shall not depart from your mouth, but you shall meditate in it day and night, that you may observe to do according to all that is written in it. For then you will make your way *prosperous*, and then you will have *good success*" (Josh. 1:8, emphasis mine).

It takes godly wisdom to enjoy success. Scripture states, "He who loves wisdom loves his own best interest and will be a success" (Prov. 19:8, TLB). Wisdom gives us the knowledge and ability to make right choices at the opportune time. True wisdom is not given to the mentally sharp; it is for all who fear the Lord and are found in Christ. In order for you to build a life of eternal significance, you must do it through godly wisdom, and that is what this message is all about.

Wisdom breeds success, which brings enduring satisfaction and rewards, "If you are wise, your wisdom will reward you" (Prov. 9:12, NIV). Not only does the Lord desire your success, but He longs to reward you for it. Again we read, "Day by day the Lord observes the good deeds done by godly men, and gives them eternal rewards" (Ps. 37:18, TLB).

The fact that God desires us to succeed has been emphasized in a good segment of the church in recent years, as it should. However, success is many times perceived the way society defines it, rather than the way God views it. It's seen through the eyes of the temporal rather than the eternal. This creates a blur in understanding, which results in misguided pursuits. We will all one day stand before the Judge of the universe, Jesus Christ, and if we've made our life count through godly wisdom, we will be rewarded eternally.

If we've been misguided in our affairs, we will either be punished or suffer eternal loss. So it's wise to spend a few hours finding out what He is looking for.

This is the focus of this book: Making your life count not only today, but throughout eternity. The Bible is clear about how to do this. If we are to be motivated by the eternal, let's start off by getting an understanding of it.

ETERNITY

Read carefully these two Scriptures:

> "No one can begin to understand eternity."
>
> JOB 36:26, TLB

> "He has put eternity in their hearts."
>
> ECCLESIASTES 3:11

Eternity. What is it? How can it be defined? How can it be understood? One dictionary defines it as *infinite time*,[1] yet another, *the state of existing outside of time*.[2] How can one dictionary define eternity to exist within the state of time, and another as outside time? And why has it gone unquestioned? Wouldn't we question one of two science books if they define something in our world to exist in different states? Suppose one book defined a fish to be a vertebrate living in water while another reports they live in environments free of water. We would immediately conclude one to be wrong and throw it out. Yet why do we not question and throw out one of the dictionaries' definitions of eternity?

The truth is that eternity cannot be mentally comprehended. Our minds are finite, prohibited from grasping perpetual or everlasting concepts. Allow me to illustrate. Take a moment and imagine where the end of the universe is. Think of its outer limits. If you can, then what do you find at the external boundary? A wall? What's it made of? How thick is it? Would the outer side of the wall be the exact point of the end of the universe? If so, what is beyond the outside of the wall? More space? Wouldn't this constitute a continuation of the universe? Where is the end? Can your mind take in the endlessness of the universe? Just stop and think about it.

Or what about a bottomless pit? Can you imagine falling into a hole in which you never stopped falling? You would never hit or even see the floor; you just keep falling and falling forever. Two things, not just one, short-circuit our mental reasoning here: first, no bottom; second, an endless time of falling. It's hard to comprehend, and it sounds like a concept from science fiction, yet there is such a place referenced seven times in Scripture.

What about God Himself, man's Creator? Pause a moment and think of His beginning, or I should say, "No beginning." Scripture declares that He is, "from everlasting to everlasting." If He wasn't born, if no one created Him, then how did He begin to be who He is? How did He evolve? The truth is He didn't evolve into God, for the Psalmist declares, "Before the mountains were brought forth, or ever You had formed the earth and the world, even from everlasting to everlasting, You are God" (Ps. 90:2). Meditate on this a while. If you do, you'll frustrate your intellectual reasoning since, as Job wrote, "no one can begin to understand eternity."

PLACED IN OUR HEARTS

What is in truth declared unreachable to our natural mind is placed in our heart by the Creator. Eternity is known in our heart. It is born in every human being. This is why "the fool has said in his *heart*, 'there is no God' " (Ps. 14:1, emphasis mine). Notice Scripture does *not* say, "The fool has said in his *mind*." There are many atheists who emphatically deny the existence of God, but in their heart they know He exists, for it is planted there.

They've not yet hardened their heart to a complete degenerated state.

I have a friend who, years ago, was a staunch atheist, or so he thought. He wouldn't allow anyone to witness to him; in fact, he ripped a Bible from the hands of a coworker one day and threw it on the ground and stomped on it, cursing the man and his Bible. He accused this Christian man of being weak and brainless.

Later, after years of confessed atheism, he suffered severe chest pains. Doctors opened him up for exploratory surgery. They immediately closed him up and told him he had less than twenty-four hours to live.

While he lay on the bed that night, he realized he was going to his eternal abode and it was not at all where he wanted to end up. How did he know that since he would not allow anyone to share the Scriptures with him? Could it be he had eternity planted in his heart, just as Scripture states of all mankind, "For the truth about God is known to them instinctively. God has put this knowledge in their hearts" (Rom. 1:19, NLT).

That night his heart stopped. He left his body and descended into deep darkness. The darkness was so thick he felt he was wearing it, not a glimmer of light could be seen. After falling for what seemed to be quite some time, he heard the horrifying screams of tormented souls. He was pulled by a strong force right up to the gates of hell when suddenly he was able to retreat back to his body. He had been revived.

The next morning he called for the only Christian man he knew. His friend came and proclaimed the good news of salvation through Jesus Christ. Once he'd received Jesus Christ into his life as Lord and Savior, his friend prayed for his healing. Three weeks later he walked out of the hospital and is still alive at the writing of this book. He's a walking miracle.

As an atheist, he proclaimed there was no God, yet eternity was planted in his heart. The fool, on the other hand, is the one who has not just denied God mentally, but has resisted in his heart to the point of a seared conscience. He is beyond reach. It's one thing to hold firm to a belief in your intellect, that can be changed; but it is quite another thing to completely harden your heart. *The New Unger's Bible Dictionary* gives this definition: "In Scripture the 'fool' primarily is the person who casts off the fear of God and thinks and acts as if he could safely disregard the eternal principles of God's righteousness."[3]

A fool can actually acknowledge God mentally, but he denies His existence in his heart, which is reflected by how he lives. The fear of God is what keeps our heart within reach of the Holy Spirit; if lost, there is no hope left for us. Paul said, "Men and brethren, sons of the family of Abraham, and those among you who *fear God*, to you the word of this salvation has been sent" (Acts 13:26, emphasis mine). Only those who fear God are capable of hearing the Words of eternal life.

ETERNITY DEFINED

Eternity has been planted in our hearts, even though it's impossible to comprehend with our minds. So in defining it, I ask you to listen with your heart; in fact, the same is necessary to benefit from this entire book. How do you do this? First of all, acknowledge your need for the Holy Spirit to help you and ask for His assistance, which we have already done (see Introduction). He will commune with your innermost man, not head. Second, stop to ponder and meditate when your heart is stirred or gripped by a statement of truth. Don't race through this book; if you do, the benefit to you will be limited. To receive the full impact of God's eternal word to you, apply these two steps and you will be changed forever. David says, "Your word I have hidden in my heart, that I might not sin against You" (Ps. 119:11). Don't just read for a mental understanding, which can be easily forgotten or lost, but let His Word be hidden in your heart through contemplation and prayer.

Eternity is everlasting; there is no end. However, it's not just a matter of ceaseless time, as it is not subject to time. Eternity transcends time. To speak of eternity in terms of merely perpetual duration is to miss the full picture. To capture the best view of eternity, we must look at God Himself. He is not limited in power, knowledge, wisdom, understanding, and all glory, just to name a few. He is self-existent; forever was and forever will be God. He is called the "Everlasting Father" (Isa. 9:6). Young's literal translation reads, "Father of Eternity."[4] He is called the "King of eternity" (1 Tim. 1:17, AMP). All that is eternal is found in Him; in fact, eternity itself is found in Him. All that is outside of Him is temporal and will change. No matter how good, noble, powerful, or enduring it may seem, it will eventually cease. Even the earth and universe will change, but He will not:

> Lord, in the beginning you laid the foundation of the earth, and the heavens are the work of your hands. Even they will perish, but you remain forever. They will wear out like old clothing. You will roll them up like an old coat. They will fade away like old clothing. But you are always the same; you will never grow old.
>
> HEBREWS 1:10-12, NLT

Not only will He never cease, but He remains eternally the same. Scripture declares:

> "All flesh is as grass, and all the glory of man as the flower of the grass. The grass withers, and its flower falls away, but the word of the Lord endures forever." Now this is the word which by the gospel was preached to you.
>
> I PETER 1:24-25

He is eternal; therefore, what He speaks is eternal. He cannot lie, nor can what He says be broken. If it weren't so, then all would collapse into utter darkness, for He is light and upholds all things by His Word. There can never be a change to what He says, or else He would no longer be eternal. That is a sure foundation upon which we can build our lives.

ETERNAL JUDGMENTS

Many today are not building their lives on the eternal—God's Word—but rather cultural thinking, tradition, assumptions, and emotional feelings about who God is. This doesn't just apply to people who are not Christians, but to many believers as well. It's a scary thing to believe something temporal as being the eternal truth. If this is done, your foundation is faulty and setting you up for a sure fall. You'll believe a lie and are in a deceived state.

I am amazed at how many people I meet who base their lives on what's not eternal. Some will tell me of God and their belief in His Son, but whom they declare just isn't the One revealed in His Word. The deception runs deep. How can they believe what they have simply imagined within their own minds, shaped by a society that has already been declared contrary to God's nature? Jesus said:

> He who . . . does not receive My words, has that which judges him—*the word that I have spoken will judge him in the last day*. For I have not spoken on My own authority; but the Father who sent Me gave Me a command, what I should say and what I should speak.
>
> JOHN 12:48-49 (EMPHASIS MINE)

There is a Judgment Day, which has been appointed from the foundation of the world (Acts 17:31). That day will not bring new revelations of truth; rather, it will measure all things by what has already been spoken. His Word, which we currently possess, will judge us in that last day. It is eternal. It is final. There are no exceptions, alterations, or revisions. Wouldn't it benefit us to know and live by what He says, rather than assume what He said?

The judgments made in that day are called *eternal* (Heb. 6:2).

In other words, the decisions made that day, which will be based on how we lined our lives up with His eternal Word, will determine how we spend the rest of eternity! There will never be any changes to those decisions, for they are called *eternal judgments*.

So many, both believers and nonbelievers, are ignorantly allowing the appointed judgment to hasten toward them without cause for investigation. They've taken a false hope in concepts that are not found in the Bible. Some think God will take into account all the good they've done and if it outweighs the bad, they will find favor. Others who profess a new birth experience have thought that they will not stand before Jesus as Judge because He is their Savior. They believe they are exempt from any form of judgment. They will be most surprised. Then there are some who think everything will just pan out. They are trusting in an unscriptural mercy.

None of these concepts are what the New Testament reveals and teaches. These notions and many others that people have devised in their own imaginations are temporal, not eternal, and will not stand in that day. There will be stunned men and women, and I personally think there will be more professing Christians than unbelievers who are shocked on Judgment Day.

CONFIDENCE AT THE JUDGMENT

We don't have to go into judgment with fear, but we can go with confidence:

> And as we live in God, our love grows more perfect. So we will not be afraid on the day of judgment, but we can face him with confidence because we are like Christ here in this world.
>
> 1 JOHN 4:17, NLT

Notice the words "as we live in God, our love grows more perfect." The key that will give us confidence on Judgment Day is the love of God being made perfect (or matured) in us. Now here is where many in the church falter. They see the love of God in the light of the temporal, not the eternal. There is love and goodness, which are admired by society and many in the church but determined by human measures, and are contrary to the love of God. Let me illustrate a few that are common.

"We love each other so much and are planning to get married." This is often stated when two people are having sex outside of marriage. Not only is this sin even if they do follow through and get married, but many times I've witnessed those who make such statements end up not getting married. They've forgotten the clear exhortation, "Marriage should be honored by all, and the marriage bed kept pure, for God will judge the adulterer and all the sexually immoral" (Heb 13:4, NIV). Notice He does not say, "The adulterer and sexually immoral who don't attend church." No, it is all who practice this lifestyle.

"I know it wasn't quite the truth, but it will help close the deal and we will make sure that they get fair treatment." Businesspeople often say this when they want to secure a sale that they really believe is good for the people but they need to twist the facts a little to get the customer to move forward. Not only is this the sin of lying, but almost always the deal is very good for the one making the statement. Have they forgotten the warning that states, "All liars (those who knowingly convey untruth by word or deed)—[all of these shall have] their part in the lake that blazes with fire and brimstone" (Rev. 21:8, AMP).

"What I said about him is the truth." This is often said when people are talking in a negative light (gossip or slander) about a fellow worker, friend, boss, etc. They may act as if they love or are concerned, but in fact it is still slander. The fact is, you can be 100 percent right and still be wrong according to eternal standards. If you recall, Noah's youngest son, Ham, reported accurately to his brothers his father's nakedness and drunken state. However, a curse came on his lineage and lasted generations as a result of his dishonoring his father. Have those who gossip and slander forgotten the exhortation to believers that states, "Don't grumble about each other, my brothers and sisters, or God will judge you. For look! The great Judge is coming. He is standing at the door!" (James 5:9, NLT).

The examples are endless, but the common denominator is that they are contrary to God's eternal will. The scary fact is that many who live in this manner and make such seemingly harmless statements may attend church, be very kind in their mannerisms, and be looked upon as model citizens. But how do they measure up to the eternal? John gave the answer on how to perfect (mature) the love of God earlier in his letter:

> Whoever says, I know Him [I perceive, recognize, understand, and am acquainted with Him *(Jesus Christ)*] but fails to keep and obey His commandments (teachings) is a liar, and the Truth [of the Gospel] is not in him. But he who keeps (treasures) His Word [who bears in mind His precepts, who observes His message in its entirety], truly in him has the love of and for God been perfected.
>
> 1 JOHN 2:4-5, AMP (EMPHASIS MINE)

Recall that it is the perfected (matured) love of God that gives us confidence to stand before our Judge. John makes it clear that the love of God is perfected in keeping His commandments, not in behaving in a way that is good in society's eyes. Keep in mind that Eve was not drawn to the *evil* side of the tree of the knowledge of good and evil, rather the *good* side! "The woman saw how *beautiful* the tree was and how *good* its fruit would be to eat" (Gen. 3:6, TEV, emphasis mine). There is a *beautiful* and *good* to the eyes and human reasoning that are contrary to the eternal love of God. It is not eternal and will not endure.

Scripture also states that we cannot observe a percentage of God's commands and believe that we will have confidence on Judgment Day. It is when we carefully observe all of His word, in its entirety, that the love of God is matured. This is why God gives us grace; it empowers us to be able to obey His Word completely, in a way that is acceptable to Him. "Therefore, since we are receiving a kingdom which cannot be shaken, let us have grace, by which we may serve God acceptably" (Heb. 12:28).

The key is to know what the King desires and looks for, not what seems good to society or human reasoning. For this reason God tells us, "Do not be conformed to this world, but be transformed by the renewing of your mind, that you may prove what is that good and acceptable and perfect will of God" (Rom. 12:2). What may seem good to our culture may be an affront to God's desires—the eternal.

Allow me to illustrate. I'm currently sitting in a hotel in Singapore, where I'll be preaching to close to twenty thousand people this weekend. I've been to this great nation many times. I've also preached the gospel in the Netherlands a few times. In the Netherlands, it is not against the law to have in your possession or smoke marijuana. The people there can smoke it legally and not fear penalty. However, in Singapore if you are caught with a certain amount of drugs (and it is a small amount), you will be arrested and severely punished. If caught with certain drugs, the punishment is death by hanging! When you fly into Singapore, it is written right on the entry card, "Death to Drug Traffickers under Singapore law."

Now can you just imagine a young Dutchman who regularly smokes marijuana travels to Singapore and shares his pot with Singaporeans? He gladly states to these newly found friends, "Hey, guys, this stuff is great. It calms you, gives you an enjoyable buzz, and takes your frustrations away. Would you like some? I'd love to share it with you."

He is immediately arrested. He's in shock. "Why are you arresting me?" is the first question out of his mouth to the officers.

Judgment day arrives; he stands in the court before the judge believing with all his heart this is some kind of fluke. The judge pronounces his guilt and punishment.

The man in shock says, "Your honor, where I come from it's fine to share marijuana with your friends."

The judge then says, "You're not in Holland, you're in Singapore, and in this nation it is against the law!"

The Dutchman's confidence is gone; he has nothing to stand on. There can be no recourse as he is standing before the highest court of the land, doomed with no defense.

While I was in Singapore several years back, there was a young American who was arrested for vandalizing an automobile. He was arrested, judged guilty, and sentenced to several strokes of Rotan. This is a punishment that inflicts permanent physical damage whipping a person on the hind side with a type of bamboo plant treated with chemicals. Even President Clinton tried to get the young man's sentence lightened. However, he had no success. The young man broke the laws of Singapore and had to serve his sentence.

All of us will stand before the highest court of the universe. This court's decision will be *eternally* final. There will be many who will be shocked, but they don't have to be. Are you ready? According to the Word of God, we can go before the Judge of the universe with confidence. This book is designed to help you prepare. If that young Dutchman would have taken time to learn and prepare to enter Singapore, he would have avoided severe penalty. How much more important for us, for the decision which is made at the Judgment Seat will be forever.

REWARDS

There will be more than one judgment; there will be one for unbelievers, another for believers, and even one for angels. The decisions made will vary. There will be loss and punishment; there will be rewards. We'll go into this in depth in upcoming chapters, but let me point out again that the decisions made will be eternal; this cannot be overemphasized (try again to mentally grasp never ending). It is God's will that we know this in advance and that we labor for the rewards. Paul says,

> Do you not know that in a race all the runners compete, but [only] one receives the prize? *So run [your race] that you may lay hold [of the prize] and make it yours.* Now every athlete who goes into training conducts himself temperately and restricts himself in all things. They do it to win a wreath that will soon wither, but we [do it to receive a crown of *eternal* blessedness] that cannot wither. Therefore I do not run uncertainly (without definite aim). I do not box like one beating the air and striking without an adversary. But [like a boxer] I buffet my body [handle it roughly, discipline it by hardships] and subdue it.
>
> 1 CORINTHIANS 9:24-27, AMP

He clearly says, "I do not run uncertainly (without definite aim)." Another version says it like this, "So I run straight to the goal with purpose in every step" (NLT). That is exactly what every human being should do, run with certainty and purpose to win. We are not competing against others, only ourselves.

DRIVEN BY ETERNITY

Just thinking everything will pan out for the good at the Judgment Seat is not enough. We have no excuse, for God has made His will available to us. There will be scores of people who've done well in relation to those with whom they've compared themselves, yet they've not allowed the eternal to direct and fuel their lives; hence the title of this book, *Driven by Eternity*.

The word *driven* means "to propel." It also means to "guide, control, or direct." Another definition is "to supply the motive force to." What is guiding and motivating our life on this earth?

Is it the eternal or is it the temporal? Is it based on divine wisdom? Or are we comparing ourselves with others or have we listened to flattery, tradition or myths proclaimed in certain pulpits or schools? Will what we've built our lives upon stand before Him at the Judgment Seat, or will our efforts be forever lost? Remember, we already know what will be the standard at judgment: "the word that I have spoken will judge him in the last day" (John 12:48).

There are going to be many who will be shocked when they stand before Jesus Christ at the judgment. The greatest number of these will not be unbelievers, but rather professing Christians! Yes, they will be those who took security in a part of what the New Testament teaches but neglected to carefully search out the entire picture. My question to you is this: Do you want to find out the truth after the *eternal* decision has already been made and it's too late to change, or do you want to know now the standard by which you will be judged?

The next chapter will open with an allegory that will continue into the following chapter. Read it carefully and remember the details, for we will refer back to it often. The story will then conclude in chapter 8, and the truths will be discussed through the rest of the book. The book revolves around this allegory, so don't skim it, and you may want to refer back to it as the teaching progresses.

Most of what is shared in this book God has sharply dealt with me about personally. I will share many of my own faults, which have been scrutinized by the Holy Spirit under the microscope of His truth. My hope is that it will stir you to carefully search the Scriptures that you may have a firm foundation to stand upon on Judgment Day. I will share some of the greatest misconceptions in our society that cause men and women to grow further from the One they profess as Savior. You will be shocked, shaken, and chastened at times, but it will all be followed by promise, hope, and comfort.

If you are courageous, desire the truth, and have a heart for God, then let's proceed. You'll be glad you did! Take to heart the following exhortation:

> God's gift has restored our relationship with him and given us back our lives. And there's more life to come— an eternity of life! You can count on this. I want you to put your foot down. Take a firm stand on these matters so that those who have put their trust in God will concentrate on the essentials that are good for everyone.
>
> TITUS 3:7-8, MES

Chapter 2

THE KINGDOM OF AFFABEL—
LIFE IN ENDEL

~

And He taught them many things in parables (illustrations or comparisons put beside truths to explain them), and in His teaching He said to them . . .
MARK 4:2, AMP

There was once a world similar to our own, yet in many ways different. In this world there were no independent nations, only the one great kingdom named *Affabel*. Though this kingdom spanned the entire known world, it had a single capital city from which all leadership was administered. It was called *The Great City of Affabel,* which we will refer to from this point on as simply *Affabel*.

This enchanted city was presided over by a remarkable king named Jalyn. King Jalyn was adored and greatly admired by his subjects. He exuded a depth of love that seemed inexhaustible. He was strong and wise, yet at the same time kind and quick to laugh. Though his bearing was regal, Jalyn was also quite personable. To be with him was to find oneself encompassed in an atmosphere of goodness. His presence raised every aspect of life to a higher level. His vision and foresight were astounding, and he had an uncanny ability to see beyond the actions of people into the motives of their hearts.

Jalyn's father who founded Affabel was known as the Founding King Father. Once the order was established, he turned all leadership over to his son. The residents of this great city helped administrate the rule of Jalyn to the outlying territories of the kingdom. This was accomplished by a hierarchical system of authority and leadership in the ruling city.

The city was enormous, with a landmass of approximately two hundred square miles. It was so well planned that even though it was densely populated, it never felt overcrowded. There was a composite of suburbs, town residences, and villas. Those located in the flatlands, which lay toward the western end of Affabel, were the modest homes of the laborers. (Their modest homes would be considered extravagant in our world.) Even though their jobs were labor intensive, these residents were thankful just to inhabit the king's city. The mountainous terrains of the northern and southern borders were home to the artisans. These were the ones skilled in the creative arts of music, writing, artwork, and design. These homes had beautiful vistas and were more expansive than those of the laborers.

The most inviting section of the city was the eastern district, which contained an abundance of beautiful villas. This area was known as the *Regal Center*. This large neighborhood is where the king resided and spent most of his time and was home to those who worked closest to the king. It was here his administration and coleaders socialized and worked together. The Regal Center was poised like a jewel on a cliff overlooking the shores of the *Great Sea*. A constant gentle breeze blew up from the azure ocean and refreshed the city. These waters were fringed by the most pristine white beaches, which were only exceeded by the beauty of the royal gardens. These gardens wove themselves throughout the Regal Center. It was without doubt the most desirable place of residency. Each home was only exceeded in elegance by the king's royal palace.

In the midst of Affabel stood the tree of life. Only the king's subjects were privileged enough to partake of its wondrous fruit. The fruit was not merely delicious and lovely to behold; it had within its fragrant flesh the power of the miraculous.

THE COMMUNITY OF ENDEL

To the west of Affabel's flatlands lay the Outer Wilderness, which stretched for almost sixty miles to the Great River Adonga. Once you crossed the Adonga, you would find yourself in another part of the kingdom, called *Endel*. At birth, the children of the citizens of Affabel were brought immediately to the province of Endel. Before their first week had passed, they were entrusted to the care of the King's Nurses. Once these young citizens, or *Endelites*, reached the age of five years they were brought to the *School of Endel,* where they received training for a period of ten years. There they learned the ways of Affabel and of the great King Jalyn. Only the King's Nurses and Teachers of the School had enjoyed the opportunity to meet Jalyn. Every five years or so, he would visit Endel in secret to confer his heart for the school and children. Though he never made his presence known to all, even so, all around Endel his goodness was evident in every aspect of the community.

The ten years in the School of Endel was to prepare the students for the life ahead of them. At the age of fifteen years they would have a short season to apply all they had been taught. In this span of time they would be entrusted with portions of wealth and responsibility. How they stewarded their young lives and resources determined how and where they would spend the rest of their lives; which in their world was one hundred and fifty years. Though the season of testing was exactly five years, none of the students were aware of its duration. All they were told was it would not exceed ten years. At the end of this time, each would appear before the king to give account of their life choices.

This span of testing determined their allegiances. Those who followed the ordinances of Jalyn with their words and actions acknowledged his leadership. These were admitted as residents of Affabel. Their choices secured for them rewards accordingly. If, however, during the season of testing they rebelled and lived only for and by the rule of themselves, they were exiled to the land of *Lone*. Lone was a desert land of utter darkness, where loneliness and hopelessness reigned. There they suffered torment and imprisonment for their life's duration.

The first person banished to this desolation was Dagon, who became the founding dark lord of Lone. Though he had rebelled against Jalyn many years before, his influence yet lingered in the land of Endel. Inhabitants of Endel who acknowledged Jalyn's lordship broke free of the dark power of Dagon. However, those who refused to serve Jalyn remained under this fallen lord's sway.

To isolate any further infiltration of darkness in his kingdom, the great King Jalyn was compelled to establish a decree to protect both the integrity and social infrastructure of Affabel. All who followed in the way of Dagon and refused to acknowledge Jalyn as king by word and action were banished for the remainder of their lives to the land of Lone.

So begins our story. We will follow the lives of five students of Endel: two ladies and three men. Their names are as follows: *Independent*, *Deceived*, *Faint Heart*, *Selfish*, and *Charity*. Let me introduce each.

INDEPENDENT

Independent constantly questions the existence of Affabel. He really can't believe someone he has never met or seen called Jalyn would require not only his allegiance but such strict adherence to a list of rules. He suspects it to be a scheme to keep him and others under the control of the teachers. In contempt, he refuses to attend classes and learn of this imaginary kingdom.

Independent ridicules others for believing such nonsense. He intends to live as he sees fit and remain free of the laws of Jalyn. The only exception will be if these edicts serve his purpose, then he'll adhere, but only because it's his idea. He has no qualms about letting others know he won't be yielding his life to the will of another.

DECEIVED

Deceived doesn't question the existence of Affabel. He believes in King Jalyn and even delights in his promises. He mentally and verbally agrees to the teachings and policies, yet large portions of his lifestyle conflict with those teachings. He celebrates his allegiance to the king and his teachings and participates in the school's functions when they are delightful, but if he doesn't see any self-benefit, his outlook quickly changes. His lifestyle is contrary to that of a true follower of Jalyn, and due to his strong personality he subtly draws others into his ways. He never really stops to consider his pending season of testing and judgment.

Deceived gets along well with Independent, even though they disagree about Jalyn's existence. Deceived is fun and they both have similar interests, so Independent likes his company.

FAINT HEART

Faint Heart is the most enthusiastic of all the students. She speaks up frequently in class and consistently makes some of the best grades. She is very active and usually the one who initiates extracurricular activities to help promote the students' involvement in the community. Anyone who assessed the students would say she was the most passionate for the cause of Jalyn.

SELFISH

Selfish also believes in Jalyn and his teachings. He does not doubt the existence of Affabel and is quite vocal, as well. He believes Jalyn is such a wonderful ruler and kind judge that he will be gracious to all who profess allegiance. He is focused on his limited perception of Jalyn's teachings and character. He has forgotten that Jalyn is a just and holy leader as well as a loving and merciful one. So Selfish has developed a distorted view of who Jalyn really is. He believes that Deceived, Faint Heart, and Charity will no doubt be a part of this glorious kingdom, though he has some concerns about the sheer resistance of Independent.

Selfish believes all who acknowledge Jalyn verbally and live a life that doesn't break any major laws will gain entrance to Affabel. However, in keeping with his name, he's largely self-seeking, and often the good he does is motivated by personal benefit. At times he is motivated by compassion, but when push comes to shove, Selfish looks out for his own best interest.

CHARITY

Our final young lady, Charity, is one who takes to heart and obeys all of King Jalyn's laws. Not only has she learned his principles but searches to know his heart behind each edict. She spends a lot of time seeking to know and understand the will of Jalyn. This means long hours of study and freely giving herself for the good of the school and community of Endel. She knows once she reaches the age of fifteen, she will have a short amount of time to carry out the wishes of the great king in Endel. Her aim is to live completely for Jalyn's glory, and she will not allow what would benefit her to get in the way of her primary purpose.

Charity loves Jalyn and longs for the day they will meet. She fervently obeys him and frequently speaks with others of his goodness. For this she is often ridiculed and isolated. Though she has suffered because of her stance of unwavering loyalty to Jalyn's laws, nothing will deter her from being faithful to the king.

THE GRADUATES

All five of these Endelites turned fifteen. The appointed day arrived, and they graduated along with two thousand other students. Each was entrusted with a specific commission and a corresponding sum of startup cash. This amount was predetermined by Jalyn and was distributed by the headmaster upon graduation. Among our five students the distribution looked like this: Independent received fifty-five thousand dollars; Deceived and Faint Heart received forty thousand dollars each; Selfish received the most, seventy-five thousand dollars; and, finally, Charity received twenty-five thousand dollars. With their money in hand, the young citizens were released with some final instructions.

THE SALESMAN

Independent immediately went on a partying binge to celebrate his newfound freedom. Though he rarely attended classes, he still felt as though they hung over his head. He had heard some of Jalyn's laws on the few occasions when he attended. At times he had wondered if maybe some of it was true. If so, he wondered if his bad behavior would affect how much he would be given once schooling had expired.

Independent is amazed at how much money he received, even though he violated the school's policies. He'd received fifteen thousand more than Faint Heart and more than twice as much as Charity. He thought, *What a waste! Charity and Faint Heart spent all their time in those useless classes and put in so many extra hours, and now they have little to show for it.* This dynamic actually affirmed his belief that Jalyn didn't exist. He reasoned that their parents, who disappeared so many years ago, had left the money. This now furthered his views that it was all a scam of the school to control their young lives and keep them from being independent free thinkers.

After a couple weeks of celebrating, Independent realized he had to set up a business. He had already run through his money more rapidly than planned. He started a car lot and realized he was a great salesman. Business went amazingly well. Many of the new graduates used part of their startup cash to buy used or even new cars from Independent's lot. As his finances multiplied, he expanded into other business ventures and found success in those as well. As his assets increased, he expanded and enhanced his personal lifestyle. He realized quickly that money was an amazing source of influence, and it seemed to have the power to purchase happiness. His wealth, assets, and rapidly expanding lifestyle had the power to attract women, which made life even more invigorating.

Independent didn't attend the weekly community gatherings. But he was still considered a very good citizen by most because they appreciated his support of community projects. It appeared life couldn't get any better for this hard-working Endelite.

THE BUILDER AND DEVELOPER

Deceived celebrated for a couple weeks as well. Though he didn't receive as much as some of the others, he was glad to have more than Charity. This too affirmed his own distorted perception of Jalyn as a king of such extreme mercy that certain issues really didn't matter. He had been sexually loose with two girls he'd dated in the school, even though it was contrary to the teachings he had received. He saw no conflict in this because he firmly believed in Jalyn and his kingdom. He had formed his own approach to life: "As long as I continue to affirm my allegiance to Jalyn and do not hurt anyone too severely, I will remain in good standing with the king." He reasoned that Jalyn understood that everyone has needs and no one is perfect. All his faults would be covered at the judgment by Jalyn's mercy and grace because he believed in him with all his heart.

After a few weeks, Deceived started his own business, just as

Independent had done. He became a homebuilder. In the beginning, it was a struggle to find customers. His model was excellent in every way, but he just couldn't find committed buyers. Some thought his prices were too high; others just couldn't afford to buy such nice homes. Desperate, he lowered his prices. He would still use his nice model home to draw customers. He would continue to make all promises he had previously made, but he started putting in much lower grade materials than what he had previously featured or promised. In fact, some of his materials violated the codes and standards. He rationalized that the lawmakers who set these marks were overly cautious. He was sure the materials he had chosen would hold up under any stress or weather conditions. Because these seemed to be such amazing bargains, interested Endelites had started signing contracts faster than he could build them. Business had finally taken off.

After a couple years, he decided to turn to land development. He was tired of complaining customers. He felt that once the land was sold, he'd be done with it all. He wouldn't have to deal with fixing warranty items any longer. Deceived came across some land for roughly a thousand dollars an acre. It seemed almost too good to be true. Further investigation revealed it was a flood plain. This information was only known by a handful of people, all of whom were his friends. He persuaded a city councilman who was a buddy of Independent's to approve his development without proper geological testing. After all, there hadn't been any floods in his lifetime; so was there really a problem? The deal went through without a glitch. After this, it seemed life couldn't get any better for the young entrepreneur.

THE TEACHER'S ASSISTANT

Immediately following graduation, Faint Heart got together with a few girlfriends for a weekend of shopping. She thought it would be good for two reasons, first, she could spend time celebrating with her closest friends; and second, she could get the clothes and accessories she would need for her new career. Faint Heart's deepest desire was to be a teacher's assistant at the School of Endel. Her interview was the following Friday.

On the second day of shopping, one of Faint Heart's friends, *Gossip*, shared with her how a mutual friend, *Slander*, had told the headmaster that Faint Heart had slept with one of the young male students. This could severely hinder her chances of being brought on as a teacher's assistant. It was an absurd lie without an ounce of truth in it. She had kept herself pure the entire time of schooling. She felt certain Slander had done this out of sheer envy and possibly even hatred.

Faint Heart was furious. Deeply offended, her thoughts were consumed for the remainder of the weekend by the treachery of this supposed friend. She vowed to make Slander pay for what she'd done.

The day of the interview arrived and to Faint Heart's surprise she was chosen for a position. The headmaster informed her that he had indeed heard the rumor, but after some investigation was convinced it wasn't true. Not only did she get a position, she was assigned as an assistant to one of her favorite teachers. His name was *Double Life*; he was one of the most gifted teachers of Jalyn. Faint Heart was amazed that she was chosen to work with such a dynamic leader. The semester began, and things were going extremely well, but she still carried a nagging offense against her former friend. No matter how well it went, it seemed she could not really get over Slander's treachery.

Even though things looked great, trouble was brewing below the surface. Double Life's name was indicative of who he was. He lived one way as a teacher, but quite another in his private life. His judgment would be the most severe because as a teacher he had been privileged to personally see Jalyn. (The teachers' judgments did not come at twenty years of age, as with the others, but rather when they were thirty. Double Life was only twenty-five at this time.)

One evening when Faint Heart and Double Life were alone together, he made a pass at her. She was shocked and outraged and left his presence immediately. He didn't give up, but persisted over the next several weeks. She began to question her reaction and listen to his persuasion because he was such a great and knowledgeable man. She enjoyed his attention. He was gentle and kind and was considered to be one of the nicest looking men in the community. She finally gave her virginity to him, and the two entered into a passionate affair. Faint Heart had never known such exhilarating feelings of passion and love in any relationship. Each time she saw him, her breath was taken away. Thoughts of rendezvousing with him on their set evenings consumed her and temporarily averted her attention from the deep and now hidden offense she still carried with Slander.

However, after four months, Double Life suddenly dumped her. Devastated, she had to know why. Finally, he told her that he had heard from others Slander's report of her past affair with a fellow student. This was not the real reason; he had just lost interest in Faint Heart. He was already flirting with another young lady in the community. Girls were hard-pressed to resist the seductive and persuasive powers of this prominent teacher.

Faint Heart was outraged. How could she go on seeing him each day? She immediately resigned her position at the school. After several days of sulking, she opened a Beauty Salon with what she had left of her forty thousand dollars. She stopped going to the weekly gatherings at the school, even though Jalyn's word stated not to forsake the assembling together of his people. She didn't want to associate with hypocrites, and most of them seemed to be just that. She grew harder by the day. She rarely mentioned the school or Jalyn. Gone was the passion she'd previously expressed so freely in conversation. However, when asked, she would confess her allegiance to Jalyn, but deep in her heart she blamed him for allowing such a corrupt man to be a teacher in his school. By the time the days of testing were over, she was a very offended and bitter woman; though if asked she would emphatically deny it. She spent the rest of her days trying to get even with those who had hurt her so deeply.

THE MAYOR OF ENDEL

And now we turn to Selfish. He was simply amazed by the amount of money he'd received. He celebrated but knew enough of Jalyn's teachings and steered away from the drinking scene. After a few days' break, he started investing. His trading proved profitable, and he quickly multiplied his startup cash. As he grew financially, he steadily increased in popularity with his peers.

He bought a house in one of the nicest neighborhoods and invited the influential and powerful to his home. Government officials, professional athletes, business executives, and other notables enjoyed the wealth of his hospitality. He was quickly becoming one of the most connected men in the community.

After three years, he decided to run for mayor of Endel and easily won because of his financial clout and social connections. Once in office, he found himself faced with many decisions. One of these had to do with the School of Endel. Due to the increase in population, there was an urgent need for more space. This meant buying land, securing contractors, building expenses, as well as everything necessary to outfit the school. The first step was for the community to raise money. In the weekly city gatherings, Selfish heard of their need for more funding. At the end of the fund raising drive, he had given just under a thousand dollars.

Then came the tough decision. The school finally had enough to buy a particular plot of land; it was an amazing deal, and the price was within their budget. However, there was a large department store that wanted to purchase the same land. The city council was divided; the school was a nonprofit organization, so it would not yield any tax revenue. On the other hand, the store would bring in huge sums of tax revenue and provide additional jobs for the residents. Since the council was split, the deciding vote had to be cast by the mayor. Selfish was conflicted. The owners of the department store had been very supportive of his campaign by contributing large sums of money, as well as leveraging their influence on his behalf. They had been guests in his home on frequent occasions.

Selfish voted in favor of the department store. He justified his choice to the public by stating it was for the overall good of the citizens of Endel. He had paved the way for more employment opportunities as well as increased the city revenue. He recommended the school should explore their options of expanding their current facility, even though he knew this was not feasible. His choice disappointed the sincere followers of Jalyn, but the community at large applauded his decision.

His two-year term was coming to a close, and it was time for reelection. Selfish was on the verge of completing his season of testing, though unaware. Feeling a bit remorseful, Selfish made a personal contribution to the School of Endel of five thousand dollars. With this he promised to find another plot of ground suitable for them to build. This helped regain the confidence of many of the followers of Jalyn. It looked as though the young leader would easily win a second term.

THE RESTAURANT OWNER

Upon graduation, Charity gave three of her twenty-five thousand dollars as a contribution to the School of Endel's land drive. She was thankful for all she had learned from her teachers and wanted to express it. With the remaining twenty-two thousand, Charity was eventually able to start a restaurant. She loved anything to do with the culinary arts. Coupling this with the fact she was a savvy businesswoman, a restaurant appeared to be the best way to utilize her gifts and serve her community. She was able to bring in some of the best chefs in the land and by coordinating their knowledge she assembled an outstanding menu. Her restaurant was an immediate success.

Though Charity won awards for her restaurant, she always credited her success to Jalyn's wisdom. In interviews she repeatedly thanked her former teachers and praised her fine employees. She refused to acknowledge her success as her own or to boast about her efforts. She knew it was only because of Jalyn.

Charity used her prosperity to help both the community and the School of Endel. She contributed food to the school's soup kitchen for the needy. Often she would set aside an evening and work the outreach food line. She enjoyed serving hot meals to the poor. She made a commitment to give 25 percent of all her restaurant profits to the school. At the end of the five years, she had given over two hundred thousand dollars.

Charity was always helping others who were working hard but just found it difficult to make ends meet. In addition to financial aid, she was quick to share Jalyn's principles of wisdom and success. She constantly told those she aided how she would never have made it had it not been for Jalyn.

Even though Charity's restaurant was successful, she was never included in the socials at the home of Selfish. Neither was she asked to participate in leadership roles in the community. She was seen as too radical in her adherence to Jalyn, along with the fact that she was a woman. Being excluded among the influential Endelites didn't deter or discourage Charity. She was focused on reaching the less fortunate. She loved the weekly gatherings at the school and was always offering to help by giving or through serving in various roles. Charity was a fulfilled young woman.

THE APPOINTED JUDGMENT DAY

The final day of testing arrived. Those who were about to be judged knew it could happen sometime in the next five years because the first five years had already passed. No one imagined it would be so soon. The day began just like any other, but it ended very differently. Late in the night, the Royal Guards of Affabel swept two thousand graduates away. Their secret exodus happened while the other Endelites slept.

These two thousand young citizens were ushered through a secret passageway. It was a deep tunnel, which brought them beneath the Adonga River. Once through the channel, they traveled an additional two days across a barren wilderness. Throughout the journey, the Chief Guard provided their every need from their store of food, water, and supplies. The guards were kind, yet reserved. All their energy was focused on the task before them. Though they would answer some questions, the Endelites posed others that were not permitted to be answered. Their standard reply to these questions was, "All will be made known soon." This only served to heighten the travelers' curiosity. They almost didn't notice the discomfort of the wasteland as they sojourned toward the long-awaited great city. As the third day dawned, they crested a hill and there, silhouetted by the morning sun, was the majestic city. Affabel was even more magnificent than any of them had dared to imagine.

As they approached the city, this revelation of its wonder grew and expanded. Even from their approach from the flatlands, it was apparent the city was without compare. Endel was puny in comparison to the outskirts of the city. As they entered the central portion of the city, they discovered in Affabel everything was vibrantly alive. It was such a magical place that the birds not only sang, but had the gift of language. Their wondrous and melodic songs interpreted the beauty they beheld and served to further magnify the glory of the city. This did not come as a total surprise for the Endelites, who had heard the horses of the Chief Guard speak. These noble beasts not only spoke to each other, but they conversed with their riders as well. It was obvious there was an affectionate relationship between these horses and their riders. It was now apparent all the creatures within Affabel had been gifted with speech and the capacity for affection and joy.

In every direction the young Endelites turned, they beheld breathtaking vistas. They were enraptured with the awe of Affabel. The air alone was invigorating. It brought both clarity of mind and strength to their travel-weary bodies. The water that flowed throughout the city intrigued them. Somehow it seemed more substantive, as though it glistened with life. Threads of enchanting music permeated the atmosphere and soothed their excited souls with an abiding sense of peace. Everything ranging from the smallest plants to the very air seemed more than alive— they possessed the ability to give life. Each element was full to overflowing in this miraculous land.

The young citizens could not help but extend their hands and touch everything within their reach as they passed through the concourse of the great city. They longed to run free and explore but somehow knew this wouldn't be permitted at this time. They were led straightaway into a large anteroom of a massive auditorium. Here the males and females were separated; they were allowed to refresh themselves in fragrant baths or showers and were given robes in preparation for their audience with the king. They were all too happy to discard their dusty clothes of Endel. Their old garments seemed awkward and strangely out of place in this radiant city.

A deep desire to dwell in this city wove itself into the fiber of each Endelite. They had the strangest sense of homecoming. After bathing and dressing, they again gathered as a group for a meal. This breakfast banquet was set up in a magnificent courtyard, where they were allowed to eat and fellowship for a short time.

The superstructure they'd been escorted to was so vast it appeared to have unlimited capacity. Without an issue at least one hundred thousand people could be contained within the marble walls. After eating, the group was separated again, this time by name. Charity, Selfish, and approximately five hundred others were brought to an adjacent hall on the right. Faint Heart, Deceived, and Independent were led with the remaining fifteen hundred to another auditorium on the left. As they entered the halls, they noticed each had a name ascribed over the threshold.

The name was strange and in a language unknown to the young Endelites. The name of one auditorium was the "Hall of Life"; the other, the "Hall of Justice."

As he crossed the threshold, Independent found himself strangely disturbed, almost to the point of being terrified. He reached back into his school memories and tried to comfort himself with what he had briefly heard of Jalyn. It all seemed so confusing now. He found himself regretting the fact he had missed so many classes. Obviously he had been wrong because both the city and the king existed. He tried to block his rising fear and focus on what he remembered of Jalyn's love and merciful nature. At that moment he did not want to consider Jalyn's justice and holiness, even though both were what now fought for his attention. He attempted to reassure himself with the ways he had been a good citizen and supported the volunteer services of the community.

Taking a deep breath, Independent began to look around to take stock of the company he was in. He could not help but notice he was among some of the worst in Endel. He recognized thieves, swindlers, and drunkards. There were both those who rarely worked and those who worked everything to their advantage. His fear mounted and, just as panic threatened to overwhelm him, he caught sight of Faint Heart. He closed his eyes and released a sigh of relief. He remembered her immediately as one the most outspoken and enthusiastic followers of Jalyn in his class. Hadn't he even heard she had worked at the school? If she were in this hall with him, it would most likely turn out for his good.

As he moved in her direction, he bumped into Deceived. Another good sign! Though he had lost touch with Faint Heart, Independent knew Deceived was a strong believer. They used to even argue about Jalyn. His mood had totally changed as he embraced his old friend. Deceived was both boisterous and positive in his manner. They engaged in conversation as all fear subsided. Jalyn's mercy must have been even vaster than they had known.

Look how freely he had forgiven the ones Independent had never even imagined could have made it. How could this be anything but true? Wasn't the great teacher Double Life just a little way off from them? Now he was certain all would be well.

However, he was slightly troubled by the absence of Charity and Selfish. Another thing he found difficult to ignore were some who wept and cried in the corners of the room. Maybe they were just overwhelmed by Jalyn's goodness.

The other hall was filled with emotions as well. Friends who had lost touch after graduation were thrilled to again be reunited. There was an overriding excitement that soon dominated every conversation: They would soon behold Jalyn! Their time had come to enter their true purpose and promised destiny. They were all abuzz with the wonder of the city. They had always known it would be a better place than Endel, but their initial impression exceeded their abilities of comprehension. It was more than they could take in.

Could it possibly be true they'd spend the rest of their lives in such a glorious place? To have such an honor any one of them would willingly clean floors! All who waited in this hall knew they'd followed Jalyn but still wondered how they'd fair against his righteous judgments. As time passed, a solemn attitude overtook the room. Had they been faithful? Time would soon tell. Yes, excitement intertwined with a measure of fear as these humble servants waited to see their king.

THE SUMMONS

The first judged were those waiting in the Hall of Life. However, we will return to this later. For now our story will take us in with those in the Hall of Justice.

It was midday. The inhabitants of the Hall of Justice were restored to a level of comfort and confidence that all would be well for them. Anything that seemed confusing or out of step they attributed to Jalyn's mercy or the mystery of his ways. This reasoning comforted them.

The first of the fifteen hundred Endelites to be called was Independent. Four Royal Guards came to escort him to the Great Hall of Judgment. In an attempt to lighten the solemn mood, he smiled and winked at one of the guards who happened to make eye contact with him as they left the room. He was surprised this drew no response. As he heard the hall door shut behind him, he found the questions returning. His heart beat against his chest like a drum. It was so loud he imagined the guards heard it, but if they did they gave no sign. He wished Deceived could have come with him. He would soon stand before the Judge and preferred to not be alone. Independent was rapidly losing confidence.

Before they entered the Great Hall, one of the guards briefed him in protocol. Independent nodded, though he feared he would not remember what was said. His pulse was now rushing in his ears and threatening to impair his hearing. The guard nodded in acknowledgment of Independent's understanding of procedure, and the great doors of the hall were thrown wide open.

As he took his first steps into the enormous hall, he discovered his body was trembling. Beads of sweat collected on his usually cool brow. He was completely disoriented because what he saw blew his mind!

Chapter 3

THE KINGDOM OF AFFABEL— THE DAY OF JUDGMENT I

—

*Jesus constantly used these illustrations when speaking to the crowds.
In fact, because the prophets said that he would use so many, he
never spoke to them without at least one illustration. For it had
been prophesied, "I will talk in parables; I will explain
mysteries hidden since the beginning of time."*
MATTHEW 13:34–35, TLB

The Great Hall was more spectacular than anything Independent had imagined to encounter. If given the chance to report the experience to the other fifteen hundred still waiting, he
would have had no words or frame of reference to describe its
grandeur. Its architecture made anything he'd known in Endel
obsolete. The auditorium was filled with quite possibly one hundred thousand people in attendance. He had never seen this many
in one place at one time.

As he stepped closer, Independent caught a glimpse of the
citizenry of Affabel. First he noticed they were regal with radiant
faces. Then almost as an afterthought he was taken aback by their
astounding beauty. It was as though they were from another

world. (This transformation was because they all were permitted to eat from the tree of life.) He wondered, *Is it possible these are former Endelites?* Then he caught sight of one he knew. Her name was *Goodness*. She was a few years older than him, and he remembered how she was constantly ridiculed for her homely appearance. Now she was gorgeous. Her features were the same, making her recognizable, but somehow she was now more beautiful than any person he had ever known in Endel. In fact, every one he beheld, even the least in beauty, was far more attractive than any he had ever seen.

After recovery from his initial shock, he noticed all of those in attendance were focused on an area just ahead of him. It was like nothing he had ever seen. It was a throne. But this description did not do it justice for it was indeed a most glorious throne. His eyes took in the one who sat upon it, and in an instant he realized the source of all the majesty of the city. It all proceeded from him. *This must be Jalyn*, thought Independent. Suddenly he profoundly believed in the one he'd so emphatically denied.

Jalyn's features were handsome yet stern, at least at that moment—wonderful but frightening would be a more accurate description. His whole appearance was enthralling, yet with every step Independent took toward him, terror grew steadily in his heart. Any confidence he'd once had was now completely gone. What would become of him? Independent tried to maintain composure by repeating to himself that he was approaching a merciful leader. He was conflicted because he was beginning to doubt he would receive a favorable judgment.

As he continued his approach, he was ordered to remain on a narrow platform halfway up. Towering above him on his throne was Jalyn. He was the essence of resolute in purpose and he addressed the assembly:

"All . . . shall recognize and understand that I am He who searches minds (the thoughts, feelings, and purposes) and the [inmost] hearts, and I will give to each of you [the reward for what you have done] as your work deserves."

REVELATION 2:23, AMP

Independent was listening with the others when suddenly Jalyn was looking him straight in the eyes and asking, "Give an account of your stewardship."[1]

Before Independent could utter a word, a huge screen above the throne began to play back his life in Endel from the first day of school until the previous day. Each deed, word, and motive was displayed and revealed to this crowd of witnesses. He was awed by this revelation he now possessed of Jalyn, "Not a creature exists that is concealed from His sight, but all things are open and exposed, naked and defenseless to the eyes of Him with Whom we have to do."[2]

Independent cringed as he watched his foolish, wicked, and selfish ways replayed. Encountering all this before such a large assembly was unanticipated, embarrassing, and shocking. What had seemed insignificant and even harmless in Endel now looked ghastly before this glorious judge and the regal citizens of Affabel. He was horrified by his own behavior. How could he have been so misdirected, so insensitive, so foolish? He strained for a glimmer of hope; he felt there were more good deeds in number than his bad.

When the replay of his life was over he was relieved, even though he expected a terrible scolding and some form of punishment. He would be happy to be least in the assembly. He felt certain Jalyn would see that his good outweighed the bad.

Jalyn then asked the Chief Scribe, "Is Independent's name found in the Book of Life?"

Without hesitation the Chief Scribe answered, "No, my lord."

Jalyn then spoke. "Independent, you are guilty of choosing an evil nature and are to be taken to the forsaken land of Lone to spend the rest of your life in the torment of utter darkness, hopelessness, and loneliness."

Shocked, Independent cried out, "Lord, why?"

"You did not believe in me," responded Jalyn. "Your teachers taught, 'If you do not believe that I am He, you will die in your sins'[3]; and they also taught, 'And there is salvation in and through no one else, for there is no other name under heaven given among men by and in which we must be saved.' "[4]

Independent continued, "But lord Jalyn, what about my good works? Didn't they outweigh my evil?"

Lord Jalyn replied, "It is not a matter of how little or much you break the law for, 'the person who keeps every law of God but makes one little slip is just as guilty as the person who has broken every law there is.' "[5]

Independent mustered some boldness and countered, "How then can anyone be saved?"

Jalyn didn't immediately respond to his question, but rather glanced over to a female citizen of Affabel who seemed to be an underruler to Jalyn, for she sat on a similar but smaller throne. The woman spoke, "Did not your teachers tell you that '*Jalyn* saved you by his special favor when you believed. And you can't take credit for this; it is a gift from *Jalyn*. Salvation is not a reward for the good things we have done, so none of us can boast about it.' "[6]

Jalyn followed her saying, "Long ago I paid the price for the laws that had been and would be broken by the citizens. It was impossible for any one to not sin against me or to redeem themselves from their treasons, but because I loved all, I paid it myself. So my salvation is a gift that cannot be earned; you couldn't have done enough good deeds to merit citizenship in Affabel. It comes through believing in me. Yet you rejected what I did to save your life."

Stunned, Independent was silent for a few moments, and then soberly replied, "I see."

He felt as though he was about to drown in a sea of hopelessness. Groping for something to latch on to, he questioned, "Then all I did was for nothing?"

Jalyn responded, "Again it is written, 'The dead know nothing. They have no further reward, nor are they remembered. Whatever they did in their lifetime—loving, hating, envying—is all long gone. They no longer have a part in anything.'[7] And again, "For the evil have no future; their light will be snuffed out."[8]

Independent, was taken aback by Jalyn's words and remained speechless. He regretted all the classes he skipped. Perhaps if he had attended he might have heard the truth and not made this fatal mistake with his life.

In the moments of silence that followed, another thought came to him. It was the one he'd comforted himself with all day, he rallied his courage again, "Yes, what you have said is all true, but, Jalyn, you are a merciful king! How can you send me away if this is so?"

Jalyn responded, "I am a merciful king, and that is exactly why I'm sending you away. By choosing to spend your time in Endel the way you did, you permanently chose your nature, that of the dark lord Dagon. How could I be merciful, true, and loving if I allowed your immoral fiber to pollute the purity of this great city? I would put the innocent of Affabel in harm's way. Your chosen nature would soon manifest and thus corrupt thousands of pure lives. You have chosen your own way. You will be recompensed for it exactly as the one you followed, Dagon. If I give you less than I gave him, then I would be an unjust leader, and that I am not!"

Jalyn then addressed the entire assembly and quoted the ancient sayings of his father, " 'He who despises the word will be destroyed, but he who fears the commandment will be rewarded.' "[9]

What transpired next left the assembly solemn. "Then the king said to the servants, 'Bind him hand and foot, take him away, and cast him into outer darkness; there will be weeping and gnashing of teeth.' For many are called, but few are chosen."[10]

Screams of horror and the agony of dread seized Independent as he was bound by the Chief Guard and carried toward the side door of the auditorium. Not a sound could be heard among the thousands in attendance. They watched in sorrow as one who had so unwisely wasted his life was carried out to his lifelong punishment.

Once out of the building, he was placed in another large waiting room. Here were thousands of small-barred cells, which held the condemned until the number of all who would be sentenced to exile was completed. Over the entrance to this area these words were written:

Blessed are those who do His commandments, that they may have the right to the tree of life, and may enter through the gates into the city. But outside are dogs and sorcerers and sexually immoral and murderers and idolaters, and whoever loves and practices a lie.

REVELATION 22:14-15

Independent stared at the words; rage boiled within him. He was now under the complete influence of his nature. Any good that was in his character before was now completely swallowed up by the very moral fiber he chose. His behavior was rapidly deteriorating into that of a mad dog. Without the influence of the king, he was given completely over to a reprobate mind.

DECEIVED BEFORE JALYN

A few hours passed. Many had already been called out of the Hall of Justice; still waiting amongst the few hundred were Deceived, Faint Heart, and Double Life. Deceived still carried an optimistic attitude, and his demeanor kept the others hopeful as well.

The doors opened and the four Royal Guards once again appeared, this time calling for Deceived. Tension gripped him, and he began to quiver; his time had come. To cover his nervousness, which he was clever at doing, he said to those who yet remained, "Well guys, my number's up!"

After being briefed on protocol; the doors to the Judgment Hall swung open and Deceived was escorted down the main aisle. He experienced similar feelings as Independent. He likewise saw the size and beauty of the hall and the countenances of the citizens. As he walked down the aisle, he recognized several whom he had known from the School of Endel who had graduated a year or two before him. He recognized more citizens than Independent had since Deceived almost never missed a meeting at the school.

One person he recognized who didn't attend classes was a man named *Ruthless*. He was known as one of the most notorious wicked men in the community. Deceived stopped in his tracks wondering, *What is he doing here?* The Chief Guard motioned to Deceived that it was fine for him to speak to this man.

Deceived walked over to him and asked, "Are you Ruthless?"

The man responded, "I was once known as Ruthless, but Lord Jalyn changed my name at his Judgment Seat to *Reconciled.*"

Deceived blurted out, "How in the world did you ever get in here? You were considered a wicked man by most in our community. You never went to school and you opposed Jalyn more than anyone I knew?"

Reconciled replied, "Yes, this is true; but I hated who I was and what I did. Since I didn't attend school, I had never heard Jalyn's life-changing word. However, a week before my Judgment Day I went for a meal at Charity's restaurant. She knew my life was a wreck and somehow detected my pain. She paid for my dinner with one condition, that I stay and talk with her. She then spent two hours telling me of Jalyn, his goodness, his salvation, and of this place called Affabel."

Reconciled continued, "She explained it was not too late for me to give my life to this great leader. I could still be forgiven unconditionally and accepted as a citizen in his kingdom. I was overwhelmed by Jalyn's love and pledged the rest of my life to his lordship. Though I was only able to serve him for a week in Endel, I did so with all my heart. I went to those I had oppressed or stolen from and asked their forgiveness. I gave back more than what I'd taken."

Deceived was speechless. He looked back at the guard, who nodded his head in affirmation. Reconciled then stepped back into his place, and Deceived proceeded toward the throne.

As he walked, he couldn't help but ponder what he had just heard. He had been told of the great mercy of Jalyn, but had now witnessed it in a manner that was staggering. This man had been one of the worst he had ever known, and now he was as regal as the others. Deceived was convinced more than ever he would find favor with Jalyn because he was such a strong believer in him.

Once Deceived stood before the throne, he was given the same order as Independent: "Give an account of your steward-ship."

Just as with Independent, he witnessed his life on the big screen from the first day of school till the day prior. What a relief to see his faithful school attendance and outspoken support of Jalyn before the assembly. However, he was soon appalled. His lifestyle accused him. He had justified his ways, but as they came to light before this majestic judge and morally pure witnesses he was embarrassed and ashamed. When the revelation of his sexual promiscuity was made known before this regal assembly, he wanted to crawl into a hole and hide.

Not only were his acts brought to the light but his intentions and motives as well. How could Jalyn know these things? How could he judge Deceived for things no one even knew? His deepest secrets were no longer hidden. The entire assembly be-held his lust for gain in his business transactions, in the sales of his homes, and in land development. They saw the slander and gos-sip he habitually used to get what he desired. It seemed everything he did was motivated by his desires for more. He wanted his own way in everything, and everything for himself. There was no arguing with the facts. However, he comforted himself in that none of this really mattered because he believed in Jalyn and professed his allegiance to him.

Once his life had been fully reviewed, Jalyn then turned to the Royal Scribe and asked, "Is Deceived found in the Book of Life?"

The Scribe responded, "No, my lord."

Jalyn announced, "Deceived, you are guilty of denying me, and are to be taken to the forsaken land of Lone to spend the rest of your life in the torment of utter darkness, hopelessness, and loneliness."

Deceived was paralyzed with utter shock. His mind raced, *No, this is a mistake. This cannot be happening! I'm a believer in Jalyn. What does he mean, "Denying me?"*

He blurted out, "How have I denied you!"

Jalyn then said, "Did you not listen when your teachers warned of those who 'claim they know *Jalyn*, but they deny him by the way they live'?"[11]

Again Deceived countered, "But, great king, I attended your school. I was faithful to not miss classes, and I was involved in many activities. I even called you lord!"

Jalyn immediately said, "Why do you call me, 'Lord, Lord,' and yet don't do what I tell you?[12] Did you not hear my words when I said, 'Not all who sound religious are really godly people. They may refer to me as "Lord," but still won't get to *Affabel*. For the decisive question is whether they obey my Father. . . . At the Judgment many will tell me, "Lord, Lord, we told others about you and used your name. . . ." But I will reply, "You have never been mine. Go away, for your deeds are evil." ' "[13]

Deceived was frantic, "But I had faith . . . I believed in you, so according to your word I should be saved!"

Jalyn was patient, but resolute. He looked to a citizen in the assembly, a former teacher in the school who now sat on a smaller throne, "Read to Deceived what you taught in your classes."

This gentleman read from the sacred writings: "Dear brothers and sisters, what's the use of saying you have faith if you don't prove it by your actions? That kind of faith can't save anyone. . . . It isn't enough just to have faith. Faith that doesn't show itself by good deeds is no faith at all—it is dead and useless. Now someone may argue, 'Some people have faith; others have good deeds.' I say, 'I can't see your faith if you don't have good deeds, but I will show you my faith through my good deeds.' Do you still think it's enough just to believe that there is one *Jalyn*? Well, even the demons believe this, and they tremble in terror! Fool! When will you ever learn that faith that does not result in good deeds is useless?"[14]

Jalyn reiterated, "You say you had faith, yet faith is not faith unless it is accompanied by corresponding actions of obedience. It is not enough to say you believe, for even the demons believe but are certainly not saved. Those who truly believe will exhibit a changed nature and no longer produce the fruit of an evil one. You continually bore the fruit of the evil lord Dagon, which was only evidence that you truly never really believed in me from your heart."

Deceived was having a hard time comprehending all that was said and countered, "But what about this evil man, Ruthless? I was better than him! How could you let him in and keep me out? You are not being fair!"

Jalyn responded, " 'You say: The Lord isn't being fair! Listen to me. . . . Am I the one who is unfair, or is it you? . . . If a wicked person turns away from his wickedness and obeys the law and does right, he shall save his soul, for he has thought it over and decided to turn from his sins and live a good life. He shall surely live—he shall not die.' "[15]

Frustrated and angry, Deceived ranted on, "But I shared your word and witnessed to people about you. I even volunteered and substitute taught at your school!"

Jalyn, now stern, replied, "Recite my laws no longer and stop claiming my promises, for you have refused my discipline, disregarding my laws. You see a thief and help him, and spend your time with evil and immoral men. You curse and lie, and vile language streams from your mouth. You slander your own brother. I remained silent—you thought I didn't care—but now your time of punishment has come, and I list all the above charges against you."[16]

Deceived was silent. His mind was reeling, but he had nothing more to say in his defense.

A few moments passed; "Then the king said to the servants, 'Bind him hand and foot, take him away, and cast him into outer darkness; there will be weeping and gnashing of teeth.'"[17]

As the Chief Guard approached, Deceived hurled profanities toward Jalyn, the guards, and the very citizens of Affabel. Enraged, he thrashed violently. Any good within him was swallowed up by the revelation of his true nature.

He was bound hand and foot and carried out of the auditorium as he cursed the entire way. Like Independent, he was held in the cage until the judgment of all was complete.

Once Deceived was out of the auditorium, Jalyn addressed the gathering of witnesses: "There is a generation that is pure in its own eyes, yet is not washed from its filthiness."[18]

FAINT HEART BEFORE JALYN

Less than one hundred were left in the Hall of Justice; Faint Heart and Double Life were in this number. Faint Heart stayed as far away from Double Life as she could, as there yet remained a bitter resentment toward him. He avoided her as well.

The four Royal Guards entered and summoned Faint Heart. She was nervous about where she was going, but grateful to leave Double Life behind. Like the others before her, she was led to the entrance of the great hall, briefed on protocol, and ushered in.

As she passed by the citizens of Affabel, she too recognized many who had gone on before her. Most were not as outspoken and passionate about their faith as she had been while in school. Faint Heart was amazed to see a number present whom she'd thought would surely be absent.

Faint Heart approached the throne and noticed the smaller thrones surrounding it. She recognized a few teachers and others she would have expected to see as leaders in the kingdom. However, there were many more who surprised her sitting on these thrones. They were the lesser-known citizens of Endel. There were some present who had been wealthy as well. *How could the rich be in such places of honor?* she thought to herself.

Before her mind could answer she heard Jalyn's voice: "Give an account of your stewardship."

The huge screen displayed her life. Faint Heart was delighted with the review of her schooling period. All her volunteer work, extra study, and class leadership bode well for her. She was proud of her boldness and diligence. However, the mood changed with showing of her response to Slander's lie. It was clear she had refused to let go of her offense. Her heart issues were exposed, and it wasn't pretty.

Then her affair with Double Life began. She had never repented of her involvement with him. She had always felt the victim and laid all the blame on Slander and Double Life. This caused her to never take responsibility for her choices. As her life unfolded, she watched anger, bitterness, and a desire for revenge multiply. Though she had managed to suppress some of it, she had never dealt with the root. It revealed itself not only in her perpetual offense with Double Life and Slander but that she actually blamed Jalyn for her hardships as well. How could he have allowed a man like Double Life to teach in his school? Her resentment and unforgiveness was being exposed as hard and relentless.

As the review concluded, it was clear she was an embittered woman who lacked goodness toward others. However, even with all this revealed before the great assembly, she was confident her previously strong commitment would secure her favor with the king. She dreaded a little scolding but never saw what was coming.

Jalyn turned to the Royal Scribe, "Is Faint Heart's name found in the Book of Life?"

The Chief Scribe responded, "No, my lord."

Jalyn pronounced his judgment, "Faint Heart you are guilty of falling away from righteousness and denying me by treason, and are to be taken to the forsaken land of Lone to spend the rest of your life in torment of utter darkness, hopelessness, and loneliness."

Faint Heart was stunned beyond description. Hers was even a greater shock than any of the others before her. This couldn't be happening! She was trapped in a bad dream; no, a nightmare, and somehow she must wake herself! Maybe she had misunderstood.

In disbelief she questioned, "Jalyn, did you say I am to be taken to the dreaded land of Lone?"

"Yes Faint Heart, you heard correctly," replied the king.

"How can this be, lord Jalyn? I believe in you. This was clearly shown in my life review. I had a good life to back my beliefs. I know my heart became hardened and the love within me died, but that wasn't my fault. It was the fault of Slander and Double Life. They caused me to grow cold."

Jalyn responded, "Did you forget my warnings through your teachers? 'Such will be the spread of evil that many people's love will grow cold. But whoever holds out to the end will be saved.'[19] You did not endure to the end."

Faint Heart continued, "But, Lord Jalyn, I am a righteous person because of my belief in you. I may have lost my witness, but I always believed that once a person was saved, they would always be saved and could never lose it. Even some of the teachers proclaimed this. According to them, no one could pluck me out of your hand."

Jalyn responded, "Yes, this is true. No one can pluck you out of my hand, but I never said you couldn't walk away. You alone hold that power. For did you not read in the sacred writings, 'If people have escaped from the corrupting forces of the world through their knowledge of our Lord and Savior *Jalyn*, and then are again caught and conquered by them, such people are in worse condition at the end than they were at the beginning. It would have been much better for them never to have known the way of righteousness than to know it and then turn away from the sacred command that was given them.'[20] If I stated it would have been better for them not to have known the way of righteousness because they are now worse off than before being saved, how could you believe it was impossible to lose salvation? If it could never be lost, then how could they be worse off than before?

"Why did you listen to teachers who taught contrary to what my word states? I recorded it carefully so all could know the way of righteousness. Why did you allow yourself to be deceived? If you had believed what I said, you would have confronted the bitterness in your heart. Instead you allowed it to grow unchecked out of your false comfort of unconditional security and now face a judgment that could have been averted."

Faint Heart pleaded, "But what about all the good I did?"

Lord Jalyn replied, "Again, did you not read what I clearly stated through my Prophet? 'If righteous people turn to sinful ways and start acting like other sinners, should they be allowed to live? No, of course not! All their previous goodness will be forgotten, and they will die for their sins. Yet you say, "The Lord isn't being just!" Listen to me. . . . Am I the one who is unjust, or is it you? When righteous people turn from being good and start doing sinful things, they will die for it. Yes, they will die because of their sinful deeds.'[21] It is just as it was written; your goodness and righteous acts are forgotten and will not be credited to you."

Still grasping, Faint Heart said, "But lord, you said if I confessed you as my Savior my name would be written in the Book of Life. How is it possible it is no longer there? Why can't your scribe find my name? How could it have been erased?"

Lord Jalyn patient, but resolute answered, "Did you not hear what was stated earlier? 'He who endures to the end shall be saved.'[22] Those who endure all the way to the judgment are those who overcome; and I clearly said, 'He who overcomes shall thus be clothed in white garments; and I will not erase his name from the book of life.'[23] If I stated I will not erase their name from the Book of Life, it means it can be erased. Otherwise, I would have said, 'If you confess me as lord, your name will be forever secured in the Book of Life.'"

Faint Heart pleaded, "How can you send me to Lone, the place where the living dead are sent?"

Jalyn turned to one of the underrulers, "Read the ancient writings that have been made known to the citizens of Endel."

The ruler turned to Proverbs 21:16 and read, "A man who strays from the path of understanding comes to rest in the company of the dead" (NIV).

Faint Heart was rendered speechless. "Then the king said to the servants, 'Bind *her* hand and foot, take *her* away, and cast *her* into outer darkness; there will be weeping and gnashing of teeth.' For many are called, but few are chosen."[24]

As the Chief Guard approached, she cursed Jalyn. She was overtaken by the violence of her bitterness and twisted by her twice fallen nature (see Jude 12). She was like a late autumn tree pulled up by its roots with no fruit of righteousness remaining.

She was bound hand and foot and carried toward the side door of the auditorium. Likewise, she was held in one of the cages. Once she'd left the auditorium, the Chief Scribe enlightened the congregation of witnesses:

"Dear friends, if we deliberately continue sinning after we have received a full knowledge of the truth, there is no other sacrifice that will cover these sins. There will be nothing to look forward to but the terrible expectation of *Jalyn's* judgment and the raging fire that will consume his enemies. . . . For we know the one who said, 'I will take vengeance. I will repay those who deserve it.' He also said, 'The Lord will judge his own people.' It is a terrible thing to fall into the hands of the living *Jalyn*."[25]

THE JUDGMENT OF DOUBLE LIFE

The last person to be called out of the Hall of Justice was Double Life. He knew the laws of Jalyn and already knew his judgment would not be favorable. He would soon discover just how much his transgression had cost him.

He felt faint as he was escorted into the judgment hall and had to be assisted by the guards in order to approach the Judgment Seat of Jalyn.

His life was reviewed, and he too heard the woeful words that his name was not found in the Book of Life.

Jalyn firmly announced, "Double Life, you are guilty of treason, falling away from righteousness, and being a stumbling block, and are to be taken to the forsaken land of Lone, where you will receive the greatest punishment and torments."

Double Life listened in horror then pleaded, "Lord, but I was a teacher in your school. I gave my life for your cause."

Jalyn answered, "You were a teacher, but did you not read from the books you taught? 'Dear brothers and sisters, not many of you should become teachers in the *school*, for we who teach will be judged by *Jalyn* with greater strictness.' "[26]

Double Life countered, "How was I a stumbling block?"

Jalyn's tone became harder. "You caused many of my little ones to stumble and fall permanently. Faint Heart is just one example. She was entrusted to your care; I gave you authority to protect her, not to use her for your own advantage. You used your influence to satiate your lust and violated her and others. A sister already wounded her, and you, who should have brought healing, took advantage of her. You shipwrecked her faith. She has been sentenced to Lone. Surely you remember the warning I gave, 'Whoever causes one of these little ones who believe in Me to stumble, it would be better for him if a millstone were hung around his neck, and he were thrown into the sea.' "[27]

Double Life pleaded, "But Jalyn, I know I'm to be banned to Lone, but why am I to receive the greatest torment? Why are you so hard on me? I was one of your servants not an unbeliever. I wasn't like Independent, who would have nothing to do with you. Why?"

Jalyn still firm and resolute, "You knew and taught the ancient writings. Why do you ask these questions of me? I will remind you so you may remember these words. The ancient writings are clear: 'But if the servant thinks, "My master won't be back for a while," and begins oppressing the other servants . . . the master will return unannounced and unexpected. He will tear the servant apart and banish him with the unfaithful. The servant will be severely punished, for though he knew his duty, he refused to do it. But people who are not aware that they are doing wrong will be punished only lightly. Much is required from those to whom much is given, and much more is required from those to whom much more is given.' "[28]

Jalyn continued, "Independent was far less aware of his transgressions, but you had both awareness and knowledge. His punishment, though severe, will be lighter than your own. For you, I've 'reserved a place . . . in the deepest darkness.' "[29]

Jalyn then commanded the Chief Guard, " 'Bind him hand and foot, take him away, and cast him into outer darkness; there will be weeping and gnashing of teeth.' For many are called, but few are chosen."[30]

As the Chief Guard approached, Double Life spewed profanities at Jalyn, the guards, and the citizens of Affabel. He was violent and even tried to break free to physically attack Jalyn. His true nature was completely revealed. Any good within was swallowed up by his duplicity.

He was bound hand and foot and carried out the side door

of the auditorium, cursing the entire way. He joined the other fifteen hundred who were immediately transported to the land of Lone.

As soon as Double Life exited the auditorium, the Chief Scribe closed his book and shouted: " 'The judgments you have made are just. . . . They are getting what they deserve!' Then I heard a voice from the altar saying . . . , 'True and just indeed are your judgments!' "[31]

THE FORSAKEN LAND OF LONE

The fifteen hundred condemned and caged Endelites were escorted by Royal Guards on a two-week trip to the blighted land of Lone. This journey brought them into the Great Desert of Fire, where the heat that rose from the parched earth was unbearable. Suddenly in the middle of nowhere, where the heat was the most unbearable, a very large and foreboding structure loomed in the distance. As they approached, they were able to read the sign: "The Forsaken Land of Lone."

Upon closer inspection, they realized the large structure had no windows or openings, just one large door at the base. Passing through the door, each heard what seemed like thousands of screams coming from the inside. Within moments they could make out the pleas directed to the Chief Guard, which came from those imprisoned near the entry, "Hasn't it been long enough? Please ask for mercy on our behalf. Our punishment is too much to bear!"

"How long have they been in this place?" Independent asked a guard.

"Their time ranges from one year to one hundred and twenty nine."

Deceived was shocked. He had somehow hoped all that had transpired in the past two weeks would turn out to be a nightmare or scare tactic. He inquired of the same guard, "This is truly where I will spend the rest of my life?"

"Yes, it is exactly as you were forewarned in Endel."

Those slated for the greater punishment were placed higher in this metal building, where the heat was the greatest. Those who didn't know the truth but still committed things worthy of exile were placed in the lower portion of the enormous metal building. However, even this placement was unbearable for even a day, let alone for more than one hundred years!

The agony of Double Life's abode was unimaginable. He was taken to a dungeon underground, near the hot sulfur rocks. The smell alone was unbearable, and with no venting the heat was more intense than any other location. It was not in the building, but deep within the bowels of the earth. This was without a doubt the greatest place of suffering and torment. Here he would suffer all alone. The area was large enough to separate those who shared the same measure of condemnation. They were unable to hear any voice but their own.

Once the condemned were securely imprisoned, the Chief Guard made their way to the entrance. When the massive iron door shut behind them, not a fragment of light could be found within the confines of the structure. These poor souls would spend over one hundred and twenty five years in utter darkness and loneliness. The only hope they had of light would be once a year, when a new round of prisoners was brought in. Yet not all even saw this, only those who were near the great door. Others, like Double Life, would never again see the light of day. For him, the blackness of darkness was reserved as punishment.

REFLECTIONS

These four regretted for the rest of their existence their choice not to listen to the truth. Alone they continually pondered the foolishness of not carefully heeding the words of Jalyn, which had been accessible in the land of Endel. They would have done anything for the chance to go back and change their destiny. Oh, how they wished they had not listened to the majority or popular opinion of the day. They would spurn their own foolish reasonings and embrace the ancient writings, which never varied or could be broken.

They were tormented by the images of that most remarkable kingdom. In their continual anguish they could still see the beauty of the city, even though they'd only experienced it a few moments. This magnified their torment with its contrast. The fiery heat, acrid stench, and darkness only served to punctuate the truth. Beauty had been theirs for the choosing, and they had forsaken it all with their folly.

Chapter 4

ETERNAL HOME OF
THE DEAD

———

*And when His disciples asked Him the meaning of this parable, He
said to them, To you it has been given to [come progressively to]
know (to recognize and understand more strongly and clearly) the
mysteries and secrets of the kingdom of God.*
LUKE 8:9-10, AMP

In the next four chapters we'll break from the allegory and
focus on the specific truths revealed by the judgment of Independent, Deceived, Faint Heart, and Double Life. We'll then finish the allegory by discussing Selfish and Charity and for the
remainder of the book focus on the truths revealed by their lives.
The better part of this book will focus on the eternal rewards of
those who follow Jesus Christ.

FOUNDATIONAL TRUTH

In our allegory, Jalyn represents Jesus Christ and the King Father
is Almighty God the Father. Dagon is Satan; life in Endel represents a human being's life on this earth; and Affabel reflects the

heavenly city of God. The forsaken land of Lone represents the Lake of Fire, where every individual without the saving grace of Jesus Christ will spend eternity. The individuals discussed in the previous chapter represent various scenarios of those who will be forever condemned; God's Word makes this very clear.

Yes, you read that correctly, forever condemned. In preparing to write this message, I struggled with how to bring you the reader to the place of being able to relate to what Scripture refers to as "eternal judgments." Read carefully the following:

> Therefore let us go on and get past the *elementary* stage in the teachings and doctrine of Christ (the Messiah), advancing steadily toward the completeness and perfection that belong to spiritual maturity. Let us not again be laying the foundation of . . . eternal judgment and punishment. [These are all matters of which you should have been fully aware long, long ago.]
>
> HEBREWS 6:1–2, AMP

As you can see, I left out the other five foundational doctrines, some of which are repentance from dead works and faith toward God, in order to emphasize that eternal judgment and punishment are *elementary* teachings of Christ.

One dictionary defines elementary as "constituting the basic, essential, or fundamental part."[1] It's the essential part we must have right from the start to build upon; it's a foundation. To understand, consider our education system. In elementary school, we get the basic tools used to further build our education, such as reading, writing, and arithmetic. Lacking these as a foundation, we will never have the ability to develop a proper education in our life. The same is true for believers; if we do not have eternal judgments firmly established in our understanding, then we will not be capable of building a proper life in Christ. It would be compared to trying to advance your education without being able to read.

Yet, I've discovered after almost twenty years of traveling that many—and I'm including devoted followers of Jesus Christ—are unaware of these issues. Notice the writer states, "These are all matters of which you should have been fully aware long, long ago." He didn't say we are to be acquainted with these issues, but to be *fully,* or *completely,* aware. His words, "long, long ago" only emphasize that these are foundational to our basic faith, as the ability to read and write is to our education.

We'll see shortly why "eternal judgment" is an elementary doctrine we must have in order to build a healthy Christian life. Keep this in mind as you continue to read because without this understanding it may be too difficult to take in what we're about to discuss and you may succumb to the thought, *What's the point?*

HELL—FIGURATIVE OR REAL

Before I began to write, I wrestled with this thought: *How do I communicate to a generation who "live for the day" the reality of eternal decisions that will shortly be made for our lives by the Judge of the universe?* After several days of struggle, in prayer the thought arose, *Jesus, to communicate spiritual truths to the minds of human beings, told stories.* Thus the idea of the allegory of Affabel.

When writing this story, upon coming to the judgment of these individuals and their lifelong punishment in the land of Lone, I trembled within myself. In fact, I wrote the final part of the previous chapter while flying home one Sunday evening. I preached three times that day; my assistants were sound asleep, but I couldn't stop typing. Upon arriving home well after midnight, I couldn't sleep, fearing for all those who will eventually one day find themselves in an unspeakably worse situation called the Lake of Fire; and, according to Jesus, it will be the majority:

> Go in through the narrow gate, because the gate to hell is
> wide and the road that leads to it is easy, and there are many

who travel it. But the gate to life is narrow and the way that
leads to it is hard, and there are few people who find it.

MATTHEW 7:13-14, TEV

While lying in bed, I reflected back a couple years when I
was asked to preach the gospel in a top security male prison in
South Africa. I remember walking into that dreadful place; the
smells, the revolting living conditions, cells that held twenty to
thirty men with bunks inches from each other, condoms hanging
on the walls are just a few of the horrors I witnessed. I had been
in several prisons ministering in America, but never had I seen
such despairing conditions in all my life. Our prisons looked like
country clubs in comparison.

I couldn't imagine living a week in that vile place, let alone
forty to fifty years (most of the prisoners were there for life). You
could see utter despair on the faces of those who were not believers in Jesus. I could almost hear their thoughts, *At least one day I'll
get out of here through death.* Yet on the other hand, they were terrified by the unknown reality of dying. It was a very terrible
quandary indeed. They were in a complete state of hopelessness. If
you lived in the free world, which all of them had, and you were
facing this place for the rest of your life, it would be sheer torment.

While there, I thought that as horrific as this is, it is beautiful compared to hell. At least these inmates had companions and
sunlight streaming through a few barred windows in this prison;
in hell, there are neither companions nor light, except for the fire
which is never quenched. In the Lake of Fire, there is no relief,
forever and ever; souls will be in perpetual anguish! In hell, the
people cannot think, *One day I'll get out of this place.* They've received *eternal* punishment!

Because it is one of His elementary teachings, Jesus discussed
hell frequently, much more often than what is mentioned today
from pulpits. He didn't see bringing up its description—the torment involved, as well as the fact that it was never ending—as a
lack of compassion. Rather He saw it as essential to reaching us

as the Good Shepherd. His addressing and teaching on it, there-fore, was motivated by love, since all He did and taught was out of a heart of compassion. So my question is: Today, are we doing the best service to people by not mentioning it from our pulpits? Is that true love?

There are several names given to hell in Scripture. *Sheol* (Old Testament only), *Hades*, and *the grave* are a few of the names given to the intermediate chambers of death. *Gehenna* and the *Lake of Fire* are the names given to the eternal hell. We will discuss the difference between the intermediate and eter-nal shortly.

Scripture tells us hell is a real place, not figurative, as our so-ciety has endeavored to promote. In Numbers 16 the earth opened up and three families were physically swallowed into Sheol before multitudes of witnesses. In the New Testament, we are told concerning the Antichrist and his False Prophet: "Both of them were hurled alive into the fiery lake that burns and blazes with brimstone" (Rev. 19:20, AMP). They didn't die with just their souls taken to this place; rather, their physical bodies and souls were cast into the Lake of Fire.

LAZARUS AND THE RICH MAN

In the Gospel of Luke, Jesus tells of an actual incident of a rich man who lived entirely for himself; neglecting a beggar daily laid before his house. We know this is not a parable because Jesus opens the story with, "There was a certain rich man." Second, He uses Abraham's name and gives a specific name to the beggar, Lazarus. It was not customary for Jesus to give first names or mention actual people in His parables.

After both died, Lazarus was carried by angels to Abraham's bosom (which was the holding area of comfort for the Old Tes-tament Saints, until Jesus made the way for them to come into the presence of God in heaven). The rich man died and found himself in Hades. We read:

And in Hades, where he was in great pain, he looked up and saw Abraham, far away, with Lazarus at his side. So he called out, "Father Abraham! Take pity on me, and send Lazarus to dip his finger in some water and cool off my tongue, because I am in great pain in this fire!"

LUKE 16:23-24, TEV

Notice that the rich man was in great pain. Other translations use the words *agony, anguish,* and *torment.* In other words, the suffering was very great. Hell is a place of conscious torment. Also notice that he recognized Abraham as well as Lazarus and they could also recognize the rich man. People are very much human beings in hell; they still have their reasoning facilities, emotions, wills, physical features, as well as senses. This man could see, hear, and feel pain. They also have some form of flesh; you can see the rich man's intense desire just to have his tongue cooled off. Jesus says that both body and soul are eternally destroyed in hell (Matt. 10:28). In other words, people's flesh will be continuously afflicted and marred by its fires and worms.

Also notice that the rich man was pleading for mercy, just as those who were begging for mercy in the dungeon of Lone in our story. Hell is a place of no escape, forever! There is nobody who will ever come from the outside to comfort its inhabitants, even though it's greatly longed for. It also seems this reality never completely sinks in. For Abraham had to remind this rich man, "There is a great chasm separating us. Anyone who wanted to cross over to you from here [*to bring comfort*] is stopped at its edge, and no one there can cross over to us" (Luke 16:26, NLT, emphasis mine). I know an individual who experienced hell; she later reported that everyone she saw cried out that it was too much to bear. This is exactly what you hear this rich man cry out in the above verse. Continuing to read:

But Abraham said, "Remember, my son, that in your lifetime you were given all the good things, while Lazarus got all the bad things. But now he is enjoying himself here, while you are in pain. . . ." The rich man said, "Then I beg you, father Abraham, send Lazarus to my father's house, where I have five brothers. Let him go and warn them so that they, at least, will not come to this place of pain."

LUKE 16:25, 27-28, TEV

You've heard of the old saying, "Misery loves company." Why doesn't it apply here? Why didn't this rich man want others there with him? The answer is that in hell there is no companionship or fellowship. Some think there will be parties in hell; others think they will enjoy their friends. If that were so, he would have wanted all his closest comrades to join him, yet he was desperate to see that they would not come to this place of torment. Hell is a place of utter loneliness and hopelessness. It also is a place of eternal remembrance, which I personally believe is one of its great torments.

Hear how Abraham responds to his plea for his brothers:

Abraham said, "Your brothers have Moses and the prophets to warn them; your brothers should listen to what they say." The rich man answered, "That is not enough, father Abraham! But if someone were to rise from death and go to them, then they would turn from their sins." But Abraham said, "If they will not listen to Moses and the prophets, they will not be convinced even if someone were to rise from death."

LUKE 16:29-31, TEV

There is such a powerful truth that is conveyed here. Many would like extraordinary experiences to prove to themselves or others the validity of the gospel. Yet Jesus shows us nothing is greater than the Word of God to produce the belief it takes to follow God completely to the end. Don't misunderstand me—

most would be startled and changed for a short while but would not be permanently convinced in their heart by experiences.

When I was a teenager, a profane young man and party animal, my dad took me to see the movie *The Ten Commandments* starring Charlton Heston. I vividly remember fixing my eyes on that huge screen when the earth opened up to swallow the people into hell; it shook me tremendously. I walked out of that theater, and my life was changed. I straightened up and walked differently for about a week, only to return to all my old ways. Why? Because I hadn't heard the Word of God, repented of my ways, and committed my life completely to Jesus in order for His grace to change me.

My friends and I had other extraordinary experiences that shook me as well, but I wasn't changed by any supernatural experiences. It wasn't until one of my college fraternity brothers came to my room and presented the Word of God through the gospel of Jesus Christ that my life was changed. We are specifically told, "So then faith comes by hearing, and hearing by the word of God" (Rom. 10:17); and "For you have been born again, not of perishable seed, but of imperishable, through the living and enduring word of God" (1 Pet. 1:23, NIV). For this reason it is so important that we teach and preach the Word of God, not just our experiences.

On the other hand, after clarifying this, let me now stress this fact: *If experiences complement or help amplify the Word of God, they are tremendous, and even needful.* Testimonies play a huge part in communicating the gospel, but it is the Word of God received and believed that will cause us to abide forever.

"WHY AM I GOING THIS WAY?"

So now allow me to share a testimony that will complement what we have seen thus far in Scripture. My wife and I sat in the living room of a friend one evening, and he shared with us what happened to him as a young man. He was raised in the Caribbean and during the rainy season fell into a pit used to gather rainwater for construction. His brother jumped in and tried to save him but couldn't, so he got out and ran for help, for our friend couldn't swim. By the time help arrived, he had been dead for about one half hour.

He told us that once he left his body, all of his senses were intact. He found himself being pulled rapidly downward into a very deep darkness. He said the darkness was so deep he couldn't see his hand in front of his face; it was so dark he felt as if he were wearing it. He said, "The fear was so great I thought it cannot get any worse, yet the more I fell the more intense it became. I have never experienced fear like that on the earth; there is no way to describe it in words."

He said, "Then I saw the flickering lights, and I knew I was headed for hell. I started screaming, 'Why am I going this way, I'm a Christian!'" His mother and father were strong believers, but he was simply going to church because his parents told him he had no choice. When he shared this story with us, he said at the time he could not explain how this could happen to him.

He then reported hearing screams of fear and torment. I vividly remember him saying, "John and Lisa, there are some screams that are ordinary. Then there are other screams that make your blood freeze in its veins. These are the screams I heard. Then I came face to face with a creature that had scales who kept saying to me, 'Come to me, you are mine.' I was fighting with the creature. At first I couldn't say anything because of the fear, but then I yelled, 'Let me go, let me go.'

"Then suddenly I found myself screaming in my body and bit the doctor who had his finger down my throat (so I was told by my mother after I explained to her my experience). At the same time, my mother was sitting outside the operating room (now at the hospital) and crying out to God, 'Father if you give my son back to me, I will give him to You forever!'" Our friend later in life pioneered a ministry in the Caribbean.

You may question his experience; however, there have been

quite a number of men, women, and children who have undergone similar occurrences. Since these near death experiences (NDEs) occur frequently in the presence of doctors, this has triggered a few to research it. One is a man named Melvin Morse, a doctor who has conducted extensive study on children who have had NDEs. He studied two groups of children. The first group of 121 patients consisted of those who were critically ill but not near death. They were on artificial lung machines, in intensive care, or heavy medication and ranged in age from three to sixteen years of age. Not one of them reported leaving their bodies.

The second group, which consisted of twelve children of a similar age group, had heart failures from drowning, car accidents, cardiac arrest, etc. Out of this smaller group, every one of the twelve had out of body experiences. Some briefly saw their bodies and described to doctors the procedures they were using while working on them.

Some may think our friend's experience was hallucinated; however, the studies done on these other children would strongly show otherwise. Besides how could he have hallucinated when he was clinically dead for almost thirty minutes?

HADES VERSUS THE LAKE OF FIRE

Our friend, as well as the others I know who have experienced hell, saw the intermediate place of torment, called Hades. This is not the eternal abode of those outside of salvation; rather, it's a waiting place of torment until the Great White Throne Judgment. After judgment, the permanent place where human beings and fallen angels will spend forever and ever is called the *Lake of Fire*. This is clearly seen in the following Scripture:

> Then I saw a great white throne and the One Who was seated upon it. . . . And the sea delivered up the dead who were in it, death and Hades surrendered the dead in them, and all were tried and their cases determined by

what they had done [according to their motives, aims, and works]. Then death and Hades were thrown into the lake of fire. This is the second death, the lake of fire. And if anyone's [name] was not found recorded in the Book of Life, he was hurled into the lake of fire.

REVELATION 20:11, 13-15, AMP (AUTHOR DELETED TWO PARENTHETICAL STATEMENTS FOR CLEARER READING)

I first want to point out that all those who were in the intermediate place of torment, Hades, were brought before the judgment. Once judgment was complete, everything that offends and all those who practiced lawlessness will be hurled into the Lake of Fire, including the fallen angels, and yes, even Hades itself.

A VISION OF THE LAKE OF FIRE

My wife and I have friends who are Greek. The wife, whose name is Joy, is a third generation minister. Her grandmother was born and raised in Greece and from a young age started seeking God. Her questions to those around her were met with apathy and downright mockery. She wanted to go to a church but she was told that "there is no God" and to stop with that nonsense.

One day, as she was dancing a folk dance with her friends in the village square during a Greek festival, a voice spoke to her and said, "Efrosyni, seek the eternal dance, this dance has no value."

She was startled! *Who said that?* she wondered. Immediately, she quit the dance and told the rest of the girls that what they were doing was no good. Nobody understood what was going on. Nevertheless, she hurriedly left the square and started toward her home. As she ran, a tremendous burden began to come on her; like a heavy weight on her back.

She ran inside the home, went straight to her bedroom, fell on her knees, and started to cry. She wanted to talk to that voice. Who was talking to her, what were the words that were spoken to her, what was He trying to communicate? Those were the questions that tormented her mind, but not for long.

No sooner had she touched the floor than she felt something like fire come into the room, engulfing her. She fell backward and came into a vision. In the vision she saw an angelic being come to her dressed in white. He lifted her and transported her to a place where light was dim. He left her there. When she focused, she realized in total amazement that she was standing in front of the scene of Golgotha. The Lord was hanging on the Cross, blood dripping from his wounds. She saw the agony on His face as He was being tormented.

At the same time, she heard screams coming from a distance. She turned to see where they were coming from and saw a great chasm between the Cross and the place across the chasm, where huge waves of fire belched from the earth. It was an ocean of fire. She could hear the screams of what seemed like multitudes of people, and they were cursing God. At that moment she felt a force pushing her head down through a gaping chasm in the earth, and the voice she had heard before spoke to her and said, "This is where you too belong."

She was terrified! She started to cry and plead for mercy. She fell at the foot of the Cross carrying on her back the great burden she felt before. She stayed there crying for quite some time. When the voice, full of love and compassion, spoke to her again, it said, "He did it for you! He died for you! If you ask for forgiveness and accept His sacrifice for you, you won't have to go there [meaning the lake of fire]!"

At that, she cried even more, responding immediately to what the voice said. She asked for forgiveness, and immediately the burden she had been carrying was lifted and rolled over to the foot of the Cross.

She looked up and saw the Lord Jesus standing in front of her, dressed in His glorified form. He picked her up and carried her toward the most beautiful green hill. She was now able to communicate with Him through her mind. She would ask a question, and He would answer. It was amazing! She asked Him where they were going, and He said, "To meet your heavenly Father!"

As they approached the top of the mountain, she could see a light coming out of a gate. Beautiful, angelic music and singing were also emanating from flowers and trees everywhere. They reached the top and entered the gate. It was incredible. The beauty was indescribable! They went straight to the throne. She did not see God's face, for it was shrouded, but she saw a great big book and a hand coming out of the clouds. It started to write. She leaned forward to see what was being written, and to her amazement she saw her name written down in the Book of Life! (Although she did not know at that time what we know as "Book of Life.")

When the heavenly Father wrote her name in the Book of Life, he said, "Welcome to the family!" and gave her a kiss on the forehead. At that moment, she saw the angels forming circles as they began dancing and singing and making a great joy! She could recognize her name being sung by the angels as they were dancing. She joined them. Then she remembered what the Lord said to her to "Seek the eternal dance!" It was much later that she found out that what the angels were doing was a great celebration to her honor because she had been saved.

After a while, the Lord spoke to her and said that it was time for her to return to earth because He had a great work planned for her. She would have to go through fiery trials for His name's sake but He would be with her, and when all this was done she would return to be with Him forever. At that, she found herself back in her room. She was greatly disappointed to he back on earth after the amazing heavenly trip she had just experienced, but she had no choice in the matter.

When the rumor spread in the village about her experience, the persecution began. It started with her father, who threatened to kill her with an ax if she didn't renounce what she believed.

She told him that she could never renounce what she had experienced. The persecution greatly intensified until one evening her sister came to her and warned that certain people were planning to come the next morning and bring her to the village square, where the Greek Orthodox church was. They would bring out the icon of Mary, and if she didn't bow down to worship it and kiss it, they would pour gasoline all over her and set her on fire.

She didn't believe that they would go that far, but it seems that they had determined to do that because the same night an angel of the Lord came to young Efrosyni and woke her up by tapping her on the shoulder. Once awake, he told her to get dressed and go to the front door. She obeyed, and when she reached the porch, she felt someone lifting her off the ground. She was physically transported from her home to safety in a different village miles away.

UNIMAGINABLE TORMENT

Joy's grandmother didn't see Hades, but the Lake of Fire, which is also called "the second death." Her destiny changed because she chose to follow Jesus Christ with all her heart. Scripture tells us:

> But cowards who turn back from following me [Jesus], and those who are unfaithful to me, and the corrupt, and murderers, and the immoral, and those conversing with demons, and idol worshipers and all liars—their doom is in the Lake that burns with fire and sulphur. This is the Second Death.
>
> REVELATION 21:8, TLB (EMPHASIS MINE)

Notice it is a lake that "burns with fire and sulphur." Sulfur is a nonmetallic substance that burns with great heat and produces a very unpleasant smell. Many who have described hell have told of its dreadful aroma; "unbearable" is the description used. In fact, those I know who have experienced this place of the dead tell me there is no possible way to describe in our vernacular the torment and horror to the senses.

Also notice the term *second death*. Jesus says, "He who has an ear, let him hear what the Spirit says to the churches." (What He is about to say is to the churches, not the unbelievers); "He who overcomes shall not be hurt by the *second death*" (Rev. 2:11, emphasis mine). You may find it strange that He would say this to the churches. However, notice in the above verse we see there are three main categories of people who will burn in the lake of fire: the first are those who turned back from following Him; the second are those who were unfaithful to Him; and the third were the sinners who never walked with Him at all. The first two groups would describe those who were once in the church. Recall the first three individuals we discussed in our allegory: Faint Heart, Deceived, and Independent. Two of them were active in the School of Endel, a type of the church. We will go into this in depth shortly.

The *second death* is anguish in the Lake of Fire for the rest of eternity. Again, think of the first chapter when we discussed eternity—forever and ever, no end, no relief, no coming out! Some think that it will eventually end, yet this is clearly contrary to what the Word of God teaches, for it states, "They will be tormented day and night forever and ever" (Rev. 20:10).

To further show it is never ending, Jesus said this about all who don't obey His word: "And these will go away into *everlasting punishment*, but the righteous into eternal life" (Matt. 25:46). Notice the words *everlasting punishment*. In other words, the punishment never ends; it's eternal! Jesus tells us:

And if your eye causes you to stumble and sin, pluck it out! It is more profitable and wholesome for you to enter the kingdom of God with one eye than with two eyes to be thrown into hell (Gehenna).

MARK 9:47, AMP

70

As you can see here, He is talking about the Lake of Fire, Gehenna. Now see what He says from a different translation:

And if your eye makes you lose your faith, take it out! It is better for you to enter the Kingdom of God with only one eye than to keep both eyes and be thrown into hell. There "the worms that eat them never die, and the fire that burns them is never put out."

MARK 9:47-48, TEV

Notice the worms that eat them never die; which mean they continually have something to eat. Let's compare this to the natural. Once a person physically dies, the worms eat the flesh until it is consumed, only bones are left, and then the worms die. These worms in Gehenna never die because what they consume never ceases to exist either. One of the individuals who saw hell reported they saw huge worms eating the flesh of the people tormented in the flames, yet no matter how long they had been in hell, they still had flesh that was being consumed.

Yes, you are getting it right—this place is unimaginable! What we must keep in mind is that God didn't originally create the Lake of Fire for human beings. Hear what Jesus says to those who are hurled into this dreadful place:

Then He will also say to those on the left hand, "Depart from Me, you cursed, into the everlasting fire prepared for the devil and his angels."

MATTHEW 25:41

It was created for the devil and his fallen angels, not mankind. However, the devil is deceiving and bringing many with him to eternal punishment. It is similar to what we saw in the allegory; the influence of Dagon resulted in many being deceived, and the wrath of Jalyn, which was originally intended for

Dagon, had to be administered to those who succumbed to his influence. Otherwise, Jalyn would not have been just.

GOING WELL FOREVER

We saw how vivid the wrath of Jalyn was in the previous chapter; Scripture declares that the man or woman who drinks of "the wine of the wrath of God . . . shall be tormented with fire and brimstone in the presence of the holy angels and in the presence of the Lamb. And the smoke of their torment ascends forever and ever" (Rev. 14:10–11). Think of forever and ever. Remember our discussion of eternity in the first chapter. Try to comprehend never ending? You can't do it mentally, but you can in your heart. For this reason, God lamented over an entire generation who wouldn't listen to Him by saying:

> Oh, that they had such a heart in them that they would fear Me and always keep all My commandments, that it might be well with them and with their children *forever*!
>
> DEUTERONOMY 5:29 (EMPHASIS MINE)

Notice the word *forever*. If they were only motivated by that which endures, driven by eternity! Notice He said, "Always keep all My commandments," He didn't say, "*For a season of time* keep *all* My commandments." Nor did He say, "*Always* keep *some* of My commandments." No, it is *always* keep *all!* We are commanded to obey His will entirely as well as continuously.

You may think, *I haven't kept all his commandments.* I will be found guilty at the judgment! Yes, that is absolutely correct. The law of God identifies and proves that every human being falls short of God's righteous standard and will be found guilty at the judgment. No one can ever stand before God and say, "I have lived a life worthy of Your Kingdom and do not deserve to be punished eternally."

The reason for this shortcoming is in the beginning, in the

garden; man willfully disobeyed God and in doing so took on the nature of sin. By his act of treason, he made himself a slave to Satan, bound to his domain, and in no way could redeem or save himself. This fallen nature would be passed down to every descendant of Adam, which is all mankind, for we are born with our parents' nature.

Out of pure love, God made a promise that even though man was fully responsible for his fallen state, the Lord would send a Savior to rescue us. That Savior is Jesus Christ. It was foretold hundreds of years before His birth that He would be born of a virgin (Isa. 7:14). His Father is God and mother was a virgin named Mary, a descendant of King David. This would have to be so, for if both parents were human Jesus would have been bound to the nature of Adam, a slave to the sin, could not have lived a perfect life, and, therefore, could not redeem us. However, He had to be born of woman because it was a man who fell and it would have to be a man who would pay the price for the treason. So Jesus was 100 percent God and 100 percent man.

When Jesus went to the Cross, He took all our sins upon Himself and shed His blood to death, paying the price for sin. However, because He lived a perfect life of righteousness, the Father raised Him from the dead and seated Him on His right hand. King David, who also was a prophet and an ancestor of Jesus, foresaw and wrote over a thousand years before what would happen after Jesus' crucifixion. Peter quotes it on the day of Pentecost by declaring:

> Therefore, being a prophet [King David], and knowing that God had sworn with an oath to him that of the fruit of his body, according to the flesh, He would raise up the Christ to sit on his throne, he, foreseeing this, spoke concerning the resurrection of the Christ, that His soul was not left in Hades, nor did His flesh see corruption. This Jesus God has raised up, of which we are all witnesses.
>
> ACTS 2:30-32

Jesus was raised from the dead to free us. Notice he was not left in Hades, which automatically tells us He was there. When was He there? Sometime between the Cross and the Resurrection. Jesus tasted death, or hell, for everyone so that we would not have to receive our just eternal punishment. Now when we renounce our self-focused life and give ourselves completely to His lordship, what He did for us, shedding His blood and tasting death, becomes the ransom to buy us back as well as our justification before God. Now we are made in right standing with His righteousness and can stand confidently before His throne of judgment. Praise God forevermore!

For this cause we are implicitly told, "God saved you by his special favor when you believed. And you can't take credit for this; it is a gift from God. Salvation is not a reward for the good things we have done, so none of us can boast about it" (Eph. 2:8-9, NLT).

If you have never before repented and given yourself completely to the Lordship of Jesus, then at this point immediately turn to Appendix B in the back of the book, where I explain God's plan for your salvation and pray with you to receive Jesus Christ as your personal Lord and Savior.

Most believers are well versed in what I've written in these last few pages. However, what I'm about to discuss in the next couple chapters I've found many believers do not fully understand. In fact, many professing Christians will be shocked at the simple truths revealed in the Scriptures that we will see in the coming pages. We shall also discover in the upcoming chapters why eternal punishment is foundational knowledge every believer must have for healthy growth.

Chapter 5

JUDGMENT OF DECEIVED

We know that the judgment of God is according to truth.
ROMANS 2:2

Jesus came to save us from paying the eternal penalty of sin, which was originally intended for Satan and his cohorts. His life being given for us reveals the amazing love of God.

Think of it: The Lord created mankind along with the animals, birds, insects, sea creatures, and all the rest of the earth including its atmosphere perfect in the beginning. We read, "Then God saw everything that He had made, and indeed it was very good" (Gen. 1:31). He then placed a perfect creation into the hands of man to guard and keep. As the Psalmist declares, "Heaven belongs to the Lord alone, but he gave the earth to man" (Ps. 115:16, TEV). It would be Adam's responsibility to protect not only himself, but all creation from the archenemy of God, Lucifer.

God didn't desire robots in the garden that couldn't freely choose to love and obey Him, so out of a myriad of trees, one was placed in the midst of the garden with the following command, "You may eat the fruit of any tree in the garden, except the tree that gives knowledge of what is good and what is bad. You must not eat the fruit of that tree; if you do, you will die the same day" (Gen. 2: 16-17, TEV). The death He spoke of wasn't physical death, for Adam didn't experience physical death until years afterward (also a result from his disobedience). Instead, the Lord showed man he would be cut off from the life of God and take on the nature of Lucifer, which is death.

After a period of time, Lucifer deceived Eve by perverting the character of God in her eyes. He was able to get her focus off all the available trees and onto the one prohibited. Once she judged the tree as good, beneficial, and pleasant, she ate because she now perceived the Lord as a "taker" instead of the "Giver" He is. Yet mankind still hadn't fallen. It wasn't until her husband partook of it that God's creation took on the nature of death. For this reason his sin was greater—she was deceived; he wasn't (see 1 Tim. 2:14).

Consequently, not only Adam but all creation he was placed over immediately took the nature of death. Prior to Adam's treason, animals didn't devour and eat flesh, nor did they die. Tornados, earthquakes, hurricanes, famines, disease, and pestilence didn't exist. This all resulted from man not guarding what God entrusted to his care. Now not only mankind had the nature of death, but all creation as well. We read:

Against its will, everything on earth was subjected to God's curse. All creation anticipates the day when it will join God's children in glorious freedom from death and decay.

ROMANS 8:20-21, NLT

Nature wasn't cursed with death by its own choice, but rather by man's insubordination to God. He didn't protect what was entrusted to his care. Adam subjected not only nature, but himself, his wife, and all future offspring to what was originally Lucifer's curse, separation from God. What treachery; what treason! At this point God could have said, "Mankind, whom I loved, blessed, and created perfect, chose Lucifer over Me; let them all go to the Lake of Fire and We (Father, Son, and Holy Spirit) will begin all over; create another universe with beings who will stay loyal and love Us as we will love them."

If the Lord had done this, He would have been perfectly just in His decision. Yet out of His amazing love, He made a promise to mankind to send a Redeemer who would deliver us from the bondage we placed ourselves under. That Redeemer would be His Son, with whom He created the heavens and earth. So in other words, He would pay our terrible price for sin and the nature of death when He didn't do anything but love us from the start. This is amazing love.

Thus the reason for Calvary. I find it amazing when Christians are stumped over a nonbeliever who says, "How can a loving God send people who have not heard the gospel to hell?" My simple answer is, "It's not His fault, but our own." Jesus paid the terrible price to free mankind and afterward told us who already understood this good news to go into the entire world and tell those who hadn't heard that we have been redeemed from our curse, which we brought upon ourselves and upon all creation. We will have to give an account for our generation; God has done His part!

WE TAKE ON GOD'S NATURE

Not only is the judgment of our sins paid for by Jesus, but we take on a new nature which is in the likeness of God's, no longer a slave to sin. When a person gives his life entirely to Jesus he becomes a brand new Creation.

> When someone becomes a Christian, he becomes a brand new person inside. He is not the same anymore. A new life has begun!
>
> 2 CORINTHIANS 5:17, TLB

We literally die when we receive Jesus Christ as Lord. Our old nature is put to death; crucified with Christ in God's eyes. A brand new person with the nature of God is born. Thus we are born again. Now we are free from the nature that once dictated our lives. As Scripture clearly shows, "And just as Christ was raised from the dead by the glorious power of the Father, now we also may live new lives. . . . Our old sinful selves were crucified with Christ so that sin might lose its power in our lives. We are no longer slaves to sin. For when we died with Christ we were set free from the power of sin" (Rom. 6:4, 6-8, NLT). We now can live according to Christ's nature, not the one we were bound to due to Adam's treason.

It is complete ignorance for a Christian to disdain an individual who has not received Jesus as their Master for his or her lifestyle. This person's spiritual DNA is to sin, and that is just what he does. What is freaky and completely unnatural is a "believer" who habitually or willfully sins. The reason I put *believer* in quotes is a person who practices sin may declare Jesus as his Savior and Lord but in reality He is not; for if He truly were, that person would manifest a godly nature in his life. Jesus made this clear by saying:

> Different kinds of fruit trees can quickly be identified by examining their fruit. A variety that produces delicious fruit never produces an inedible kind. And a tree producing an inedible kind can't produce what is good. So the trees having the inedible fruit are chopped down and thrown on the fire. Yes, the way to identify a tree or a person is by the kind of fruit produced.
>
> MATTHEW 7:17-20, TLB

What He states is not complex and definitely unalterable. The cause is not the fruit, but the nature of tree; however, it shows up at the fruit level. If you approach a bush that contains healthy blueberries, you know it is a bush that is good for food. On the other hand, if you find poisonous berries, it is not a good bush. The proof, or evidence, that a tree is good or poisonous is by the kind of fruit it produces. Even so, Jesus says the way to identify if a person is a genuine Christian is not by what they say, how religious they may seem, or how often they attend Christian gatherings, but rather by what they do! Is their fruit selfless and Kingdom focused, or is it selfish and focused on the world, such as the Apostle John describes in his letter:

> Don't love the world's ways. Don't love the world's goods. Love of the world squeezes out love for the Father. Practically everything that goes on in the world—wanting your own way, wanting everything for yourself, wanting to appear important—has nothing to do with the Father. It just isolates you from him. The world and all its wanting, wanting, wanting is on the way out—but whoever does what God wants is set for eternity.
>
> I JOHN 2:15-17, MES

It took Lisa and me a long time to convince our children of this. They would attend Christian schools and observe numerous classmates who regularly attend church with their parents and professed to be Christians but were habitually producing self-gratifying fruit, as seen in the above Scripture, rather than Christlike fruit. These classmates lived lives for themselves rather than seeking and delighting in doing the will of God. Our children's situation at school is only one of countless examples I could give. This problem is found in homes, the business world, even churches and ministries. There are many who confess to being Christians yet produce fruit that clearly indicates otherwise.

THE TYPICAL "CONVERSION"

The gospel we've preached has been lopsided with emphasis placed on accepting Jesus by praying a sinner's prayer. We confess

Him as "Lord," and once done we are saved eternally. Yet this is not what Jesus teaches. He says, "Not everyone who says to me, 'Lord, Lord,' will enter the kingdom of heaven" (Matt. 7:21, NIV).

If we would just listen to His statement without filtering it through years of unbalanced preaching, teaching, writing, and singing on the grace of God, we would see it contradicts our modern gospel. His words couldn't be clearer—not everyone who has prayed the sinner's prayer, confessing Him as their Lord, is going to heaven. And if they are not going to heaven, there is only one alternative, which we saw last chapter.

Let's rehearse a typical evangelistic service. The preacher preaches a "come to Jesus and get 'blessings'" message. He tells how Jesus will give us joy, peace, prosperity, happiness, health, heaven, and so forth. Don't get me wrong. It's God's desire to bless us, but Jesus never used the blessing to entice people to follow Him. Then after the forty-five-minute-or-so sales pitch, he then asks the audience to bow their heads and asks if they were to die tonight would they go to heaven? He even encourages everyone to look to the person to their left and right and ask the same question in order to help recruit them. "If they can't say yes," he says next, "take them by the hand and bring them forward."

As the candidates come forward, songs are sung, such as "Just as I Am." In other variations, the audience just claps and smiles with the instruments playing a jubilant tune for their march forward.

Once all are up front, the minister asks them to bow their heads and repeat a common prayer such as, "Father, I confess I am a sinner, forgive me of my sin. This day I ask Jesus into my life as my Lord and Savior. Thank You for making me Your child. In Jesus' name, Amen."

The audience cheers, the music plays, and the new "converts" go back to their seats, "just as they were." Except now they are deceived. Nothing has been said concerning repentance from disobedient lifestyles, denying their own desires in order to embrace the will of God, and losing their lives for the cause of Christ. They've confessed Jesus as their "Lord," but there's been no heart change. Jesus is now just a part of their lives. Well let me inform you, the King of kings and Lord of lords doesn't come into anyone's life as second, or even first, among rival lovers. He only comes in as our complete and total King with no person, thing, or activity vying for His place in our hearts. He must be Lord, which means Supreme Master and Owner; meaning we don't own our lives any longer.

Think of it, would you marry someone who informed you that they would be loyal to you along with their other lovers but that you would be first? How much more the King of the universe? Will He accept a bride who says, "You are first of all my other lovers?" There is no covenant relationship, no joining together as one. What deception!

These "new converts" have not allowed the Cross to slay their self-seeking life and make room for the new nature of Jesus to be formed within. They've just been sold on a better life here and the promise of heaven. It's interesting, in many countries of the world where Christians are persecuted, they come to Jesus knowing they are losing their lives. Today in Western societies we come to Jesus for a better life and Heaven. But we must lose our lives as well.

Today, many typical Evangelicals in our society live in deception as a result of the type of gospel we've preached. New converts may be energized by their newfound "faith," participate in Christian activities, attend church, even get involved in an outreach because it is all fresh and exciting. It's like being in a new club, trying a new sport, attending a new school, or working a new job. There's freshness about it, but they have not done what Jesus commanded all true followers to do, which is to count the cost of following Him and then make the permanent decision to pay the price of their lives given to His service (see Luke 14:27-33).

LOSS FOR GAIN

It's an exchange; we must give our entire life, and in place of it we get His life (nature). Jesus repeatedly communicates this:

> If anyone intends to come after Me, let him deny himself [forget, ignore, disown, and lose sight of himself and his own interests] and take up his cross, and [joining Me as a disciple and siding with My party] follow with Me [continually, cleaving steadfastly to Me].
>
> MARK 8:34, AMP

We are to continually cleave steadfastly to Him. It's not just a one-time prayer and then life as usual except that you are now in the "born again" club and are heaven bound. Jesus continues, "If you try to keep your life for yourself, you will lose it. But if you give up your life for my sake and for the sake of the Good News, you will find true life" (Mark 8:35, NLT). The *Amplified Bible* states it this way: "Whoever gives up his life [which is lived only on earth] for My sake and the Gospel's will save it [his higher, spiritual life in the eternal kingdom of God]."

It's a definitive exchange; we give up our rights as owners of our lives in order to follow His desires, and in return we receive His eternal life. With the gospel that is preached today, we've not emphasized this extremely important aspect of following Jesus; we've only told the benefits. In essence, we've preached the *resurrection promises* without preaching the *impact and decision of the Cross*.

It could be compared to a young man who sees a military recruiting commercial on television. He observes a classy naval man near his age dressed in a sharp uniform on the deck of a remarkable ship sailing the open seas with a beautiful crystal sky, smiling with his mates. The commercial then shows this sailor in ports all over the world, and it's all free. The young man immediately goes to the recruiter and signs up. He doesn't read the conditions of joining because he's so focused on the benefits. He is so happy; now he'll have a blast seeing the world, becoming a part of a great military, and making lots of new friends.

However, he quickly finds out in basic training that he can't sleep in till nine o'clock in the morning, as was his custom. He is ordered to cut his cherished long hair. He can't go to many social gatherings because he can't leave base except for a couple days per month. Worse of all, he is on a regimented schedule that doesn't allow time to hang out. All the while, he's cleaning bathrooms and mess halls and doing pushups and other difficult training exercises. He's lost the abundant leisure time he once had and is collapsing in bed each night from exhaustion. He's still hopeful, as he knows he'll soon be on the ship. Once basic training is over, he's assigned to a ship, but it's just as labor intensive, only now it is on the open seas. War breaks out, and now he finds himself fighting a battle for which he didn't sign up.

He enlisted because it was a life he never could have provided for himself, and it was free. Yes, it was free, but he didn't make note of the details at the recruiter's office that it would cost him all his freedoms. In many ways he's now offended. He feels cheated; in his eyes, he was sold a package that showed him only the benefits but didn't make known the personal cost.

We've preached a gospel that speaks of a free salvation, which is absolutely accurate, but we've neglected to tell candidates it would cost them their freedom. When I speak of freedom, it isn't real, but perceived liberty, for all those outside of Christ are bound to sin. They are slaves even though they may fully believe they're free. It could be compared to the movie *The Matrix*. My oldest son rented the edited version of this movie one evening and showed it to our family, and I saw an amazing parallel.

An interesting question is posed in *The Matrix*: "How would you know the difference between the dream world and the real world if you didn't wake from the dream?"[1] In this film, twentieth-century life flows on as normal, or so it seems. Late in the 21st century, man develops artificial intelligence (referred to simply as the Machines). These Machines take control of Earth, and man fights back. In the resulting power struggle, the world is decimated and the Machines are victorious. These machines discover they can manage to survive using electricity generated by the human body, so they create a grand illusion to fool humans into serving them. The world "seems" to still be normal (twentieth century), but in fact the bodies of humans are contained in chambers on large "farms" and their minds are linked into a worldwide virtual reality computer program called the Matrix. So, in essence, the freedom of their lives isn't real; rather, they are slaves.

It's at this point that the film opens with a select group of men and women who have hacked their way out of the Matrix, discovering their true identity. They form a colony called Zion in the real world (which is otherwise lifeless). A few of them re-enter the Matrix to battle the Machines and set humanity free. The battle is intense and life is not easy; but the crusaders are more interested in genuine freedom rather than living a lie of false liberty. They would rather have liberty with difficulty than slavery with deceptive comfort.

Here we see the parallel. Many nonbelievers see Christians as slaves, in bondage, losing freedoms, while they themselves are free. However, the truth is that those outside of Christ are the ones bound, not unlike those living a lie in the "farms" enslaved by a machine. They are slaves to sin.

DIFFICULT TO BE A CHRISTIAN

Not only are those who've never heard, or refuse to believe the gospel in bondage, but many typical "converts" of this generation are in bondage as well. We've created this dilemma by neglecting to proclaim the cost of following Jesus. Many assume they are free but in reality aren't and the evidence is in their lifestyles. Jesus says:

I assure you, most solemnly I tell you, whoever commits and practices sin is the slave of sin. Now a slave does not remain in a household permanently (forever); the son [of the house] does remain forever. So if the Son liberates you [makes you free men], then you are really and unquestionably free.

John 8:34-36, AMP

These words reiterate the truth of the fruit tree. If someone habitually sins, then he is a slave to it. He is not a son, for his true nature hasn't changed. He may think he is free because he confessed a sinner's prayer, yet he has not freely given up his "rights" in order to follow Jesus. He still wants his freedoms (the counterfeit) along with the benefits of salvation. You cannot have both!

As stated earlier, they may start out their "born again experience" with joy, excitement and passion because it's fresh and new. However, eventually their unchanged nature will manifest, but it will manifest in Christian circles and be cloaked in an Evangelical language and lifestyle. This is why it is most deceptive. Yet the New Testament warns specifically of this deception; Paul writes, "In the last days it is going to be very difficult to be a Christian" (2 Tim 3:1, TLB).

We are living in the last days. There is no question about it; all prophetic Scriptures reveal Jesus is soon to return. Paul foresaw our day as being the most difficult time period to be a Christian. Other translations use the words *perilous* and *terrible* in describing our times. Why is this? In examining Paul's days, we see he encountered great opposition. He received thirty-nine stripes on his back from whippings on five different occasions; three separate times he was beaten with rods; once he was stoned; and he spent years in prison. He met up with amazing persecution everywhere he turned. Yet he says our days will be more difficult to be a Christian! Why? He gives the reason:

People will be lovers of themselves, lovers of money, boastful, proud, abusive, disobedient to their parents, ungrateful, unholy, without love, unforgiving, slanderous, without self-control, brutal, not lovers of the good, treacherous, rash, conceited, lovers of pleasure rather than lovers of God.

2 TIMOTHY 3:2-4, NIV

In examining his statement, you may still wonder what point he's trying to make. How does this list differ any from his day? People in his society had all these traits; they loved themselves, money, were unholy, unforgiving, etc. Peter even said on the day of Pentecost, "Be saved from this crooked (perverse, wicked, unjust) generation" (Acts 2:40, AMP). So why is Paul singling out our generation to have these traits causing it to be the most difficult time to be a Christian? He goes on to give the reason: "For [although] they hold a form of piety (true religion), they deny and reject and are strangers to the power of it [their conduct belies the genuineness of their profession]" (2 Tim. 3:5, AMP). The NKJV states, "Having a form of godliness but denying its power."

So you can see what makes it difficult to be a Christian in our generation; there will be many (according to other references in the New Testament) who profess being *Christian, born again*, or *saved* who will not have allowed the Cross to slay their self life. They'll not have made the decision to forsake all their own rights to follow Jesus. They'll sincerely believe He is their Savior, but they'll affiliate with Him for the mere fact of what can He do for them, rather than who He is. It's no different than a woman marrying a man for his money. She may marry him for love, but for the wrong reasons. Out of this motive they'll seek Him for the sake of salvation and success in this life and believe sincerely that He is their Savior, but they will have never relinquished control of their own lives.

BLURRED LINES

The difficulty is found in the lines being blurred. Let's look at a person who is self-seeking but who confesses the born again experience, talks the language of a true believer, makes friends with the godly and is even excited about believer's gatherings; yet there is no nature change. So in essence this person is unknowingly an impostor, and the difficulty arises in the fact that his self-deception spreads like a disease. Others base their lives off of the "norm" in the Christian culture, and this "norm" is out of sync with heaven, thus making it hard to be a true believer. In Paul's day, if you were a believer your life was in jeopardy every hour. There was no question about it—if you gave your allegiance to Jesus, you put your life on the line. Paul continues:

> But you know what I teach, Timothy, and how I live, and what my purpose in life is. You know my faith and how long I have suffered. You know my love and my patient endurance. You know how much persecution and suffering I have endured. You know all about how I was persecuted in Antioch, Iconium, and Lystra—but the Lord delivered me from all of it. Yes, and everyone who wants to live a godly life in Christ Jesus will suffer persecution. But *evil people* and *impostors* will flourish. They will go on *deceiving others*, and *they themselves will be deceived.*
>
> 2 TIMOTHY 3:10-13, NLT (EMPHASIS MINE)

Paul made it clear. It wasn't only what he taught, but what he lived and his purpose in life (eternally driven, which we will get to later in this book) that proved Timothy could trust him. It wasn't his answered prayers, supernatural gifts producing the miraculous, or his excellent ability to teach the Word of God. No, it was not these traits he pointed to. It was his lifestyle. It was, and still is to be, the determining factor.

He continued by saying *"evil people* and *impostors"* will flourish. Now we all know to stay clear from an evil person; however, it's impostors, those who assume an outward identity that does not match their true nature, who are the most dangerous. They are the ones who profess and have a form of Christianity, but there is no evidence of the life changing power of grace. Notice Paul says that they will not only deceive others, but they themselves will be deceived.

This perfectly describes Deceived in our allegory. This young man was active at the School of Endel, professed to be a devout follower, and sincerely believed he was in good standing with the king. He put more emphasis on his professed allegiance than a life that revealed his loyalty. Not only was he deceived, but he deceived others. Due to the standards Deceived set, many were compromised, from the girls he slept with to the many he influenced by his *message* within the student body.

You ask, *Message? He wasn't a teacher.* Oh yes, I mean *message*, for how we live communicates much louder than what we speak. For those students in Endel who were true to Jalyn, it was a battle to not be influenced by the strong personality and lifestyle of Deceived. Those who didn't stand strong succumbed to his influence.

This is a battle not only Paul warned us about but so did many other writers of the New Testament. Jude tells us,

> My dear friends, I was doing my best to write to you about the salvation we share in common, when I felt the need of writing at once to encourage you to fight on for the faith which once and for all God has given to his people.
>
> JUDE 3, TEV

Notice the urgency in his voice. He wanted to discuss the wonderful things we share in salvation, but he had to write about something different. He had to encourage them to fight, battle, and wage war for the faith. What is the fight? He explains by saying:

> For some godless people have *slipped in unnoticed among us*, persons who distort the message about the grace of our God in order to excuse their immoral ways, and who reject Jesus Christ, our only Master and Lord. Long ago the Scriptures predicted the condemnation they have received.
>
> JUDE 4, TEV (EMPHASIS MINE)

The war is against the influences created by people who have perverted the grace of God in order to excuse their ungodly lifestyles. These assaults are more deadly than all-out persecution against the church. They're more dangerous than laws against biblical principles such as abortion and the requirement for schools to teach evolution. They're a stronger influence than any cult or false religion. They're eternally fatal!

You might ask how this applies to people in church because the people Jude references reject or deny Jesus Christ. No one could do that in our churches today and still be accepted as Christians. What would make you think they were more vulnerable in those days? Look again carefully. These people slip into our circles *unnoticed*. No one could stand up in our assemblies today or in Jude's day and confess with their mouths their denial of Jesus Christ and still be unnoticed. So how do they renounce Him? The answer is found in another New Testament book. "Such people *claim they know God*, but they *deny him* by the way they live" (Titus 1:16, NLT). They deny Him by their lifestyles, not words. In fact, they claim to know God, they confess Jesus as their Lord, but they communicate otherwise by their works. Remember, they not only deceive others, but they deceive themselves. In other words, with all sincerity they believe they're Christians.

THE TRUE GRACE OF GOD

Jude states these people distort the message of God's grace. This is so prevalent in these final days because our teachings have opened the door to this. We've taught grace as God's blanket of protection for disobedient lifestyles. You can hear this mindset often by many in the church with common statements such as, "I know I'm not living the way I should, but thank God for His grace." This is serious deception. Scripture doesn't teach grace as the big Band-Aid, but rather: *God's empowering presence within to do what truth demands of us.*

Grace has been taught as simply God's unmerited favor. It is indeed His favor and cannot be bought or earned. However, it also empowers us to obey, and the evidence that we've truly received it is our godly lifestyle. Our obedience to His Word confirms grace's reality in our lives. For this reason James says:

> Faith, if it does not have works (deeds and actions of obedience to back it up), by itself is destitute of power (inoperative, dead). But someone will say [to you then], you [say you] have faith, and I have [good] works. Now you show me your [alleged] faith apart from any [good] works [if you can], and I by [good] works [of obedience] will show you my faith. You believe that God is one; you do well. So do the demons believe and shudder.
>
> JAMES 2:17-19, AMP

James identifies a huge gap today in our teaching. We pull Scriptures out such as, "Believe on the Lord Jesus Christ, and you will be saved" (Acts 16:31). If just believing in His existence and that He's the Son of God is all that's required to be saved, then James shows the demons will be saved because they believe. That is ludicrous! To even drive his point home further, James points out that the demons shudder. In other words, the demons fear God more than some who say they have faith but lack corresponding actions of obedience.

The evidence of our truly being saved by the grace of Jesus Christ is that we will have the lifestyle to prove it. This is why John the Apostle states,

> Now *by this we know that we know Him*, if we keep His commandments. He who says, "I know Him," and does not keep His commandments, is a liar, and the truth is not in him. But whoever keeps His word, truly the love of God is perfected in him. By this we know that we are in Him. He who says he abides in Him ought himself also to walk just as He walked.
>
> 1 JOHN 2:3-6 (EMPHASIS MINE)

John clearly states the proof that we do indeed know Jesus Christ is that we keep His commandments. The one who says that he knows Jesus but doesn't keep His word is deceived, a liar, estranged from the truth, even though he confesses with his mouth his knowledge of the word of God. For this reason, John says, "My little children, these things I write to you, so that you *may not sin*. And *if* anyone sins, we have an Advocate with the Father, Jesus Christ the righteous" (1 John 2:1-2).

Notice he does *not* say, "These things I write to you so that when you do sin you have an Advocate." No, the goal is *not* to sin. We've got the power of God's grace so we can set our sights on a life like Christ ("also to walk just as He walked"), for we are free from the control of the nature of disobedience. But if we do succumb to sin, we do have an Advocate. The celebration of the believer is that we now have the ability to serve our God acceptably. "Therefore, since we are receiving a kingdom which cannot be shaken, let us have *grace*, by which we may *serve God acceptably*" (Heb. 12:28, emphasis mine).

There you have it. Grace empowers us to serve God acceptably. Why have we not proclaimed the entire Gospel, just half the story? Yes, salvation is a gift—it cannot be purchased, and it cannot be earned. This is all true. However, we forgot to tell people that the only way to obtain it is to forsake all, lay down our lives confessing His lordship, and in doing this we will be empowered to live in accordance to His nature. Just as Peter wrote:

> Grace and peace be yours in abundance through the knowledge of God and of Jesus our Lord. His *divine power* has given us everything we need for life and godliness through our knowledge of him who called us by his own glory and goodness. Through these he has given us his very great and precious promises, so that through them you may *participate in the divine nature* and escape the corruption in the world caused by evil desires.
>
> 2 PETER 1:2-4, NIV (EMPHASIS MINE)

Notice we've been given *grace* through the knowledge of Jesus Christ and that grace is His *divine power* that gives us everything we need to live in a godly manner, and that godly lifestyle is according to His *divine nature*. Thus we have been redeemed from the corruption that entered the world through Adam, and that corruption has been multiplied by the desires in men contrary to God. Don't let anyone, whether by word or action, discourage you from living in the divine nature imparted into your being. Paul clearly states:

> For the grace of God that brings salvation has appeared to all men. It teaches us to say "No" to ungodliness and worldly passions, and to live self-controlled, upright and godly lives in this present age, while we wait for the blessed hope—the glorious appearing of our great God and Savior, Jesus Christ, who gave himself for us to redeem us from all wickedness and to purify for himself a people that are his very own, eager to do what is good. These, then, are the things you should teach.
>
> TITUS 2:11-15, NIV

The grace of God teaches us to deny all ungodliness and worldly passions and to live a self-controlled, upright, and godly life. Teachers instruct and empower us, and that is exactly what God's grace does in our lives. Notice we are to teach these things. In fact Paul goes on to say, "This is a faithful saying, and these things I want you to affirm *constantly*, that those who have believed in God should be careful to maintain good works (Titus 3:8, emphasis mine).

We are to maintain good works by the power of God's grace in our lives. We didn't have grace before we were saved, nor did the Old Testament saints; this is God's gift to us through Jesus Christ. That is why Jesus tells us that in Old Testament times you were considered a murderer, in danger of hell, if you took someone's physical life. However, under grace, all you have to do is call your brother a fool, be prejudiced, refuse to forgive, or harbor any other form of hatred to be in danger of hellfire (see Matt. 5:21-22). Why? We have the power now to live according to God's nature through the power of grace.

AFFIRM CONSTANTLY

Notice in the above Scripture that we are commanded by the Word of God to affirm or teach these things *constantly*. Did you hear that? I find these things are *rarely* spoken of from pulpits or amongst believers today, let alone continuously. For this reason, we've drifted from the importance of maintaining good works through the grace of God. We in essence are allowing the power that is in us to remain dormant through the lack of belief and acknowledgment. Our faith, which accesses grace, must remain active through verbalizing our beliefs. Paul says, "That the communication of thy faith may become effectual by the acknowledging of every good thing which is in you in Christ Jesus" (Philem. 6, KJV).

If we don't affirm these things constantly, then we will drift away from the truth. This is clearly seen by the writer of Hebrews:

Therefore we must give the more earnest heed to the things we have heard, *lest we drift away*. For if the word spoken through angels proved steadfast, and every transgression and disobedience received a just reward, how shall we escape if we neglect so great a salvation.

HEBREWS 2:1-3 (EMPHASIS MINE)

By affirming these things, constantly we keep before us the urgent matters of eternity that keep us from drifting away. I remember when I used to fish as a boy. While focused on fishing, the boat, if not anchored, would drift unnoticed to us. We'd look up forty-five minutes later and wouldn't even recognize our location. The drifting occurred because we had our mind on other matters, namely fishing. This has been quite costly for some, as there have been many who've been fishing in certain rivers that led to deadly waterfalls. Countless numbers have gone over falls to their death because of drifting away from where they were first positioned.

The same is true with the important matters of eternity. If God says we are to affirm these things constantly, then this should be our emphasis. Why are we not highlighting the power of grace, which gives us the ability to maintain godly lifestyles of obedience? I find that the early church did this. I examined some of the writings of the early church fathers and found they taught things that would almost seem foreign to our teachings today, but they didn't teach contrary to Scripture. The Fathers of the first few centuries believed that works played an essential role in the evidence of our salvation. Let's look at a few examples.

The first man I'll quote is Polycarp (A.D. 69–156), bishop of the church at Smyrna and a companion of the Apostle John. He was arrested in his very old age and burned at the stake. He wrote: "Many desire to enter into this joy (of salvation), knowing that by grace you are saved, not of works."[2] This would be an accepted statement in today's Evangelical circles, as we have stressed the fact that we are not saved by our own good works. However, he also wrote to believers: "He who raised Him up from the dead will also raise us up—if we do His will and walk in His commandments and love what He loves, keeping ourselves from all unrighteousness."[3]

You won't hear this spoken often from our pulpits today. Notice the word "if." We are told we have to do His will and walk in His commandments in order to be raised up in the believer's resurrection. You'll see shortly that this is exactly what Jesus said as well.

The next man I'll quote is Clement of Rome (A.D. 30–100), a companion of the Apostle Paul and Peter and an overseer in the church of Rome. He wrote, "We are not justified by ourselves, nor by our own godliness, or works. But by that faith through which Almighty God has justified all men."[4] This too would be a widely accepted statement in today's circles of Christianity. However, he also wrote to believers, "It is necessary that we be prompt in the practice of good works. For He forewarns us, 'Behold, the Lord comes and His reward is before His face, to render to every man according to his work' (Rom 2:6-10)."[5]

Could this truth be why Paul stated while on trial, "Therefore, King Agrippa, I was not disobedient to the heavenly vision, but declared first to those in Damascus and in Jerusalem, and throughout all the region of Judea, and then to the Gentiles, that they should repent, turn to God, and *do works befitting repentance*"? (Acts 26:19-21, emphasis mine). Since Paul stressed this importance, it seems to follow suit that his companion, Clement of Rome, would do the same.

The next one I'd like to point out is Clement of Alexandria (A.D. 150–200). He was a leader in the church of Alexandria, Egypt, and was in charge of the school of instruction for new believers. He wrote about unbelievers: "Even if they do good works now, it is of no advantage to them after death, if they do not have faith."[6]

This, too, would be heartily cheered among Evangelicals

today. We know, as I've already pointed out in the last few chapters, that no matter how many good works an unbeliever accomplishes, they still cannot gain him entrance into the eternal Kingdom of God; it is by God's grace we are saved. However, look at what else Clement wrote to believers:

> *Whoever obtains the truth and distinguishes himself in good works shall gain the prize of everlasting life . . . some people correctly and adequately understand how God provides necessary power (to be saved), but attaching slight importance to the works that lead to salvation, they fail to make the necessary preparation for attaining the object of their hope.*[7]

Some of you may be thinking, *It sounds like these guys didn't read the New Testament.* But they did. Josh McDowell points out in his book *Evidence that Demands a Verdict*[8] that Clement of Alexandria took 2,400 of his quotes from all but three books in the New Testament. The same is true of the others. I have to say that many books in our Christian bookstores today have very little Scripture in them. Could it be that we have drifted due to the fact that we have not affirmed constantly what is important?

OUR INCOMPLETE GOSPEL

Unfortunately, we only quote such Scriptures as, "If you confess with your mouth the Lord Jesus and believe in your heart that God has raised Him from the dead, you will be saved" (Rom. 10:9). So we tell people all they have to do is quote the magical prayer and they're in. Yet, why don't we also quote Jesus' own words: "But why do you call Me 'Lord, Lord,' and do not do the things which I say?" (Luke 6:46). As we've seen, "Lord" means Supreme Master, it carries the meaning of Ownership. So Jesus is saying, "Don't call me Master and yet still own your own life, better to call me 'Great Prophet' or 'Teacher' so that you do not deceive yourself."

So now let's reexamine Jesus' statement with which we

opened this entire discussion: "Not everyone who says to me, 'Lord, Lord,' will enter the kingdom of heaven" (Matt. 7:21a, NIV).

As we've already stated, not everyone who calls Jesus Christ *Lord* will be in heaven. So that emphatically tells us just saying the "sinner's prayer" doesn't secure us heaven. Then my question is this, "Jesus, who will enter into the kingdom of heaven?" Jesus answers by saying, "But only he who does the will of my Father who is in heaven" (Matt. 7:21b, NIV).

Interesting. These were almost the exact words of Polycarp. So it is not confessing Jesus only, but confessing Jesus and doing the will of God that will get us into heaven. And the only way we can do His will is through the grace He gives us when we humble ourselves by denying our own lives and receiving Him as Lord. It is as simple as confessing, but the difficult part comes in yielding ourselves entirely to the reality of His lordship.

Hear now why I've stressed this point so passionately:

When the Judgment Day comes, many will say to me, "Lord, Lord! In your name we spoke God's message, by your name we drove out many demons and performed many miracles!" Then I will say to them, "I never knew you. Get away from me, you wicked people!"

MATTHEW 7:22-23, TEV

In the late 1980s, God gave me a spiritual vision. I saw a multitude so large you couldn't see the end of it. It was a sea of humanity. I knew there were no atheists in this group, no self-acknowledged sinners, no followers of other religions; rather, all confessed being Christians through the lordship of Jesus. This multitude had come to the Judgment and were fully expecting to hear Jesus say, "Enter into the joy of your Lord; the Kingdom of God." But instead they heard the words, "Depart from Me, you who practice lawlessness" (Matt. 7:23).

I beheld the utter shock and terror upon their faces. Can you imagine feeling secure in a salvation you don't possess? Can you imagine being exiled into the flames of hell forever when you fully believed you were heaven bound? Forever and ever having to deal with the memory that you, and possibly those who preached to you, took your eternal destination so lightly? Is there room for a seeker-friendly ministry that shuns the admonitions of Jesus? Can you understand why we are to proclaim the whole counsel of God, not just the positives or benefits? Yes, we love the benefits, and we should tell them and enjoy them, but not at the expense of neglecting the warnings!

I recall in a conference stating the reason for preaching these truths is that "I don't want anyone screaming at me at the Judgment, 'Why didn't you tell me the truth!', while their blood is dripping off my hands!"

After my session, a pastor immediately approached me quite upset; in fact, he was irate. He said, "How dare you put that Old Testament theology on us ministers. I won't have blood dripping off my hands for not proclaiming the entire gospel." He obviously liked the positive aspects but stayed clear of the confrontational portions of God's Word.

I then said, "Sir, look at what Paul stated to the leaders of Ephesus." Having my Bible in hand I turned to Acts and asked him to read: "Therefore I testify to you this day that I am innocent of the blood of all men. For I have not shunned to declare to you the whole counsel of God" (Acts 20:26-27).

He looked up at me in shock; his eyes and mouth wide open. He said, "All the times I've read the New Testament, I've never noticed this." We then had a friendly conversation. I mentioned that in order to present every human being mature in Christ, we must not only teach, but warn them (see Col 1:28). What is the warning? To not drift away from truth, to not be swayed by the message propagated by impostors who seduce not only themselves but countless others from godliness.

Paul had been with the people of Ephesus for quite some time. He loved them dearly and knew by the Spirit of God he would not see them again until heaven. Think of how carefully you would choose your words knowing they would be your last to those who were like your children. His parting words were:

> Keep watch over yourselves and all the flock of which the Holy Spirit has made you overseers. Be shepherds of the church of God, which he bought with his own blood. I know that after I leave, savage wolves will come in *among* you and will not spare the flock. *Even from your own number* men will arise and distort the truth in order to draw away disciples after them. So be on your guard! Remember that for three years I never stopped warning each of you night and day with tears.
>
> ACTS 20:28-31, NIV

How would they distort the truth? Possibly by words, but most likely by actions. Notice that Paul felt so strongly about this that he didn't stop warning them day and night for three years. Again, we see the emphasis; we are to affirm these things constantly.

GOD OF LOVE AND JUSTICE

In our allegory, you could feel the shock and agony of Deceived. You gasped at the foreboding dungeon of Lone. You cringed thinking, 125 years in the darkness and unbearable heat, a sweatbox of contaminated air. Yet that is nothing compared to what countless men and women will face if we don't proclaim the whole counsel of God.

If you will remember, Jalyn was both loving and just. In his judgment, love was revealed in that he couldn't permit someone who possessed the nature and character of Dagon into the city of Affabel. If he did, he would pervert and contaminate the entire city, including all its inhabitants. His love protected the innocent.

At the same time, he was just in that he couldn't permit someone who had the nature of Dagon to receive a lesser penalty for disobedience than Dagon himself. For this reason, all who did not chose to follow Jalyn had to be exiled to the same dungeon of Lone.

Even so, God's love cannot permit someone who has the nature of Satan into the eternal city forever. He would be unjust to sentence Satan and his cohorts to the eternal Lake of Fire while making exception for those who were under his rule and chose to maintain his nature. All who have his nature will be sentenced with him for eternity in the Lake of Fire. God is, and will continue to be, both merciful and just, and His glory will be known throughout the earth.

Chapter 6

THE GREAT FALLING AWAY

But whoever holds out to the end will be saved.
MATTHEW 24:13, TEV

Now we come to the truths reflected by Double Life and Faint Heart. At one time they truly followed Jalyn but eventually turned from his ways, permanently bringing forth their fatal end.

"READ WHAT WE BELIEVE" OR "BELIEVE WHAT WE READ"

I've discovered some of the truths we'll discuss in this chapter are controversial among some in Evangelical circles; however, the controversy is eliminated upon thorough investigation of Scripture. So before we begin to examine what the Bible reveals concerning Double Life and Faint Heart, let me first of all ask that you would read with an open heart and mind.

One of the greatest hindrances to people coming to know the will of God is the fact that when they read Scripture, they will *read what they believe* rather than *believe what they read*. We read what we believe when we choose to see truth through tainted lenses. This tainting occurs from incorrect knowledge gained from others or taught by our denomination or from our preconceived notions of who God is or of His ways. This is very dangerous because it can lead us into deception.

An example of this is seen in the Book of Job. Recently I picked up my Bible, and before I could open it I heard the Spirit of God say, "Go to the Book of Job and begin reading from the thirty-second chapter."

I turn immediately to this chapter and realized this was the beginning of Elihu's message. After experiencing tragedy, Job's perception of God's ways rapidly deteriorated because of his pain and misfortune. He now viewed God through his experience rather than seeking God for His wisdom (see James 1:2-8). Over time, this reasoning moved toward self-justification. Job's three friends, who spoke in earlier chapters, became errant self-made theologians attempting to interpret Job's tragedies. This made matters even worse. They found no way to refute Job's wayward reasoning, and instead condemned him.

Elihu, as the youngest, waited for a long while to hear God's wisdom from Job's three friends, but when he perceived the three men had nothing more to say, he finally spoke up, saying, "I listened patiently while you were speaking and waited while you searched for wise phrases. I paid close attention and heard you fail; you have not disproved what Job has said. How can you claim you have discovered wisdom? God must answer Job, for you have failed" (Job 32:11-13, TEV).

Elihu proceeded to rebuke all the men. He said, "Must God tailor his justice to your demands?" (Job 34:33, NLT). Oh, how accurately he spoke to the error that is so prevalent with many today. This is one of the main roots of misguided theology in the church; *we allow our experience to interpret the word of God rather than allowing the word of God to establish truth!* Elihu didn't speak human reasoning or theology formed by events or occurrences and preconceived notions of who God was, but rather, without tampering with truth, he spoke the pure Word of God. Once he concluded his sayings we read,

> Then out of the storm the Lord spoke to Job. "Who are you to question my wisdom with your ignorant, empty words? Stand up now like a man and answer the questions I ask you."
>
> JOB 38:1-3, TEV

The *Amplified Bible* records God's question as, "Who is this that darkens counsel by words without knowledge?" This is exactly what we do when we filter God's words through our experience, others' opinions, or preconceived notions of who He is. We darken His counsel, thus making it unavailable to all we influence. We actually hide the truth from those who would seek to know. This is why God was so angry with Job and his friends and is so today when we incorrectly represent His ways. We keep people from knowing the truth! The Lord then spent four chapters revealing His word to Job. Once He is through, Job contritely says:

> I know, Lord, that you are all-powerful; that you can do everything you want. You ask how I dare question your wisdom when I am so very ignorant. I talked about things I did not understand, about marvels too great for me to know. You told me to listen while you spoke and to try to answer your questions. *In the past I knew only what others had told me*, but now I have seen you with my own eyes. So I am ashamed of all I have said and repent in dust and ashes.
>
> JOB 42:2-6, TEV (EMPHASIS MINE)

Notice Job says, "In the past I knew only what others had told me, but now I have seen you with my own eyes." There is a powerful truth in this. Scripture states we are changed from glory to glory as we *behold* Him (see 2 Cor. 3:18), not as we *hear* about Him. He is the living Word of God and to see Him is to know Him, to know His ways. This is what revealed truth does to a person. We hear the word of God, but there is not a change until we are *enlightened*. When the understanding of God's Word enters our hearts, we cry out, "I see, I see"; at that moment we are enlightened and are transformed further toward His likeness.

It is this spiritual fact that motivates Paul to pray, "I . . . do not cease to give thanks for you, making mention of you in my prayers: that the God of our Lord Jesus Christ, the Father of glory, may give to you the spirit of wisdom and revelation in the knowledge of Him, *the eyes of your understanding being enlightened*" (Eph 1:15-18). Job was now enlightened like never before, even though he walked a very godly life prior to his tragedies. Now he knew God on a higher level.

Once God is through speaking to Job He then turns to Eliphaz, one of the friends, and says, "I am angry with you and your two friends, because you did not speak the truth about me" (Job 42:7, TEV).

The Lord does not take it lightly when we represent Him or His ways incorrectly. It darkens counsel and perverts His justice. For this reason I find it strange that men will so quickly speak a theology that is not backed by the overall counsel of Scripture. Oh, how frightening! How can we know the truth if we are not willing to be instructed or corrected by it?

After I finished reading the Book of Job, the Lord then spoke something to me that answered many questions. He said, "Son, did you notice that I did not come on the scene while Job or his friends spoke of Me incorrectly? My presence didn't manifest until someone stood up and spoke the truth!" I was in awe of what God had spoken to my heart, and I began to ponder that. Then I heard Him again say, "This is why so many individuals, churches, or denominations are not experiencing My presence and life-changing power. They are not proclaiming My pure Word, but rather their own filtered interpretations or reasonings, no different than Job or his friends. They are darkening My counsel with their words without knowledge."

If we will know the reality of God's presence and power, we must seek to know truth, without tampering with it. Therefore, as we continue to examine what Scripture reveals of God's judgments, don't allow preconceived notions of God, errant theology, experiences, or circumstances alter what He has already made clear. Instead, seek Him in the revealed Word of God that you may be enlightened to His ways.

FOLLOWING FOR GAIN

Let's first return to Jesus' words we discussed last chapter:

> When the Judgment Day comes, many will say to me, "Lord, Lord! In your name we spoke God's message, by your name we drove out many demons and performed many miracles!" Then I will say to them, "I never knew you. Get away from me, you wicked people!"
>
> MATTHEW 7:22-23, TEV

The NKJV states, " 'I never knew you; depart from Me, you who *practice lawlessness!*' " This version is a closer rendition to the original. The Greek word for *lawlessness* (*anomia*) means acting contrary to the law (or will) of God. Jesus also prefaces lawlessness with the word *practice*, indicating this is not a person who periodically stumbles or even a babe in Christ struggling to be free who hates his disobedience. Rather, this is one who lives contrary to what pleases God, but overlooks it, justifies it, or just plays it off. This applies to the deluded, such as Deceived, or to the unfaithful, such as Double Life. This multitude Jesus addresses will hear proclamations of judgment that will reverberate in their souls throughout eternity in the regions of the damned. It is critically important that we don't overlook or take lightly this warning of the Master.

Let's look a little closer at whom Jesus is talking to in the above Scripture. A portion of those who will be turned away from the Kingdom of God will be those who cast out demons *in the name of Jesus.* Who are these people? Could they be men and women who use the name of Jesus just to cast out demons without any other association with the Lord Jesus? To find our answer, we must look at Acts.

> A team of Jews who were traveling from town to town casting out evil spirits tried to use the name of the Lord Jesus. The incantation they used was this: "I command you by Jesus, whom Paul preaches, to come out!" Seven sons of Sceva, a leading priest, were doing this. But when they tried it on a man possessed by an evil spirit, the spirit replied, "I know Jesus, and I know Paul. But who are you?" And he leaped on them and attacked them with such violence that they fled from the house, naked and badly injured.
>
> ACTS 19:13-16, NLT

It was impossible for these exorcists to cast out a demon in the name of Jesus! There is a truth established in this account: to cast out a devil, it's not enough to have the name only; you have be in relationship with the One who bares it. You have to be a follower and servant of Jesus, unlike those we discussed in the last chapter.

You may now be thinking, *But Jesus said He had never known them; therefore, how could they have cast out devils and done miracles in His name? How can this be?* There are those who genuinely joined themselves with Jesus for the benefits of salvation, but purely out of the motive of personal gain. They never came to know the heart of God; they only wanted His power and blessings. Paul warns these are men who possess "corrupt minds and destitute of the truth, who suppose that godliness is a means of gain. From such withdraw yourself" (1 Tim. 6:5). They sought Jesus for their own benefit, so their service for Him was gain-motivated, not love-motivated. Jesus will not know them, for we read, "But if anyone *loves God*, this one is *known by Him*" (1 Corinthians 8:3, emphasis added).

He is known by God, or God knows him. This word *known* doesn't mean to merely know of someone, for God knows everything about everyone; He is all knowing! Rather, it carries the meaning of intimacy. The *Amplified Bible* brings this out, "But if one loves God truly [with affectionate reverence, prompt obedience, and grateful recognition of His blessing], he is known by God [recognized as worthy of *His intimacy* and love, and he is owned by Him]."

Jesus says to the multitude on Judgment Day, "I never *knew* you." So the ones who don't love God (which is evident because they do not give Him their prompt obedience, affectionate reverence, and gratefulness) are not *known* intimately by the Father or Jesus—even if they have looked to Him for salvation. Loving Jesus means you lay your life down for Him. You no longer live for yourself, but for Him.

Judas is an example. He joined himself with Jesus. It appeared he loved God by the great sacrifice he made to follow Him. Judas left all to join the ministry team and go on the road with the Master. Judas stayed even under the heat of persecution, and even when other staff members left (John 6:66); he didn't quit. He cast out devils, healed the sick, and preached the gospel (see Luke 9:1).

However, Judas' intentions were not right from the start. He never repented of his self-seeking motives. His character was revealed by statements such as: "What are you willing *to give me* if I. . . ." (Matt. 26:14). He lied and flattered to gain advantage (Matt 26:25), took money from the treasury of Jesus' ministry for personal use (John 12:4-6), and the list goes on. He never intimately knew the Lord, even though he spent three and a half years in His presence as a disciple. For this reason, Jesus said of him: "'Did I not choose you, the twelve, and one of you is a devil?' He spoke of Judas Iscariot, the son of Simon" (John 6:70-71).

There are those not unlike Judas who make great sacrifices for the ministry, even casting out devils, healing the sick, preaching the gospel, trusting Him for salvation, but they have never intimately known Jesus, for it was all done out of the motive of self-gain, not for the love of God. This would perfectly describe Double Life in our allegory. He followed Jalyn because he loved the influence and power it gave him. His motives were not out of love for Jalyn right from the start.

For these the greatest condemnation is reserved. Jesus says of Judas, "It would have been good for that man if he had not been born"(Matt. 26:24). He says to the religious leaders who serve God out of the motive of gain and take advantage of people in the name of the Lord, "Therefore you will receive greater condemnation" (Matt 23:14). These men and women, just as Double Life, will find themselves in the darkest and most tormenting places of Hell.

GIVING UP SALVATION

The above perfectly describes Double Life in our allegory. However, what about Faint Heart? She truly had a relationship with Jalyn, yet she didn't endure to the end? Does Scripture reveal this as well? Let's begin with the prophet Ezekiel:

> "But when a *righteous man* turns away from his righteousness and commits iniquity, and does according to all the abominations that the wicked man does, shall he live? All the righteousness which he has done shall *not be remembered*; because of the unfaithfulness of which he is guilty and the sin which he has committed, because of them he shall *die*."
>
> EZEKIEL 18:24 (EMPHASIS MINE)

First and foremost, God is addressing a *righteous* man, not one who *thought* he was righteous but never was. There is no doubt that this person is not the same as the deceived or impostor we discussed previously.

God says He will *not remember* any of his righteousness. When God forgets something, it is as if it never happened. We speak about God forgetting our sin, putting it as far as the east is from the west, and burying it in the sea of forgetfulness, which He certainly does. For He states, " 'Their sins and their lawless deeds I will remember no more' " (Heb. 8:12). God forgets our sins once we receive Jesus as Lord. The devil tries to accuse us, but God said He will remember them no more. So in His mind, it is as though we have never sinned. Well, the converse is also true. When God says a man's righteousness will not be remembered, He means He will forget He once knew him, as the relationship is terminated.

Let's now closely examine what Scripture states concerning a believer permanently walking away from their salvation. The Apostle James writes:

> *Brethren*, if anyone among you *wanders* from the truth, and someone turns him back, let him know that he who turns a sinner from the error of his way will save a soul from *death* and cover a multitude of sins.
>
> JAMES 5:19-20 (EMPHASIS MINE)

The first point to notice is found in the words, "*Brethren*, if anyone among *you*." James is not talking to people who just think they are Christians. He is speaking of a *believer* who wanders from the way of truth. In this passage, a brother who wanders from the truth is called a *sinner*. This doesn't mean he is now no longer born again; rather, he is in habitual sin and needs to return to obedience. However, if he persists in his wandering ways, James makes it clear the result will ultimately be death to the soul (a lost soul), if there is no turning back to God (repentance). Proverbs confirms this by saying: "A man who *wan-*

ders out of the way of understanding shall abide in the congregation of the spirits (of the dead)" (Prov. 21:16, AMP, emphasis mine).

Proverbs confirms James' words by showing the final abode of a man or woman who *wanders* from the ways of God without turning back to righteousness is the assembly of the dead, which is Hades, and eventually the Lake of Fire.

THE BOOK OF LIFE

The Book of Life is mentioned eight times in the New Testament. Paul and John show us that all who will spend eternity with Jesus are recorded in this book. Our names are written in it the moment we are born again. Recall Efrosyni's testimony from chapter 4. Once this young Greek girl gave her life to Jesus, God the Father wrote her name in the Book of Life and said to her in the vision, "Welcome to the family!" Paul writes to a fellow believer, "And I ask you, my true teammate, to help these women, for they worked hard with me in telling others the Good News. And they worked with Clement and the rest of my co-workers, whose names are written in the Book of Life" (Phil 4:3, NLT).

The converse is true; all those who are not recorded in the Book of Life are lost. Hear what the book of Revelations states: "Anyone not found written in the Book of Life was cast into the lake of fire" (Rev. 20:15).

John emphatically tells us the only people who will be admitted into the eternal city of God are "only those who are written in the Lamb's Book of Life" (Rev. 21:27); the rest will find themselves in the assembly of the dead.

In Revelation 3, Jesus speaks to a church—not a city, a group of lost people, or worshippers of false gods. No, he spoke to those who are truly His, and warns: "He who overcomes shall be clothed in white garments, and I will not *blot out* his name from the Book of Life" (Rev. 3:5, emphasis mine). The *Amplified Bible* records His words, "I will not *erase* or *blot out* his name from the Book of Life" (emphasis mine). Did you notice the word *erase*? The only way to have your name *erased* from the Book of Life is for it to originally be there. Only those who have been truly born again through faith in Jesus Christ are recorded in the Book of Life. The unbelievers and even the deceived, who never truly walked with Jesus, were never written in this book, so their names cannot be blotted out. He is speaking to those "in the family."

A SOBERING VISION

Kenneth E. Hagin was miraculously healed of a fatal disease at the age of sixteen and afterward served faithfully in ministry for close to seventy years before his departure in 2003. His influence in the Body of Christ is monumental, with his books numbering over 65 million in print and his school, Rhema Bible Institute, graduating over 24,000 to this date. He wrote on this subject in his book *I Believe in Visions*. He records in 1952 that Jesus appeared to him to reveal truths of Scripture. In the vision, the Lord showed him a pastor's wife with whom he was familiar. She had come to believe a lie that her abilities and beauty were being wasted in ministry. Over time she entertained the thoughts of the fame, popularity, and wealth she could have in the world. She eventually gave in, left her husband, and went out searching for the success she desired.

The Lord specifically said to Brother Hagin, *"This woman was a child of Mine";* and then instructed Kenneth *not* to pray for her. The following is taken directly from his book:

"Lord, what will happen to her?" I asked.

"She will spend eternity in the regions of the damned, where there is weeping and gnashing of teeth," He answered. And in the vision I saw her go down into the pit of hell. I heard her awful screams.

"This woman was your child, Lord. She was filled with Your Spirit and had part in the ministry. Yet You said not to pray for her. I cannot understand this!"

The Lord reminded me of the following Scripture: "If any man sees his brother sin a sin which is not unto death, he shall ask, and he shall give him life for them that sin not unto death. There is a sin unto death; I do not say that he shall pray for it" (1 John 5:16).

I said, "But Lord I always believed that the sin referred to in this Scripture is physical death, and that the person is saved although he has sinned."

"But that Scripture doesn't say physical death," the Lord pointed out. "You are adding something to it. If you will read the entire fifth chapter of First John, you will see that it is talking about life and death—spiritual life and spiritual death—and this is spiritual death. This refers to a believer who can sin a sin unto death, and therefore I say that you shall not pray for it. I told you not to pray for this woman because she sinned a sin unto death."

"This really disrupts my theology, Lord. Would you explain some more?" I asked. (Sometimes we need our theology disrupted if it is not in line with the Word.)

Jesus reminded me of the following Scripture: Hebrews 6:4-6 (KJV)

4 For it is impossible for those who were once enlightened, and have tasted of the heavenly gift, and were made partakers of the Holy Ghost,

5 And have tasted the good word of God, and the powers of the world to come,

6 If they shall fall away, to renew them again unto repentance; seeing they crucify to themselves the Son of God afresh, and put him to an open shame.[1]

There are certain qualifications listed in the above Scripture to note. First, a person must be enlightened and have tasted the heavenly gift. This would apply to those who have received Jesus, as He is the heavenly gift. Second, he is filled with the Holy Spirit. Third, he has tasted the good Word of God and the powers of the world to come. This would include the gifts of the Spirit, the anointing of God, etc. From this list we can see this would not include baby Christians, but seasoned believers.

I've had several people come up to me in the past in tears saying that they at one time told the Lord they didn't want to serve Him any longer. Later they felt deep remorse and repented. They experienced great fear when encountering this Scripture and a few others in their Bibles. However, infants sometimes do stupid things in ignorance, and the Lord knows that. The writer of Hebrews is not talking about a babe in Christ, but one who is mature.

To continue ministering comfort to these troubled souls, I tell them if they did commit the sin unto death (as seen in the above Scripture), they wouldn't have a desire to come back into sweet fellowship with Jesus. The very facts they hungered for Him and did indeed repent, accompanied by godly fruit, meant the Holy Spirit drew them back into fellowship. There would be no desire for intimacy with Jesus or to live a holy life if they permanently walk away as this woman in Brother Hagin's vision.

Jesus said this woman was truly a child of God. As a boy, Brother Hagin was raised in a denomination in which many do not believe a person can walk away from their salvation; they believe in unconditional eternal security. This is why he said, "This really disrupts my theology." As a child of God, her name was written in the Book of Life. She did not endure, but permanently returned to the world; therefore, her name was blotted out. She chose to walk away for good. For this reason the writer of Hebrews tells us that it was impossible for a person like this to be restored. She was now *twice dead*. She was once dead in sins, then inherited eternal life, but died in sin again in permanently walking away (see Jude 12).

Once a person comes to this state, they can never again be

reborn. For this reason the writer of Hebrews says it is "impossible . . . to renew them again unto repentance." So it's quite erroneous to think we can have situations in which people are born again again.

Again, let me reiterate, if a person commits this sin, they wouldn't have a desire to repent and live all out for Jesus ever again. For no one can draw us to Jesus except the Holy Spirit, and once He departs a true believer as a result of their apostasy, such as the woman Brother Hagin described above, He will not return. For this reason the Holy Spirit is longsuffering. He will not give up easily.

THE BLACKNESS OF DARKNESS

The Apostle Peter gives us further light: "For if, after they have escaped the pollutions of the world through the knowledge of the Lord and Savior Jesus Christ . . ." (2 Pet. 2:20).

First, let's examine whom Peter addresses. If someone has escaped the pollutions of the world through the knowledge of the Lord and Savior Jesus Christ, this would undoubtedly make them a Christian. They would not fall under the category of impostors discussed in the previous chapter—those who profess to know God but in reality don't—but rather these have truly escaped the corruption of this world through the saving grace of the Lord Jesus. There is no doubt he is addressing people who have truly been born again.

Continuing we read:

> . . . They are again entangled in them and *overcome*, the latter end is worse for them than the beginning. For it would have *been better* for them not to have known *the way of righteousness*, than having known it, to turn from the holy commandment delivered to them. But it has happened to them according to the true proverb: "A dog

returns to his own vomit," and, "a sow, having washed, to her wallowing in the mire."

2 PETER 2:20-22 (EMPHASIS MINE)

Peter is addressing Christians who return to the ways of the world, but notice he adds that they are *overcome* by its pollutions. To be overcome means they did not return; they never repented of their willful lawlessness. Peter states that it would have been better for them never to have known the *way of righteousness* than to have known it and turned from the way of the Lord. In other words, God is saying it is better never to have gotten saved than to receive the gift of eternal life and then permanently turn from it. This goes closely in line with what Ezekiel said: "All the *righteousness* which he has done shall *not be remembered.*"

Why would it have been better to have never known the way of righteousness? Jude answers this. As with Peter, Jude also addresses those who walk away from their salvation. He states: "Woe to them! For they have gone in the way of Cain, have run greedily in the error of Balaam for profit, and perished in the rebellion of Korah (Jude 11). Cain, Balaam, and Korah all at one time had a relationship with the Lord, and two of them were ministers. Cain's error was disobedience to God; Balaam's was the love of money; and Korah's was rebellion to delegated authority.

Jude continues:

These are spots in your love feasts, while they feast with you *without fear, serving only themselves;* they are clouds without water, carried about by the winds; late autumn trees without fruit, *twice dead,* pulled up by the roots; raging waves of the sea, foaming up their own shame; wandering stars for whom is reserved the blackness of darkness forever.

JUDE 12-13 (EMPHASIS MINE)

Love feasts were evening meals in the early church, during which members came together as an expression of their close relationship with God and with one another. The love feast usually ended with the sacrament of Holy Communion.[2] We now learn a most sobering fact: Not all who walk away from salvation will leave the organized church, as did the woman in Brother Hagin's vision. This makes them most dangerous because their influence on the babes, weak in conscience, and wounded can be fatal.

Korah would be an example of this type of person. He was an associate minister to Aaron, but said to both Moses and Aaron, "You have gone too far! Everyone in Israel has been set apart by the Lord, and *he is with all of us*. What right do you have to act as though you are greater than anyone else among all these people of the Lord?" (Num. 16:3, NLT). His influence caused the judgment of death to come upon 250 leaders and 14,700 congregation members!

Jude tells us these apostates, referred to as *spots*, remain in our congregations with a false sense of security in a grace they once walked but have now perverted in living to serve themselves and have lost the fear of God. (Notice that Korah said God was "with all of us." He too walked in a false sense of security, for the next day the earth opened up and swallowed him alive into hell.) Consequently, these apostates will still know the language of a Christian and hang out with other believers, but you will not find them among the overcomers Jesus is returning for. He is coming for a church without *spot* (see Eph 5:27).

Jude points out these people are *twice dead*. How can you die twice? Could it be that you were once dead in sin, then received eternal life through new birth, but tragically died again through persistent unrepentant sin? Remember James stated that the Christian who wanders from the truth and remains in that state, his soul shall *die*. John says there is a sin unto death for believers. Both refer to one who is *twice dead*.

Notice Jude states, "For whom is reserved *the blackness of darkness forever*." The *blackness of darkness* means the worst eternal punishment. This is clearly seen in Jesus' words discussing His coming and judgment. He says:

> Blessed are those servants whom the master, when he comes, will find watching. . . . But if that *servant* says in his heart, "*My master* is delaying his coming," and begins to beat the menservants and maidservants, and to eat and drink and be drunk, the master of that servant will come on a day when he is not looking for him, and at an hour when he is not aware, and will cut him in two and appoint him his portion with the *unbelievers*. And that servant who *knew his master's will,* and did not prepare himself or do according to his will, shall be *beaten with many stripes*. But he who did not know, yet committed things deserving of stripes, shall be *beaten with few*.
>
> LUKE 12:37, 45-48 (EMPHASIS MINE)

There is so much in these verses. Let me just point out a few highlights. First of all, notice this is a *servant*, not a heathen or sinner. He *knew his master's will*, yet did the contrary. This would not speak of Independent; he would fall under the category of those who did not know and were beaten with *few stripes*. It couldn't apply to Deceived either, for Deceived thought he was a servant, but according to Jalyn, he was never a true servant. This person Jesus refers to is called a *servant* by the Master, and he fully understood his master's will. He is one who walked away from his salvation.

Notice that he beat fellow servants. This speaks of a lifestyle of taking advantage of others for your good or pleasure. He now lives for the day. He is eating, drinking, getting drunk; he lives to serve himself. Recall Jude states that these apostates feast with other believers without the fear of God and serve only themselves. All their decisions, even if they look noble, are for their advantage.

Concerning this servant's judgment, notice he was appointed

or sent to where the unbelievers (those never saved) were, and the unbelievers only received *few stripes*, but the servant who knew his master's will was beaten with *many stripes*. Thus showing he shall receive the greatest condemnation of the Lake of Fire or the blackness of darkness forever!

BITTER UNFORGIVENESS

This would certainly apply to Faint Heart (along with Double Life). Faint Heart knew it was the will of Jalyn to forgive, yet she refused. She chose to hold fast to the offense of Slander. Her bitterness opened the door to her defilement. For this reason we read, "Looking carefully lest anyone fall short of the grace of God; lest any root of bitterness springing up cause trouble, and by this many become defiled (Heb. 12:15). In both searching Scriptures of the New Testament and through years of experience in the ministry, I've come to learn the greatest trap for pulling people away from their walk with God is unforgiveness. As with Faint Heart, it opens the door to all kinds of other errant beliefs and behavior.

In Matthew 18, Jesus tells a parable of a great king in process of settling accounts. One was brought to him who owed him ten thousand talents. A talent was not a measure of money, but a measure of weight. It was used to measure gold (2 Sam. 12:30), silver (1 Kings 20:39), and other metals and commodities. In this parable it represents a debt, so we can safely assume He was referring to a unit of exchange such as gold or silver. Let's assume gold.

The common talent was equivalent to roughly 75 pounds. It was the full weight that a man could carry (2 Kings 5:23). Ten thousand talents would be approximately 750,000 pounds, or 375 tons. So this servant owed the king 375 tons of gold. At the time of this book, the price of gold is roughly $420.00 an ounce. So put the math to it. In today's market, ten thousand talents of gold would be worth $5 billion! This is how much this servant owed the king! The point Jesus emphasizes here is that this servant owed an overwhelming debt he could never pay.

The king commanded that he and his family be sold and payment made toward the debt. The man fell at the king's feet and pleaded for mercy, which the king granted. He forgave the entire debt. When harm is done, there is a debt owed. You have heard it said, "He'll pay for this." Forgiveness is the cancellation of a debt. This man was now forgiven of the unpayable debt. So you can see in the allegory the king represents God the Father and the man forgiven of the debt represents someone who has received His forgiveness through Jesus Christ.

However, we read, "But that servant went out and found one of his fellow servants who owed him a hundred denarii; and he laid hands on him and took him by the throat, saying, 'Pay me what you owe!'" (Matt. 18:28).

A denari is a common wage of one day. Let's assume $75.00 in today's money. So the total would be approximately $7,500.00. So you can see this is not a small offense.

Now continue to read: "So his fellow servant fell down at his feet and begged him, saying, 'Have patience with me, and I will pay you all.' And he would not, but went and threw him into prison till he should pay the debt" (Matt. 18:29–30).

A fellow servant owes him $7,500, but this man, who has been forgiven of $5 billion dollars, will not release his fellow servant; he is determined to make him pay. It is important to note the offenses we hold against each other compared with our original offense against God is comparable to a $7,500 debt stacked up against a $5 billion one! No matter how badly you've been treated by another, it does not compare with our transgressions against God. You may feel no one has it as bad as you have. You don't realize how badly Jesus was treated. He was innocent, a blameless lamb that was slain and took our $5 billion debt!

A person who cannot forgive has forgotten how great a debt they were forgiven! When you realize the great death and eternal torment Jesus delivered you from, you will freely release others.

There is nothing worse than eternity in a lake of fire. There is no relief, the worm does not die, and the fire is not quenched. That was our destination until God forgave us through the death of His Son Jesus Christ! If a person cannot forgive, he is unaware of the reality of hell and has not comprehended the love of God.

Let's continue with the parable:

> So when his fellow servants saw what had been done, they were very grieved, and came and told their master all that had been done. Then his master, after he had called him, said to him, "You wicked *servant*! I forgave you all that debt because you begged me. Should you not also have had compassion on your *fellow servant*, just as I had pity on you?"
>
> MATTHEW 18:31-33 (EMPHASIS MINE)

I want to emphasize that Jesus is not referring to unbelievers in this parable. He is talking about servants of the king, or born again believers. This man had already received forgiveness of his great debt (salvation) and is called the master's servant. The one he could not forgive was a *fellow* servant. So we can conclude his fate to be that of a "believer" who refuses to forgive.

I find an amazing fact here. In all the other parables of the gospels, people would have to inquire as to the meaning. However, Jesus gives the interpretation of this parable without being asked. I believe it's because what He communicates is so far out of their norm that He had to make sure they got it. Here is His interpretation:

> And his master was angry, and delivered him to the tor-turers until he should pay all that was due to him. So My heavenly Father also will do to you if each of you, from his heart, does not forgive his brother his trespasses.
>
> MATTHEW 18:34-35 (EMPHASIS MINE)

There are three major points in these two verses I want to point out. First, the unforgiving servant is turned over to torture. Second, he now has to pay off the original debt, 375 tons of gold; and third, this is what God the Father will do to any "believer" who does not forgive his brother's offense.

Let's briefly discuss each point. First, the word *torture* means the act of inflicting extreme pain, agony of mind or body, and to twist from a normal position. A torturer is one who inflicts torture. A believer who refuses to forgive will be tormented by demon spirits. The *torturers* are given permission to inflict pain and agony of mind and body at will. I have often prayed for people in services who could not receive healing, comfort, or deliverance, all because they would not release others and forgive from their hearts. This most always in turn leads to anger and offense toward God. Now their faith becomes defiled, and their end will be fatal if there is no repentance and forgiveness.

Second point, this unforgiving servant now has to pay the original unpayable debt. He is now required to do that which is impossible! It is the debt Jesus paid at Calvary. You may cringe at this, but hear the words of Jesus in another account: "And whenever you stand *praying*, if you have anything against anyone, forgive him, that *your Father in heaven* may also forgive you your trespasses" (Mark 11:25, emphasis mine)

Notice whom Jesus is speaking to here. Notice His words *"your Father in heaven."* God is not Father to the sinner; He is *God* to the sinner and *Father* to the believer. Also, sinners do not pray. So it is clear He is addressing children of God.

Let's continue. "But if you do not forgive, neither will your Father in heaven forgive your trespasses" (Mark 11:26).

That is as clear as it can get. Which brings us to the third point; you will have to pay the unpayable debt if you refuse to forgive. Jesus says that your Father will not forgive your trespasses and will turn you over to the eternal tormentors. Is it worth it?

We are not talking about someone who is working through an offense, praying to forgive, but rather someone like Faint

Heart, who insistently refuses to forgive. Notice in the allegory her unforgiveness opened the door to all other manner of evil, and she gradually slipped away from her devotion to Jalyn. Was it worth her fatal end? Again, this is why the writer of Hebrews emphatically tells us to carefully examine ourselves and let go of any form of bitterness, for by it *many* are defiled.

Now we can understand Jesus' words concerning the latter days of the Church. He says, "Many will be *offended*, will betray one another, and will hate one another. . . . And because *lawlessness will abound*, the *love* of many will grow cold. But he who endures to the end shall be saved" (Matt. 24:10, 12-13, emphasis mine).

Notice it is not a few or even some, but *many* who will be offended in the days in which we are living. The word *many* means a vast, very large, or great number. The offense, or unforgiveness, will lead to lawlessness, and the love of a vast number will grow cold. The Greek word for *love* is *agape*, which describes the love of God shed abroad in a Christian's heart the moment they are saved. Jesus is not speaking of impostors, for they have never truly received the love of God. No, he is speaking to genuine believers, for notice he says, "But he who endures to the end shall be saved." You don't say to a sinner, or an impostor, if you endure to the end you'll be saved. They haven't started the race yet!

DEPARTURE FROM THE FAITH

Scripture warns us of the *falling away* that will occur among believers in the days we are living. Paul says, "Let no one deceive you by any means; for that Day [the coming of the Lord] will not come unless the *falling away comes first*" (2 Thess. 2:3, emphasis mine). And again he foretells, "Now the Spirit *expressly says* that in the latter times some will *depart from the faith*" (1 Tim. 4:1, emphasis mine).

Why? "For the time will come when they will not endure

sound doctrine, but according to their own desires, because they have itching ears, they will heap up for themselves teachers; and they will *turn their ears away from the truth*" (2 Tim. 4:3-4, emphasis mine). In the above Scripture, notice that Paul says they "will depart from the faith." The faith he speaks of isn't an imaginary faith; it is the true faith in Jesus Christ. For these to depart, it means they needed to be realistically in the faith at one time.

I've shared the truths of almost every writer in the New Testament concerning believers walking away from their salvation. Let me now share some of the writings of the noted early church fathers, some of whom were companions of the apostles who wrote the New Testament. I find their writings to directly correlate with the words we've seen in Scripture.

> Let us then practice righteousness so that we may be saved unto the end.
>
> CLEMENT OF ROME[3]

> Even in the case of one who has done the greatest good deeds in his life, but at the end has run headlong into wickedness, all his former pains are profitless to him. For at the climax of the drama, he has given up his part.
>
> CLEMENT OF ALEXANDRIA[4]

> Some think that God is under a necessity of bestowing even on the unworthy what He has promised [to give]. So they turn His liberality into His slavery . . . For do not many afterwards fall out of [grace]? Is not this gift taken away from many?
>
> TERTULLIAN[5]

> A man may possess an acquired righteousness, from which it is possible for him to fall away.
>
> ORIGEN[6]

Those who do not obey Him, being disinherited by Him, have ceased to be His sons.

IRENAEUS[7]

Upon hearing my stance on these truths from Scripture, some have incorrectly said to me, "John, you are an Arminian." This is a term that the dictionary describes as follows: "Of or relating to the theology of Jacobus Arminius and his followers, who rejected the Calvinist doctrines of predestination and election and who believed that human free will is compatible with God's sovereignty."[8]

To these people I simply say, "No, I'm neither a Calvinist nor an Arminian, but a Christian who believes in the Bible being the infallible Word of God." Jacobus Arminius lived long after the writers of the Scripture and even the early leaders quoted above. So could you call these writers Arminian? Obviously not, as they lived and wrote before Arminius was born. What I'm writing is not a personal thought, concept, or belief, but the truth. And God made His message of warning very clear to those of us who believe. We must be careful to not get hung up on schools of thought, but to be open to the context of the Scripture inspired by the Holy Spirit, for:

All Scripture is inspired by God and is useful to teach us what is true and to make us realize what is wrong in our lives. It straightens us out and teaches us to do what is right. It is God's way of preparing us in every way, fully equipped for every good thing God wants us to do.

2 TIMOTHY 3:16-17, NLT

It is interesting to note that those who were false leaders, whom Jesus warned and rebuked sternly, were those who congregated around schools of thought and taught in like manner. However, if you look at what was said of John the Baptist, Jesus, or others who spoke the truth, it was repeatedly reported that they "taught them as one having authority, and not as the scribes" (Matt. 7:29). For this reason, Paul instructs Titus, "Speak these things, exhort, and rebuke with all authority" (Titus 2:15). And to Timothy he writes, "Remain in Ephesus that you may charge some that they teach no other doctrine" (1 Tim 1:3). Paul also instructed Timothy to:

> Herald and preach the Word! Keep your sense of urgency [stand by, be at hand and ready], whether the opportunity seems to be favorable or unfavorable. [Whether it is convenient or inconvenient, whether it is welcome or unwelcome, you as preacher of the Word are to show people in what way their lives are wrong.] And convince them, rebuking and correcting, warning and urging and encouraging them, being unflagging and inexhaustible in patience and teaching.
>
> 2 TIMOTHY 4:2, AMP

And of himself Paul writes that, "I may speak boldly, as I ought to speak" (Eph 6:20). You can see this is a trait among all God's true spokespeople. Their authority is founded in the Word of God. They will not gather around personal feelings, schools of thought, or the consensus of the majority. The majority can sometimes be wrong. We must know that God means what He says and says what He means!

KEEP YOU FROM STUMBLING

Some have been shaken by this message of falling from grace, which is so clear in the Scripture. They've come to me in a panicked state, saying, "I thought we have eternal security."

To this I reply, "Absolutely yes! We do have eternal security! Jesus said He would not lose any the Father gives Him (John 18:9) because He would never leave or forsake us. But He didn't say that we couldn't leave Him and be lost." This usually is met with concerned looks. So I then say, "If you truly love Jesus Christ, why would you ever want out! You will not deny Him if you truly love Him!"

If you love God, you will have no trouble keeping His commandments! If serving God is an obligation, you have entered into a legalistic relationship, and it will be hard to keep His commandments. We should not serve God to earn His approval; we should serve God because we are in love with Him!

Jude goes on to tell us how to keep that love fresh, even if there is bad leaven in the church. He says, "Keep yourselves in the love of God, *looking* for the mercy of our Lord Jesus Christ unto eternal life" (Jude 21, emphasis mine). We are to look for the Lord every moment of the day (remember the servant who fell away was the one who wasn't anticipating the return of his master?). We are to long for Him and seek Him continually that He might reveal Himself in a greater way, for "everyone who has this hope in Him [the hope of Jesus revealing Himself] *purifies* himself, just as He is pure" (1 John 3:3, emphasis mine).

When you look for Him; fellowship with His Spirit, you will never want out. So there is nothing by which to be shaken? At the conclusion of the Book of Jude is one of my favorite promises in the Bible. To those who keep themselves in love with God by looking for the revealing of Jesus, He says:

Now to Him who is able to keep you from stumbling, And to present you faultless before the presence of His glory with exceeding joy, to God our Savior, Who alone is wise, be glory and majesty, dominion and power, both now and forever. Amen.

JUDE 24-25

This is my earnest prayer and desire for you!

Chapter 7

THE FOUNDATION

—

The [uncompromisingly] righteous have an everlasting foundation.
<small>PROVERBS 10:25, AMP</small>

B efore returning to our allegory of Affabel to discuss the
judgments and rewards of Selfish and Charity, we'll put a cap
on what we've discussed the past three chapters. Recall from
chapter 4 this Scripture:

> Therefore let us go on and get past the *elementary* stage in
> the teachings and doctrine of Christ (the Messiah), ad-
> vancing steadily toward the completeness and perfection
> that belong to spiritual maturity. Let us not again be lay-
> ing the foundation of . . . eternal judgment and punish-
> ment.
>
> <small>HEBREWS 6:1-2, AMP (EMPHASIS MINE)</small>

Being without a firm foundation in the truths of eternal
judgment and punishment prevents us from building a proper
and healthy life in Christ. It would be compared to attempting to
advance your education without basic tools acquired in elementary school, such as the ability to read.

Why is this so? In careful study of the Gospels you'll notice that Jesus spoke of hell and described it more than He did heaven. He did this to plant a foundation within us; the fear of God. Here's one example:

> Whatever you have said in the dark will be heard in the light, and what you have whispered behind closed doors will be shouted from the housetops for all to hear! Dear friends, don't be afraid of those who want to kill you. They can only kill the body; they cannot do any more to you. *But I'll tell you whom to fear. Fear God, who has the power to kill people and then throw them into hell.*
>
> LUKE 12:3-5, NLT (EMPHASIS MINE)

His words are strong and precise: Attaining and maintaining a good understanding of eternal judgment and punishment firmly plants and keeps the fear of the Lord in our hearts. Allow me to explain. Only God can give the eternal sentence of hell. What we have spoken in secret will be made manifest by the light of His glory at the Judgment. Not only our words, but motives, attitudes, and works will be manifest. The fear of God keeps us continually aware that nothing can be hidden from Him, even the most secret things, and we know nothing will escape His judgment—and His judgment is just. If we lack this understanding, we can become deceived into believing God overlooks or even doesn't see lawlessness, and we take comfort in an unscriptural mercy that doesn't exist, such as Deceived, Faint Heart, and Double Life did. We can easily become one of the many in these last days who will drift away from steadfast devotion and into lawlessness.

Those who lack this foundation will surely slip over to the fear of man, and we will ultimately serve whom we fear. If we fear God, we will obey Him even under pressure; if we fear man, we will yield to man, especially under pressure, and drift toward what benefits our own pleasures or fleshly desires. To yield to the flesh will ultimately lead to serious consequences. So if we lack a conscious understanding of eternal judgment and punishment, we will lack a certain measure of the fear of the Lord, for the judgments of Christ are indeed one aspect of the fear of the Lord. Paul says it like this:

> For we must all appear before the *judgment seat of Christ*, that each one may be recompensed for his deeds in the body, according to what he has done, whether good or bad. *Therefore knowing the fear of the Lord*, we persuade men.
>
> 2 CORINTHIANS 5:10-11, NASB (EMPHASIS MINE)

He wasn't referring to the Great White Throne Judgment Jesus referred to in the previous verse (in which people will be sentenced to hell), but to the believer's judgment, which we will begin to discuss in the next chapter. However, notice that Paul equates Christ's judgment seat with the fear of the Lord (however, it could also refer to the white throne). In fact, in the verse, above he actually calls the Judgment Seat the "fear of the Lord." The point is, you cannot separate the fear of the Lord from judgment, and the fear of the Lord is the key to a healthy life.

Hear the words of the Prophet Isaiah: "He will be the sure foundation for your times, a rich store of salvation and wisdom and knowledge; the fear of the Lord is the key to this treasure" (Isa. 33:6, NIV).

Holy fear is the key to God's sure foundation. Recall in the previous chapters Jesus foretelling of the multitude who would do miraculous things in His Name but would be turned away to eternal punishment. It's not surprising that He immediately followed by giving the cause of their downfall; it was their foundation. They built their life on a mindset and heart belief that couldn't weather life's storms.

"So then, anyone who hears these words of mine and *obeys* them is like a wise man who *built his house on rock*. The rain poured down, the rivers flooded over, and the wind blew hard against that house. But it did not fall, because it was built on rock" [*God's sure foundation . . . the fear of the Lord*].

"But anyone who hears these words of mine and *does not obey* them is like a foolish man who *built his house on sand*. The rain poured down, the rivers flooded over, the wind blew hard against that house, and it fell. And what a terrible fall that was!"

MATTHEW 7:24-27, TEV (EMPHASIS MINE)

Those who have endured to the end withstood the storms because of their firm foundation. The fear of the Lord is that foundation; it provides stability for us. It is a storehouse of the riches of God; His salvation, wisdom, and knowledge are all hidden in it.

FEAR OF THE LORD

What is the fear of the Lord? Is it to be scared of Him? Absolutely not, for how can we have intimacy with the Lord (which is His earnest desire) if we are afraid of Him? God came to reveal Himself to Israel, to have fellowship with them as He had with Moses, but they all ran back and refused to draw near. Moses said to the people,

"*Do not fear*, for God has come to test you, and *that His fear may be before you*, so that you may not sin."

EXODUS 20:20 (EMPHASIS MINE)

Notice his words sound like they contradict themselves. Rather, Moses differentiates between being afraid of God and the fear of the Lord; there is a difference. The one who is afraid of God has something to hide (recall what Adam did when he disobeyed in the Garden; he hid from the presence of the Lord). On the other hand, the one who fears God is afraid to be away from Him (he runs from disobedience).

The fear of the Lord is to honor, esteem, value, respect, and reverence Him above anything or anyone else. It is to love what He loves and hate what He hates. What is important to Him is important to us; what is not important to Him is not important to us. When we fear Him, we will *tremble at His word*; which is to obey Him instantly—when it doesn't make sense, when it hurts, when we don't see the benefits—and we see it to completion. So yes, the manifestation of the fear of the Lord is *obedience* to His Word, ways, or laws.

Scripture tells us the fear of the Lord is the beginning of wisdom, or we can say it like this: It's the *foundation* of wisdom. Wisdom, which we will discuss in great depth in future chapters, is the knowledge and ability to make the right choices at the opportune time. Those who make wrong choices under pressure lack wisdom, and wisdom's source is the fear of the Lord.

Scripture tells us that our lives can be compared to building houses; first comes the foundation, next we build the structure. We read, "Through wisdom a house is built" (Prov. 24:3). If we are building our lives with the ability to make right choices, then we will build a healthy life that will be able to stand with confidence before the Judgment Seat. The very beginning or foundation of this wisdom is the fear of the Lord.

KEEPS US FROM DEPARTING

Christians wouldn't backslide if they had the fear of the Lord firmly planted in their hearts. We wouldn't slip or drift away from our steadfast devotion to Jesus. We wouldn't take His Word for granted or treat it casually. We wouldn't flirt with sin, which causes believers hearts to harden and eventually fall away (see Heb. 3:12-13). We would always know that what is done and spoken in secret would be proclaimed publicly at the Judgment Seat. Hear what God said to Jeremiah about New Testament people:

They shall be My people, and I will be their God; then I will give them one heart and one way, that they may *fear Me forever*, for the good of them and their children after them. And I will make an everlasting covenant with them, that I will not turn away from doing them good; but I will put *My fear in their hearts so that they will not depart from Me.*

JEREMIAH 32:38-40 (EMPHASIS MINE)

Notice God says, "*Fear Me forever . . . that they will not depart from Me.*" I recall a meeting in Malaysia, where the Spirit of the fear of the Lord manifested strongly. People were from all over the Eastern Hemisphere; Bible school students, pastors, and many others packed the auditorium where I was speaking. Toward the close of the service, many were weeping uncontrollably and lying on the floor all over the front near the platform. The terror of the Lord was so awesome in that atmosphere. I thought, *John Bevere, you make one wrong move, say one wrong thing, and you are dead!* Would that have happened, I don't know, but I can say a man and woman made a wrong move in a similar atmosphere in the New Testament and died. The result of their immediate judgment was, "So great fear came upon all the church and upon all who heard these things" (Acts 5:11).

After the meeting a couple from India approached me and said, "John, we feel so clean inside."

I responded, "Yes, I do too."

A few days later I was in my hotel room and found the Scripture, "The fear of the Lord is clean, *enduring forever*" (Ps. 19:9, emphasis mine). The Holy Spirit immediately spoke to my heart, "Lucifer was the lead worship angel in heaven; he was anointed, beautiful, and blessed. But he didn't fear Me; *he didn't endure forever.*" I contemplated this, I then heard, "A third of the angels who surrounded My throne and saw My glory, didn't fear Me; *they didn't endure forever.*" I was struck by what He revealed, and again I heard, "Adam and Eve walked in the presence of My glory; they fellowshipped with Me, But they did not fear Me; they didn't *endure in my presence forever.*"

The fear of the Lord gives us staying power. It keeps us consistently obedient to God's Word. Believers are warned: "Therefore, since a promise remains of entering His rest, let us *fear* lest any of you seem to have come short of it" (Heb. 4:1, emphasis mine). It's interesting that he says "fear" instead of "love." It is the fear of God that keeps us from drifting back into sin, not the love of God.

FAMOUS EVANGELIST

I will never forget the time I visited a famous evangelist who was serving his last year of a five-year prison sentence. His case was made known to the world and brought much reproach on the kingdom. However, in his first year of prison he had a genuine encounter with the Lord. When I walked into the prison four years later, one of the first things he said to me was, "John, this prison wasn't God's judgment on my life, rather His mercy. If I would have kept going the way I was living, I would have ended up in hell for eternity."

He now had my attention. I knew I was speaking to a broken man of God, a true servant of Christ. I knew he started out in the ministry very much in love with Jesus. His passion was evident. I wondered how he ended up so far from the Lord while still in the height of his ministry.

So I asked him, "When did you fall out of love with Jesus?"

He looked at me and answered without hesitation, "I didn't!"

Very puzzled, I replied, "But what about the mail fraud and adultery you committed in the past seven years, all that you're in prison for?"

He said, "John, I loved Jesus all the way through it, but He wasn't the supreme authority of my life." (He didn't fear God.) Then he said something that riveted me, "John, there are millions of American Christians just like me. They call Jesus their

Savior and love Him, but they don't fear Him as their supreme Lord."

A light went on inside me at that point. I realized we can love Jesus, but that alone will not keep us from falling away. We must also fear God as well. Recall Moses' words: "God has come to test you, and *that His fear may be before you, so that you may not sin*" (Exod. 20:20, emphasis mine). It is the fear of the Lord that gives us the staying power to not drift away from our obedience to God, as did Lucifer, a third of the angels, Adam, and the many in the church who will fall away in these last days.

COMPLETE YOUR SALVATION

For this reason Paul tells us to

"Work out (cultivate, *carry out to the goal*, and *fully complete*) your own salvation with *reverence* and *awe* and *trembling* (self-distrust, with serious caution, tenderness of conscience, watchfulness against temptation, timidly shrinking from whatever might offend God and discredit the name of Christ)."

PHILIPPIANS 2:12, AMP (EMPHASIS MINE)

We carry out and complete our salvation with reverential *fear and trembling*. This keeps us under the awareness that every thought, word, and deed will be made manifest at the Judgment. Having this consciousness keeps us humble, cautious, sober minded, tender, aware of temptations to disobey, and always keeping away from what may displease God.

Notice that Paul doesn't say we fully complete or finish our salvation with "love and kindness." The fear of the Lord gives strength to not fall away from His grace into a life of lawlessness. Consider Paul's words to the Romans. He discussed how Israel's falling away resulted in the Gentiles' salvation. He called Israel the natural branches and New Testament Gentile believers the wild branches. Hear what God says through this apostle: "Well said. Because of unbelief they were broken off, and you stand by faith. Do not be haughty, but *fear*" (Rom. 11:20, emphasis mine).

Notice he doesn't say, "Do not be haughty, but *love*." No, he refers to the fear of God. Why? You'll again see in the next two verses it's what gives us the strength to continue in His love:

> For if God did not spare the natural branches, He may not spare you either. Therefore consider the *goodness* and *severity* of God: on those who fell, *severity*; but toward you, goodness, *if* you continue in His goodness. *Otherwise you also will be cut off.*
>
> ROMANS 11:21-22 (EMPHASIS MINE)

We as believers are to consider the goodness (love) and the severity (judgment) of God. If we do not *fear* God, we will not continue in His goodness and can be cut off. Again, emphasizing God's warning to us: "Therefore, since a promise remains of entering His rest, let us *fear* lest any of you seem to have come short of it" (Heb. 4:1, emphasis mine).

The fear of God keeps us from coming up short by falling away. The love of God, on the other hand, keeps us from legalism, which also destroys intimacy with God. Our love for God also fuels our motives and intentions, keeping them passionate and accurate. We must have both the great forces of love and fear in our lives to maintain a healthy relationship. For this reason Paul calls God our "Heavenly Father and Abba" (meaning Daddy), but he also says our God is "a consuming fire." He is Love, but also He is Just and a Holy Judge. To not fear Him is to lack enduring stability, and Jesus repeatedly says, "He who endures to the end shall be saved" (Matt. 10:22).

OUR INFLUENCE

The other critical reason we must have a firm understanding of the elementary doctrine of eternal judgment and punishment is our influence on others. If we lack the fear of the Lord, we will communicate, by either words or actions, an unbalanced Gospel; this will result in those we influence being susceptible to slide back or even permanently fall.

Without this foundation, if we are a gospel teacher, preacher, or pastor, we will convey only the principles found in the Scriptures of how to live a blessed, prosperous, happy life. These principles found in Scripture will work, as they were intended, producing health, financial success, peace, better relationships, etc. However, without the foundation of eternal judgments, we will shy back from preaching the cross, the price to follow Jesus. We will preach merely seeker-friendly messages while excluding the important point of laying our lives down at all costs.

There is an excellent example of this found in the Gospels. On a certain day a young man who had great possessions came to Jesus in the midst of His disciples and asked, "What shall I do that I may inherit *eternal* life?"

I used to have a logical concept of this encounter between Jesus and this wealthy man. I imaged a man getting out of his latest model luxury chariot, surrounded by servants, clothed with a fashionable expensive designer outfit. He comes to Jesus, stopping short to keep his distance, hands on his hips, with a slightly arrogant tone asking what he needed to do to inherit eternal life. Yet one day God opened my eyes and I read, "Now as He was going out on the road, *one came running, knelt* before Him" (Mark 10:17, emphasis mine).

I was shocked. Now my image changed. I now saw Jesus in the midst of a large number of His staff members, and probably one of the richest men of the community running up to and collapsing at Jesus' feet, almost out of breath, crying out, "What must I do to be saved!" I saw intensity and sincerity in this man.

Jesus then gave him the highlights of adhering to the word of God in regard to treating others. He said, "You know the commandments: 'Do not commit adultery,' 'Do not murder,' 'Do not steal,' 'Do not bear false witness,' 'Do not defraud,' 'Honor your father and your mother' " (Mark 6:19). The Master gave him the fifth through tenth commandments, which deal with man's relationship with man, but omitted the first four, which deal with our putting nothing before God and submitting ourselves to His lordship.

To this, the rich young man replied, "All these things I have kept from my youth. What do I still lack?" (Matt. 19:20). He did keep all the principles and commandments of the Word of God. I believe this was the reason for his success. Executing the principles of God's Word will produce results (see Josh 1:8). This is true not only for churchgoers, but for those outside the church as well. There have been many unsaved people who have reaped the benefits of the laws and principles of God. One that comes to mind was a man who had a fatal disease. God's word states, "A merry heart does good, like medicine" (Prov. 17:22). Upon learning this he began to watch a steady diet of the Three Stooges. He laughed himself to health. It worked, even though he may not have been a Christian. I know of non-Christians who are very successful in their businesses because they give frequently to charities. They are reaping the benefits of the laws of sowing and harvesting made so clear in Scripture.

This young man in the Gospels obeyed the principles of Scripture and was successful. However, it is interesting to note, he still had an awareness something was missing in his life. I personally believe this was because of his integrity; he had not deceived himself. He called Jesus "Good Teacher," rather than "Lord." I respect him so much for this, for how many today call Him Lord (Supreme Master) but do not do what He says. Recall His statement, " 'But why do you call Me "Lord, Lord," and not do the things which I say?' " (Luke 6:46).

Many lack the awareness of their need of eternal life today *in the church* because they deceive themselves. They call Jesus "Lord," when in reality they still own their own lives. This is made clear by the Apostle James, "If anyone among you thinks he is religious, and does not bridle his tongue but deceives his own heart" (James 1:26). A person whose heart is deceived is out of touch with spiritual reality.

This man, because of his honesty, stayed in touch with reality. Therefore, he knew he lacked eternal life, even though he was raised in synagogue, learned and obeyed the principles of God in dealing with others, and the principles of God's Word worked. Now hear Jesus' response to him:

> Then Jesus, looking at him, *loved him*, and said to him, *"One thing you lack*: Go your way, sell whatever you have and give to the poor, and you will have treasure in heaven; and *come, take up the cross, and follow Me."*
>
> MARK 10:21 (EMPHASIS MINE)

The first point to notice is that Jesus *loved* him. If you love someone, you will tell him the truth, not flatter him. Many ungodly salespeople will flatter people to blind their discernment. You may think they love you more than your family members do because they are telling you what you want to hear, when in reality they are just trying to get something from you. When you love others, you will seek their benefit, even if it hurts.

Jesus, out of His love, attacked the area in this man's life that kept him from unconditional obedience to God: his wealth. To take up our cross does not speak of sacrifice, or even suffering, although it probably will result in suffering. It speaks of obedience. If we die to our own lusts, agendas, and ambitions, then we will never have a conflict in obeying God. If we haven't; eventually we will come to a place where friends or our flesh will desire to go one way while God's directive will be to go another. If we haven't taken up our cross already, we will go our way while still calling Jesus Lord, thus deceiving ourselves. With this man it was his wealth, but with others it may be sports, food, friends, security, music, etc.

Notice what happened:

> But he was *sad* at this word, and went away *sorrowful*, for
> he had great possessions.
>
> MARK 10:22 (EMPHASIS MINE)

Wow! Did you see that? This man came running to Jesus,
knelt down, and fervently asked how to inherit eternal life. How
many times have you had this happen in your neighborhood?
How many times have you seen this in a service? What desire!
What passion! What enthusiasm! Yet Jesus' response to this seeker
caused him to walk away sad and sorrowful.

Can you imagine Jesus doing this today in our "seeker
friendly" church culture? The businessmen of the worship center
have been working on the wealthiest man in the community.
They've given him a Bible with his name engraved in gold. He
agrees to come to a service. Jesus gets up and teaches in line with
the fear of the Lord, as He did above. The man leaves sad, sorry
that he came, and tells the men of the worship center, "I'm not
going back to that church. I've worked hard for what I have. I've
got a good reputation in the community, and I've been honest.
What does He mean forsake all and take up the cross; that is too
extreme."

Can you see the businessmen's response? They call an emer-
gency board meeting and say, "Jesus, you are too radical! Don't
you realize we have been working on this man for six months.
He was excited to come to our service. He wanted to receive
eternal life, but after you got done teaching he never wants to
come back! Couldn't you have just eased him into the message
of the Cross after a couple years of him being saved? All you had
to do is get him to believe in you and confess the prayer of salvation, and he would have been a Christian! You keep preaching
like this and we won't have anyone left in the church!"

The manner in which Jesus addressed this seeker is quite
contrary to what normal Evangelical Christianity has become in

the twenty-first century. Are we better than Him? Have we come up with greater tactics of winning people than the Master Himself? Has our revelation progressed beyond His? I speak foolishly to make an important point. Could it be we've omitted a major aspect of the gospel and therefore have slipped into an unbalanced gospel? We've taken the Cross out of salvation and only offered its benefits. Notice Jesus didn't say to this upstanding citizen, "All you have to do is believe in Me; believe that I am the Savior, and you will receive what you seek—eternal life." No, He didn't do what has become so common today because Jesus was well versed in eternal judgment and punishment: "His delight is in the fear of the Lord" (Isa 11:3).

AN ETERNAL PERSPECTIVE

If we are not driven by eternity, we will live and communicate more to benefit this life, instead of seeing life from an eternal perspective. We will teach people to live for the day rather than to live as the patriarchs, who "waited for the city which has foundations, whose builder and maker is God" (Heb 11:10). Yes, there are rewards in this life for obeying the principles of God; we've taught them well, but let's not forget we are temporary residents on this earth. We are to succeed in this life, but by the standards of Heaven, not of our culture. Our real home is not here. Read carefully the motive of these saints who gave up this world to follow God:

> These all died in faith, not having received the promises, but having seen them afar off were assured of them, embraced them, and confessed that they were *strangers* and *pilgrims* on the earth. For those who say such things declare plainly that they seek a homeland. And truly if they had called to mind that country from which they had come out, they would have had opportunity to return. But now they desire a better, that is, a heavenly country.

Therefore God is not ashamed to be called their God, for He has prepared a city for them.

HEBREWS 11:13-16

The homeland these saints looked for is the city of God, the New Jerusalem, to which we will turn our attention for the remainder of this book. Those who will live in this city are called *overcomers*. Their reward shall be infinitely better than the very best this life here on earth can offer.

Chapter 8

THE KINGDOM OF AFFABEL— THE DAY OF JUDGMENT II

———

*I am He Who searches minds (the thoughts, feelings, and purposes)
and the [inmost] hearts, and I will give to each of you [the reward
for what you have done] as your work deserves.*
REVELATION 2:23, AMP

L et's return to the allegory of the kingdom of Affabel to dis-cover the outcome of Selfish and Charity. We'll learn impor-tant aspects of the believer's Judgment, one of which is that not all believers will be rewarded equally.

THE BELIEVER'S JUDGMENT

This judgment took place in the morning soon after the En-delites arrived at the Great Hall. Approximately five hundred Endelites waited in the Hall of Life, anxiously anticipating their first meeting with King Jalyn. Both Charity and Selfish had found friends both old and new and were in the process of catch-ing up when suddenly the Royal Guards entered the hall. All conversations ceased as the Chief Guard addressed the group.

"Shortly you will face your king. He has always loved you and has yearned for this day when you will be united. Though you've never met, he has seen you. He has beheld your heart and discerned your fruit. He knows your hearts, your motives, your thoughts, your feelings, as well as your works. Nothing has been hidden. Know his judgment is just. None will be slighted or misrepresented."

The Chief Guard proceeded to instruct them as to how they would be ushered into the Great Hall as well as the necessary protocol once within. Once the briefing was complete, he announced, "The first to go before King Jalyn is Selfish. Step forward so we may escort you to the Great Hall."

SELFISH AND HIS JUDGMENT

Selfish surmised he had been summoned first because of his position as the mayor of Endel. He was confident he would be rewarded handsomely for his leadership in the king's outer realm of Endel. He remembered how the teachings from the ancient writings spoke of rewards and ruling positions in Affabel for those deemed faithful in Endel. He had seen the community thrive during his two-year term as mayor. He was confident as he went to face the king.

The doors of the Great Hall were opened and Selfish was escorted into the presence of the king. He was overwhelmed by the grandeur of this massive auditorium. He noticed it was almost completely full. All in attendance were standing. Selfish wondered why there were random seats vacant, but quickly dismissed it by reasoning it was due to the citizens arbitrarily seating themselves.

There, at a great distance, was the throne of Jalyn; it was more majestic than he ever could have imagined. He also noticed smaller thrones that he correctly assumed belonged to the underrulers of Jalyn. His heart skipped a beat—there were a couple seats yet unoccupied. He felt certain he would be assigned a vacant throne.

AN OLD FRIEND

As Selfish proceeded, he was taken aback by the glorious transformation in the appearance of former Endelites who now held citizenship in Affabel. After just a few steps toward the throne, he recognized an old friend in the very back of the auditorium. His name was *Social*. He had owned a restaurant that Selfish frequented. He looked to the Chief Guard as if to ask if it was all right to speak; the guard nodded his approval.

Selfish approached, and the two embraced. "How have you been, Social?" asked Selfish.

"I've been very well," replied the old friend; "but my name is no longer Social; it is now *Content*. Lord Jalyn gave me this new name just as he does with all his servants once they appear before his throne.

"Affabel is more wonderful than we ever could have dreamed. This Great Hall is but an entrance to realms of beauty, splendor, and grandeur of the magnificent city. The king is more personable, loving, and majestic than anyone you have ever met or known. I am so thankful to know and serve him. It is an honor to be in his kingdom. It is better than anything we ever knew. If I had known in Endel what I know now, I would have lived differently. I would have focused more on pleasing the king. I would have lived as a better citizen in my short stay in Endel. If I had, I would be closer to him now."

Selfish countered, "What do you mean? You were a great citizen in Endel! You ran one of the best restaurants and sponsored numerous community events. You frequently contributed both finances and free meals for fund-raising campaigns. You even sacrificed evenings of revenue to do this!"

Content shook his head, "I did those things to gain recognition and acceptance. I also knew it would draw more patrons. My motive was not to bless, but to ensure my success. I should have listened to the words of Jalyn. He told us, 'When you give a dinner or a supper, do not ask your friends, your brothers, your relatives, nor rich neighbors, lest they also invite you back, and you be repaid. But when you give a feast, invite the poor, the maimed, the lame, the blind. And you will be blessed, because they cannot repay you; for you shall be repaid at the resurrection of the just.'[1] I donated those dinners for my benefit, not for the good of the community. I wanted to move among the influential of Endel."

Selfish probed deeper. "But you frequently contributed to the School of Endel. Didn't this win you favor in the eyes of Jalyn?"

Content countered, "I did indeed contribute to the School of Endel, but not in proportion to the success of my business. I actually only gave a small percentage. I hoarded much of the restaurant's profits because I was afraid of failing. This was coupled with a desire to live the 'good life.' My true intentions were to protect myself. The little I gave was to ease my conscience. I was compelled because our teachers frequently discussed the importance of giving to the kingdom and to those in need. I ended up giving out of guilt and compulsion rather than out of compassion and love."

Content continued, "I forgot Jalyn's illustration of the widow who loved the kingdom of Affabel. Remember he said, 'I tell you that this poor widow put more in the offering box than all the others. For the others put in what they had to spare of their riches; but she, poor as she is, put in all she had—she gave all she had to live on.' "[2]

Selfish pondered the socials and dinners he held at his home; there were no poor or even less fortunate there. Then he remembered the five thousand dollars he gave to appease those who were disappointed with his choice to grant the land to the department store rather than to the school. At the time he had thought it was quite a bit, but now he was embarrassed by how little he had given. How would this fair before Jalyn?

His reflections were interrupted by Content's further comment, "If I had been truly passionate for Jalyn and his people, I would have given my time and served at the school. If all do their part, the burden is lifted, but if not it is borne by the few. If Jalyn's design was implemented, none would be overburdened. The few who took the heavy loads have been greatly rewarded. Bottom line: The little I gave I did to ease my conscience of my lack of commitment to Jalyn's kingdom.

"When my life was reviewed, it was clear to all that I lived more for my comfort, security, and reputation than for his glory. Now I'm one of the lowest citizens of this city. Even though this is the case, I am still overwhelmed by his goodness and how much he loves me. I really didn't deserve anything I received from him, but as you will shortly discover, his love and generosity are beyond comprehension. I am in debt to his extravagant kindness for the rest of my life."

Shocked, Selfish cried out, "Lowest citizen? Do you mean there is a class system here?"

Content smiled and said, "Yes, there is of sorts. We were taught this in Endel, although many of us never considered it seriously. But deep within we knew; in fact, you even considered this truth when you walked into this auditorium. I heard your thoughts; you anticipate being assigned a throne. You knew this from the ancient writings taught in class. Though I doubt you would have acknowledged you believed this while in Endel.

"Those who were faithful to Jalyn during our short stay in Endel are the leaders and citizens who hold the most interesting positions in this society. They live in the most beautiful section of the city and have the privilege of frequent interaction with the king. Those of us who lived for ourselves while in Endel are assigned positions in the outer parts of the city. It is seen in this auditorium as well. Those in the rear of this hall are those who live in the flatlands. They have been assigned the labor-intensive jobs. We are the least in the kingdom. Those who occupy the midsections make their homes in the mountains with more creative positions, while those in front and upon the thrones live in the Regal Center. This is where the king lives, and they are privileged to live and work along side him. These are the greatest in the kingdom."

Content concluded, "My friend Selfish, know that Jalyn is a

just and loving leader. Anything he gives you will be a reward. None of us would have a life such as what is found in the least parts of this city had it not been for him."

Having said this, Content stepped back into his place. The Chief Guard then motioned for Selfish to continue his progress toward the throne.

A POPULAR TEACHER

Selfish took a few more steps and noticed another he knew and admired, whose name was *Motivator*. He was formerly a teacher at the School of Endel and one whom Selfish considered outstanding. He was informative, articulate, and always inspired Selfish when he spoke. This fabulous instructor taught in such a way that the students felt uplifted and good about themselves. The other teachers were uplifting, but at times they seemed a bit stern and their words brought painful conviction. Not so with Motivator; students always felt great coming out of his class. In fact, he was by far Selfish's favorite teacher.

Selfish again glanced at the Chief Guard, seeking permission to speak to his former teacher. The guard again nodded his affirmation. Selfish approached Motivator, and the two greeted each other warmly.

Selfish couldn't help but ask, "Why are you here in these back rows?"

"This is my position and place. I am one of the least of the citizens of Affabel. I live in the flatlands and work as a plumber."

"What?" cried Selfish. "You were one of Jalyn's finest teachers! How can you be one of the lowest citizens? You should be on one of the thrones."

"There are several reasons I'm not further up in the ranks of this great assembly or ruling with Jalyn! For time's sake, I'll only share the root of my folly. Remember how all who pledge their lives to Jalyn are likened to builders? We were taught this all through school. One of our chief responsibilities in Endel was to build the lives of others. This was done by the messages we communicated, whether through speech, conduct, or our works. However, as an instructor, I was given both great privilege and responsibility. I taught students the principles and ways of Jalyn."

"Yet I failed as a teacher in so many ways. First, my teachings were unbalanced. I emphasized only the positive aspects of serving Jalyn. I motivated many of my students to only pursue success without considering the long-term effects. I didn't teach them that the truest goal of life was to please Jalyn. I taught them how to use his ways to succeed in life. Consequently, I never warned them of the pitfalls and snares of our society. The ancient writings clearly stated I was to preach the whole counsel of Jalyn. This included, 'Warning every man and teaching every man in all wisdom, that we may present every man perfect in *Jalyn*.'[3] I taught, but neglected to warn. By being an exclusively positive teacher and never giving healthy warnings, I built numerous lives that brought little glory to Jalyn." Here he dropped his head. "A good number of them are in perdition."

Seeing the shock on Selfish's face, the teacher reemphasized his point. "Yes, they fell into perdition. Many now inhabit the forsaken land of Lone due in part to my unbalanced teaching. I didn't give the students what they needed—I gave them what they wanted. I didn't want to lose their acceptance or my popularity. This caused me to build improperly. I didn't root up the weak and faulty areas in their lives. I covered it with insights that only served to fuel their self-seeking desires. Remember the warning given to instructors in the ancient writings: 'Because they lead my people astray, saying, "Peace," when there is no peace, and because, when a flimsy wall is built, they cover it with whitewash, therefore tell those who cover it with whitewash that it is going to fall.'[4] Many students erected and sheltered their lives with temporal things, and I knew deep in my conscience that these were flimsy walls, but I didn't warn them. I said all was well when it wasn't. I encouraged their course and solidified their deception. Though some made it to Affabel, I yet grieve for those at Lone. As for those who made it to Affabel embracing only the positive teachings"—looking over his shoulder, he dropped his voice to a whisper—"many are found in these back rows. Their lives were wastefully spent and their efforts consumed with fire before this Judgment Seat."

Selfish questioned, "Burned up before this Judgment Seat?"

"Yes," replied the teacher. "Do you not remember the ancient writings, 'Now anyone who builds on that foundation may use gold, silver, jewels, wood, hay, or straw. But there is going to come a time of testing at the judgment day to see what kind of work each builder has done. Everyone's work will be put through the fire to see whether or not it keeps its value. If the work survives the fire, that builder will receive a reward. But if the work is burned up, the builder will suffer great loss. The builders themselves will be saved, but like someone escaping through a wall of flames.' "[5]

The famous teacher continued, "The foundation the ancient apostle spoke of is the lordship of Jalyn, which we both know is the only way a person can enter this kingdom. However, once we truly belong to him, we should build upon this foundation. When measured by the ancient writings, my life fell short of his expectations and I failed in the area of my influence on those I taught. I didn't use my authority to impact these students for Affabel and, inevitably, I lost my reward. Remember what the great teacher of old, Paul, said concerning those he'd been called to influence, 'After all, what gives us hope and joy, and what is our proud reward and crown? It is you! Yes, you will bring us much joy as we stand together before our Lord.'[6]

"I knew well the truths of Jalyn when I first began to teach, but I allowed insecurity, the desire for the approval of others, and finally pride to sway me. It wasn't long before I strayed from what I knew. Eventually I started living what I preached. As I drifted, I lost sight of the warnings of Jalyn in my own personal life. I was deceived and did not know. The perspective on popularity and favor are very different here than in Endel. Much of what we considered great there is considered least here."

Selfish soberly asked, "Motivator, my friend told me Jalyn changes our names. What is your new name?"

The teacher smiled. "My name is *Humbled*." With that he inclined his head and stepped back to his place. Selfish turned to the Chief Guard, who nodded, affirming everything he heard from Humbled was true.

Selfish continued toward the throne. He wasn't as confident as when he was first called. He reflected on his life. What were his motives? Did he rule for Jalyn's glory or out of selfish ambition? How had he conducted his life? Was it in line with the words of Jalyn or was he likewise deceived? Did he build others, or did he use them to build his own success?

A RULER

Selfish was passing the midsection of the Great Hall. He noticed the citizens looked even more regal, if that were possible. Each looked at him which such love and acceptance. He drew comfort from their eyes and facial expressions. This helped immensely because he was feeling quite unsure about himself and what he was about to face.

It seemed to take ages for Selfish to make it to the throne. With each step he reviewed so many aspects of his years in Endel. He still was hopeful that he might be commissioned a ruler with Jalyn because of his success as mayor.

Now he was in the midst of the underrulers of Jalyn. He noticed the royal apparel and crowns upon their heads; each held a scepter. They were truly the most regal of all the citizens of this great city. He was amazed that any human could appear so glorious.

He noticed a former secretary to one of the city council members. *Why is she seated on one of the thrones?* wondered Selfish? She never stood out. She'd graduated a year before him. He really didn't know her personally because she was of a more reserved nature, definitely more of the quiet type.

She stepped forward, and the Chief Guard stopped and bowed to her. She greeted Selfish with an embrace and warm smile. "Welcome to Affabel, Selfish. I'm *Patient*. Jalyn asked me to speak with you before you come before him. I am one of his rulers in Affabel."

Selfish spoke before thinking, "A ruler? How could you be a ruler? You never did anything in Endel." He blushed with the realization of how out of line and insensitive his statement was.

Patient nodded as though she understood. "Don't be embarrassed by your statement. Deception cannot hide within this hall or the great city. You are only being honest. In Endel, you were concerned with both image and reputation. This trains many to speak deceptively while unaware of their folly. Here, words are very important, but even weightier are our motives and intentions, as they are always apparent here. You will learn this soon enough, as you are judged for every word you spoke in Endel."

"Every word?" cried Selfish. "Do you mean every single word of every conversation?"

"Yes," replied Patient, "every word. Remember the statement of Lord Jalyn in the ancient writings, 'You can be sure that on the Judgment Day everyone will have to give account of every *useless word* he has ever spoken. Your words will be used to judge you—to declare you either innocent or guilty.'[7] Useless words are vain, idle, or careless, all of which are contrary to the nature of Jalyn."

Selfish questioned, "I always thought we'd have to give an account of huge lies or great truths we'd spoken, along with the good deeds and major accomplishments we achieved." He pondered a moment then finished, "What am I about to face?"

Patient replied, "The ancient writings clearly state, 'Your reward depends on what you say and what you do.'[8] So yes, not only will you be judged for everything you did, or your works, but for every word. This includes evil, good, and, yes, even idle language that proceeded out of your mouth. However, not only your words and works be examined, but the motives behind them. You will also be judged by the thoughts you embraced. Do not forget that Jalyn's judgment is righteous, 'testing the mind and the heart'[9]; and he himself stated, 'I *Jalyn*, search all hearts and *examine secret motives*. I give all people their due rewards, according to what their actions deserve.'[10] Not only are every action and word examined, but the intentions behind them as well."

Patient continued, "This is why you are so shocked to see me on a throne. Your judgment of me was according to my accomplishments in light of Endel. Jalyn's judgment was in a different light; it is the one that you are beginning to see now and will vividly see shortly. My dear brother, you will receive a just reward for your life in Endel."

Selfish had never experienced this kind of hard truth, yet it was saturated with such love, a love that he had never known. He now knew Jalyn must be a loving, compassionate ruler. He had just experienced a measure of this from an underruler. It was correction encased in love. He realized love was not about pleasing others—it was truth.

Patient inclined her head. "Your king awaits you." With that, she stepped back to her throne and the Head Guard motioned Selfish on to walk alone before the throne. They would wait in the lower tier, where the thrones of the underrulers were located.

SELFISH BEFORE JALYN

As he was instructed, Selfish cautiously climbed the steps to the plateau just below the majestic throne. He then looked up and beheld the king himself. No one in this entire assembly was as handsome, regal, and majestic as Jalyn. His splendor was both captivating and awesome. Selfish had never seen anyone like this man. He knew immediately no one could resist his wisdom and strength.

Gazing into Jalyn's eyes for the first time, Selfish recognized the king was more tender and terrifying than he ever could have imagined. His eyes gazed right through Selfish; he felt naked, and it was clear nothing was hidden. Selfish lost all confidence of a favorable judgment, but he no longer cared. He now desired truth more than anything else.

Jalyn said, "Welcome to my kingdom, Selfish. I've longed for this moment. You are a ruler of my people in Endel; are you worthy to rule and sit upon one of the thrones in Affabel?"

This normally confident man, who was never at a loss for words, was now speechless. He once felt he could do a great job of leading, but after all the conversations, he imagined his thoughts were most likely deluded.

Jalyn asked an underruler who was close in proximity, "How many citizens did Selfish impact for the kingdom?"

Very few were named. Selfish was shocked and speechless at this revelation.

The king then asked the same ruler, "What is the number of citizens Patient impacted for this kingdom?"

"Just over five thousand, my lord," replied the ruler.

"How can this be?" blurted out Selfish. "She was just a secretary, and I the mayor. How could my number be so few and hers so vast?"

Jalyn firmly replied, "I didn't ask how many were influenced, but how many were influenced for the kingdom!"

His tone softened but remained resolute. "Your former teacher, Motivator, now known as Humbled, had more influence on people's lives than even yourself. However, very little of it extended into this realm. This is why he is not a ruler in the city. The influence that endures this Judgment Seat is in accordance with my ways and my kingdom."

Jalyn continued, "Allow me to share with you some of the ways Patience influenced over five thousand. She cheerfully gave to the school, both financially and through service. Therefore, all who were benefited by the school's ministry were credited to her."

Selfish countered, "But I too gave to the school."

Jalyn replied, "Your contributions were motivated by appeasing your conscience or by maintaining or repairing a reputation. For this you received your full reward in Endel. Patient, on the other hand, gave out of passion for the kingdom and love for the people. Patient led a man named Brutal to my service. At this moment he is in the Hall of Life awaiting his judgment. He will be renamed Evangelist because he became a great communicator of my ways. He personally influenced over a thousand lives for the kingdom. All those lives he built were credited to Patient's account because she led him to my service and supported the school that trained him."

Selfish remembered Brutal from Endel, and after a conversion he thought that Brutal was too zealous in his beliefs. He was a contributing writer for the community newspaper and frequently shared in his columns the citizens' lack of commitment toward the kingdom. He also rallied numerous Endelites to phone and email council members requesting their support for the school's expansion. He made known his displeasure when Selfish swayed the vote and denied the school the land. For these reasons Selfish had disliked Brutal. Now he felt ashamed as he realized all Brutal stood for was in line with the kingdom's advancement. How could Selfish have been so blind?

Jalyn continued to show other ways Patient had influenced the lives of Endelites for the kingdom. There were many little things that added together to count for so much. She treated everyone kindly out of a pure heart of love. She was generous to those in need. She was resolute in her firm stance for truth. When the king was through discussing Patient, he reviewed Selfish's life extensively. As Patient foretold, every motive, word, and deed was evaluated.

Selfish saw the good he had done in the king's name but was overwhelmed by how much of his life works were motivated by his own protection, reputation, and selfish motives. By the time the review was complete, Selfish felt certain he was doomed.

He cried out before the king, "I deserve to be punished the

rest of my life. I deserve Lone; I've wasted so much and produced so little in return for the talents and responsibilities I had." The pain Selfish felt was indescribable; tears were streaming down his face. This man, who'd been so confident before entering the Great Hall, was now grasping for a thread to hang on to. All he had left was the hope of mercy. But even this he really didn't believe he deserved. He braced himself in anticipation of hearing the king pronounce his judgment to Lone.

After moments of heavy silence, the king finally spoke, "Selfish, you are my servant. You believed in me and submitted to my lordship, even though you wasted so much. I love and welcome you into my kingdom for the rest of your life."

Selfish was stunned. He looked up then burst into tears, not of sorrow, but of tremendous joy. He was overwhelmed by the mercy and goodness of this great king. In just a split second, much of what he'd heard of Jalyn's character became clear. Only seconds earlier he felt doom and pain such as he never imagined could exist. He deserved nothing, only to be an outcast—he deserved to be condemned; the examination of his life showed it. Now with the most tender and kind words imaginable, he was hearing this awe-inspiring king welcome him to this majestic city. What mercy! What love! What amazing love!

Selfish had watched as just about everything he had done in Endel was burned up, but still heard the words, "I love and welcome you into my kingdom." He understood what his friend Content said as true. Anything he would receive was much more than he deserved.

The king spoke again, "Selfish, you shall no longer be known by your former name. Behold I give you a new name. In my kingdom you shall be known as *Unpretentious*. I've prepared a residence for you in the flatlands, and your occupation will be a landscaper. Though you will not be a ruler in this city, you will assist me in ruling the outer realms."

Selfish questioned, "Rule with you in outer realms?"

Jalyn responded, "All who live in this city are rulers. My

realm spreads to the farthest corners of the planet; there are many other cities in my kingdom. The citizens of these outer cities have not gone through the training in Endel as the citizens of Affabel, nor did they face the judgment. Consequently, they do not have the superior abilities the citizens of this city have. Though you will not be a leader in the city of Affabel itself, you will assist me in administrating my rule globally. Your specific assignment will be to lead through serving and training all the landscapers of the twenty cities of the continent of Bengilla."

Selfish bowed his head and wept. The kindness of the king was overwhelming.

The king walked over to a table and picked up an object, then turned and headed back toward Unpretentious. He walked down to the plateau and said, "Now, take and eat this piece of fruit."

Unpretentious took the fruit from Jalyn's hand and partook. It was the most delicious food he had ever tasted. It seemed to bring clearing into his mind and heart. His thoughts overflowed with great love and a desire to serve. As he ate, he was being cleansed from his former pain and dark thoughts. He felt invigorated, happy, and full of hope and faith. It didn't take long for him to conclude the fruit was from the famous Tree of Life the teachers spoke of in class. A huge smile came over Unpretentious's face as Jalyn watched in pleasure.

Jalyn then said, "Turn and face your family."

Unpretentious cautiously turned. He still felt a slight amount of shame knowing everyone had heard and seen the details of his life. When he was turned completely, the crowd roared with applause and shouts of joy, music played, and citizens even danced. Unpretentious could hardly believe the love and acceptance he was feeling from these regal citizens. It was the medicine that brought complete healing from all his errors in Endel. He was now fully clear.

He turned and caught the most glorious and joyful smile on Jalyn's face. It was then he noticed his eyes. They looked at Unpretentious with a love and warmth such as he had never seen before. Now he could hear Jalyn's thoughts, as Patient and the others could hear his, they were thoughts of acceptance, delight, and anticipation of years of bliss to come for this citizen he loved so much. Unpretentious fell to his knees and thanked the king. The king raised him to his feet and gave him a huge hug and again with a smile said, "Welcome, friend."

He then was escorted to his place toward the rear of the auditorium to await his fellow Endelites' judgment. Every tear had now been wiped away. There was no more sorrow, pain, or crying; the former things were passed away.

CHARITY AND HER JUDGMENT

The morning progressed, and all the citizens were called out of the Hall of Life with the exception of Charity. She remained alone. This was not a burden because the room was filled with several beautiful books by authors from the city. She was reading the Second Chronicle of Affabel when the Chief Guard came to call her. The Chief Guard spoke, "Charity, your king awaits you."

Her heart raced with joy. She would now have the privilege of beholding the one she longed to see and loved. She had waited years for this moment, and now it was upon her. The guard smiled as she approached, and they all walked together to the Great Hall.

Once the Great Hall's doors opened, she was overwhelmed by the magnificence she beheld. Her focus, however, was the distant throne of Jalyn. At this point all she could see was his outline. Her eyes swept the audience of the regal citizens of Affabel. *Oh what exceptional people*, she thought. *How could I ever call such my contemporaries?*

She noticed they all bowed as she passed. Why would these stately men and women bow to her? They were handsome and beautiful with their outfits of increasing glory as she approached the throne. They looked as though they were superhumans. How could such as these bow, especially to her?

She recognized several she knew from Endel. Their smiles were full of excitement and love for her. She wanted to stop and embrace each but sensed it was not the proper time. She noticed Ruthless and couldn't help herself. She ran over to him with a huge hug. The two rejoiced together.

After their embrace, Ruthless bowed to her and said, "Welcome to your new home."

Charity said, "Why do you bow to me, Ruthless? I'm not a god to be worshipped."

The regal citizen replied, "There is a difference between worship and honor. Only the Lord is to be worshipped, but in this kingdom, we honor those who served us well in Endel. We honor, as well, those who rule among us. We didn't understand the importance of honor in Endel. Charity, you served me in Endel. If it had not been for your obedience to the king, I would never be here; I would abide in the forsaken land of Lone. I am first and foremost indebted and grateful to the king, but I am also grateful and indebted to you. It will be my pleasure to serve and honor you the rest of my life."

He continued, "Charity, my name is no longer Ruthless. Lord Jalyn changed my name at this Judgment Seat to Reconciled. I'm one who was shown possibly the greatest mercy before our king."

Charity replied, "Reconciled, what a magnificent name. Dear friend, I didn't reach out to you in Endel so that you would serve me in return. I did it because I loved you and cared about your life and destiny."

"Your motives are exactly the reason I will honor and serve you. You will be greatly rewarded by the king. You labored out of love for Jalyn. You never reached out to gain the recognition of your fellow followers or to receive a reward. Jalyn delights in those who reach out to others with his love. It was so important we caught his heart while in Endel, not just his vision. You did both dear sister, and your heart motives were imparted to me. This is why I reached out so passionately to so many my last week in Endel. Now I've been rewarded handsomely for my labor, even though it was brief."

Charity smiled. "Reconciled, I am so happy for you. I will serve you the rest of my life."

"Charity, you already speak as one who has lived in Affabel for years," Reconciled responded. "We live to serve one another in this great city; in fact, those of us who lead are the greatest servants here. We have the heaviest responsibilities, and it's our delight. It's different than in Endel. The leaders here don't seek to be served, but rather rejoice that greater opportunities are given to minister. The greatest joy of any citizen here is to serve first our king, second our fellow citizens, especially those who touched us in Endel, and finally the citizens of the outer realms of whom you shall soon learn."

Reconciled concluded, "My dear sister, I'm proud of you; go to your king. He longs to see and reward you for your service to him."

With that, the two embraced and Charity rejoined the guard, and they proceeded toward the throne.

CHARITY BEFORE JALYN

Jalyn's features were now in clear view as Charity was roughly seventy-five feet from the throne. As she passed the rulers, she didn't even notice them bowing; her gaze was on Jalyn. She was awed by his majestic splendor.

She climbed the steps and upon reaching the plateau fell prostrate before her king. Jalyn stepped down and raised her to her feet. He spoke affectionately, "Charity, my dear servant, welcome to my kingdom. I've longed for this moment, to meet you in person."

Charity responded, "Sir, it is I who've greatly longed for this moment. You are my king. I hope now to be in your presence the rest of my life that I may serve you more fully."

The king then said, "Come and possess the kingdom which has been prepared for you ever since the creation of the world. I was hungry and you fed me, thirsty and you gave me a drink; I was a stranger and you received me in your *home*, naked and you clothed me; I was sick and you took care of me, in prison and you visited me."

Charity responded in shock, "When, Lord, did *I* ever see you hungry and feed you, or thirsty and give you a drink? When did *I* ever see you a stranger and welcome you in *my home*, or naked and clothe you? When did *I* ever see you sick or in prison, and visit you?"

The king replied, "I tell you, whenever you did this for one of the least important of these brothers of mine, you did it for me!"[11]

Jalyn then showed Charity how she had so greatly ministered to him by serving his people and obeying his laws. Her life was reviewed; each word, deed, thought, and motive of her heart. Everything was revealed. Her service, her giving to the school, the love she showed fellow citizens, her refusal to take part in careless or inappropriate activities and discussions, the persecutions she received for her passion for Jalyn, her labor to serve others through the restaurant, reaching out to wayward souls, hours of sighing and weeping for the lost, the stances she took in strictly adhering to Jalyn's ways, being excluded from socials because of her zeal for Jalyn, refusal to speak against fellow citizens or partake of gossip, and the list extensively continued.

Charity was shocked at all the ways she had affected and influenced others. Much of what she did to bring glory to Jalyn wasn't consciously planned or thought out. She just was following closely the manner of life taught from the ancient writings.

There were some things she did that were burned up. These brought Charity great sorrow and remorse for the missed opportunities or errors she'd committed. However, only a small fraction of her life's labors was lost.

CHARITY'S REWARD

After the review of her final thoughts, words, and deeds, the king looked to an underruler sitting close by and asked, "How many lives did Charity influence for my kingdom?"

The ruler replied, "My lord, 5,183 people—a little more than one sixth of the population of the community."

Charity was surprised. "How could it be so many?"

Jalyn replied, "Recall in the ancient writings that I promised to 'multiply the seed you have sown and increase the fruits of your righteousness.'[12] Charity, my kingdom works on the multiplication principle."

The king then showed in greater detail how her obedient efforts multiplied to influence the masses, even though she wasn't a leader in the community. The ripple effects were staggering. Jalyn added, " 'As it is written, He [the benevolent person] scatters abroad; He gives to the poor; His deeds of justice and goodness and kindness and benevolence will go on and endure forever!'[13] A life submitted to me will result in a scattering effect that no citizen is fully aware of until he or she stands before this Judgment Seat. For this reason many did not obey in the small matters because they saw them as insignificant, yet most often it is the seemingly insignificant matters that produce the greatest harvest in this kingdom. The key was your obedience, no matter the circumstances."

Jalyn then said, "Charity, do you see the unoccupied throne to your left, which is near mine?"

She replied, "Yes, my lord."

"This will be your throne on which to sit, and you will rule with me for the rest of your life."

Charity was in compete shock. "Lord, I'm not worthy to rule. I was simply a restaurant owner. There are so many who are more gifted than I. How could I rule with you in such a magnificent kingdom? Selfish was a great leader in our community. How about him? Please give me a job that just serves you or your people."

Jalyn responded, "Selfish is in the rear of the Great Hall and will be a landscaper in the sections of our city called the flatlands. He will also serve landscapers in selected outer cities. However, you shall be a ruler because of the love you showed me and my people. Your endurance, loyalty, and humility have secured you this honor. For do you not recall my words from the ancient writings? 'For everyone who exalts himself will be humbled (ranked below others who are honored or rewarded), and he who humbles himself (keeps a modest opinion of himself and behaves accordingly) will be exalted (elevated in rank).'[14] Not only shall you rule with me, but I've prepared a glorious home for you on the coast of the Great Sea, near my home in the Regal Center. I know how much you love water and the sound of waves, so I've granted your desire and delight. I grant all faithful servants their heart's desires."

Charity was speechless.

The king continued, "You shall be governor over ten districts in the city. There are eleven other governors along with you overseeing a total of one hundred and twenty districts in the city of Affabel. You'll work closely with me along with the other seventy-seven rulers in our city who sit upon these thrones. The other rulers have governing authority over areas such as education, manufacturing, entertainment, the arts, and various other fields. The seventy-seven rulers, my Father, and I are the ones who plan, forecast, and oversee life in Affabel. You will be one of my trusted advisors and liaisons between my citizens and me.

"Not only shall you rule with me in this city, but as with the other seventy-seven, you shall also have leadership over the cities of the outer realm. I give you charge over the twenty cities of the continent of Bengilla. You shall be prime minister of this continent. All those who live and lead there shall report to you. You will only report to me."

As Jalyn spoke these words to Charity, Unpretentious stood in the back, full of joy for his fellow classmate. However, this was mixed with a twinge of regret as he thought how he had the opportunity to influence thousands of lives for the kingdom and did not. He could have been one of these underrulers privileged to work directly with Jalyn. He was thankful for his acceptance in the kingdom of Affabel, but he realized he had wasted time in his short stay in Endel and it would affect the rest of his 125-year life.

The king then said to the Chief Guard, "Bring the Crown of the Overcomer and the Scepter of Rulership to me."

Once Jalyn received the crown and scepter, he placed the crown on Charity's head. "Well done!" the king exclaimed. "You are a trustworthy servant. You have been faithful with the little I entrusted to you, so you will be governor of ten *districts and twenty* cities as your reward."[15]

Then the king handed her the scepter and said, "You shall no longer be called Charity, for I give you a new name; you shall be called Cherished Overcomer. For did I not foretell all the citizens of Endel, 'To him who overcomes and does my will to the end, I will give authority over the *districts and* nations—"He will rule them with an iron scepter" . . . just as I have received authority from my Father.'"[16]

Jalyn walked over to the table that contained one last piece of fruit. He brought it to Cherished Overcomer and said, "My dear friend and fellow ruler, you may partake of the fruit from the Tree of Life."

As Cherished Overcomer ate, she experienced a powerful cleansing and purifying just as the others had experienced when eating this most delicious food. Her thoughts overflowed with even greater love, and her desire to serve expanded to a magnitude she had not previously known. She was cleansed from any former pain and dark thoughts of Endel. All things were made new. She felt totally invigorated, happy, and full of hope and faith. She looked up to Jalyn and smiled. Then without knowing exactly why, they laughed joyously together. This was the beginning of a lifelong companionship.

Jalyn escorted her up to his throne and said, "Cherished Overcomer, turn and face your family."

She turned to thunderous applause. Great sounds of joy and dancing overtook the audience. It was more than what had been witnessed to celebrate any other judgment. The atmosphere was filled with exuberant rejoicing and celebration. A radiant smile filled the face of Cherished Overcomer, and the outpouring of such love amazed her. Her king put his arm around her and with great joy proclaimed, "Well done, good and faithful servant. . . . Enter into the joy of your lord."[17]

Thus concludes our story of the great king, his servants, and the renowned kingdom of Affabel.

A WORD OF INSTRUCTION AND CAUTION

In this chapter we've glimpsed what the judgment of saints will look like. I cannot overstress the fact that the glory of Christ's Judgment Seat will be much greater than any glory depicted by this story. However, this allegory illustrates many truths reflected in the kingdom of God. The details of this story are not meant to establish truth, rather to amplify and convey truth. When Jesus told parables, you saw the points He made in the stories and did not stumble over the minute details that had no real relevance to the truth He was communicating. Even so, I've attempted to carefully stress the important points of the story that have relevance to the eternal kingdom of Christ. By the time you are finished with this book, you will be able to reread the allegory and most likely glean even greater depths from the teachings of Scripture in previous and upcoming chapters.

Chapter 9

HEAVEN

—

As for me, I will see Your face in righteousness;
I shall be satisfied when I awake in Your likeness.
PSALM 17:15

L et's now discuss the passing of the righteous. Just as there is
a temporary abode for the unbeliever, called Hades, and later
a final home, called the Lake of Fire, there is a residence for believers who've departed, which will also one day change locations. The present home is referred by most as *heaven*, but is
scripturally referred to as *the heavenly Jerusalem.* The final home of
the righteous will also be called Jerusalem, but it will be located
on earth. This is the city that will come down from heaven after
the final judgment. It is called the New Jerusalem (Rev 21:2).

JERUSALEM ABOVE

You have come to Mount Zion and to *the city of the living God*, the *heavenly Jerusalem*, to an innumerable company of angels, to the general assembly and church of the
firstborn who are registered in heaven, to God the Judge

of all, to the *spirits* of just men made perfect, to Jesus the Mediator of the new covenant.

HEBREWS 12:22-24 (EMPHASIS MINE)

The *heavenly Jerusalem*, or *Jerusalem above* (Gal 4:26), is a city, as depicted by Affabel in our allegory. It is built on a mountain called Zion. The Father and Son live there, as well as myriad angels. The general assembly and the church of the firstborn reside there, which respectively refer to the Old Testament saints and those in Christ who have passed on. Jesus is called the firstborn of many brethren (Rom. 8:29). So the church of the firstborn can be called the Church of Christ Jesus.

Also notice "the *spirits* of just men made perfect" are found in this city as well. Who are these people, since he has already covered both the Old and New Testament saints who've gone on to their reward? Recall that when we are reborn by the Spirit of God, we become brand new creations; our spirits are made perfect in the likeness of Christ and we are found in Him. In this verse the writer does not refer to their souls or bodies, but only their spirits. I personally believe this refers to the saints here on earth serving Jesus. Think of it: The writer of Hebrews compels us, "Let us therefore come boldly to the throne of grace" (Heb. 4:16). The throne of grace is located in the midst of the city of God, and this invitation is spoken to us who are on earth. Could it be that many who yet live here on earth are well known in the throne room because they come often through prayer?

We are spirits, with souls (which is our intellect, will, and emotions), who now live in physical bodies. Jesus said the only way we can truly worship God is in "spirit and truth" (John 4:24). Paul reemphasizes this, "For God is my witness, whom I *serve with my spirit* in the gospel of His Son" (Rom. 1:9, emphasis mine). Because our spirits have been created in the image of God and we have been born again, we now have the availability through the blood of Jesus and power of the Holy Spirit to go into the throne room of God anytime we have need or we desire to worship.

VISITS TO HEAVEN

Jerusalem above is presently located in a place called the third heaven. It is a real place, which the Apostle Paul visited before his death. He wrote:

> I will go on to visions and revelations from the Lord. I know a man in Christ who fourteen years ago was caught up to the third heaven. *Whether it was in the body or out of the body I do not know*—God knows. And I know that this man—whether in the body or apart from the body I do not know, but God knows—was caught up to paradise. He heard inexpressible things, things that man is not permitted to tell.
>
> 2 CORINTHIANS 12:1-4, NIV (EMPHASIS MINE)

Bible scholars agree Paul was talking about himself. In fact, in the New Living Translation it is recorded, "I was caught up into the third heaven fourteen years ago." Notice Paul was unaware if he was in his body or out of it. This could only be explained by heaven being a real and physical place. I find there are many who think it is an invisible area where people float around as ghosts. No, it is a physical place, and there are streets, trees, animals, buildings, water, etc.

I know several who have been to heaven and back, just as Paul, but let me share one of my favorites. I have a pastor friend who I've preached for three times. In October 1979, his first evening of ministry, he came home from the meeting only to find his wife crouched down on their staircase weeping uncontrollably. He knew immediately something was seriously wrong. He soon learned that his ten-year-old son brought a small television set into the bathroom to watch a football game while taking a bath. He accidentally pulled the TV into the bathtub and was electrocuted.

My friend found his son; he had no pulse, his flesh was cold and blue, and his eyes were fully dilated, which indicated no brain activity. My pastor friend received paramedic and first aid training while working as a deputy sheriff for the Los Angeles County Sheriff's Department and had witnessed many deaths. If he had walked into a similar situation as a police officer, he would have pronounced the victim dead and called the coroner.

Now he was a believer who knew the power of prayer. He started praying and doing CPR on his son. After a few minutes the paramedics arrived, so he left the medical work to the experts and continued to pray. They were there for forty-five minutes without any success in bringing his son back. The EKG machine had been a flat line the whole while. The paramedics were now becoming restless waiting for what they thought was a fanatic to give up.

My friend finally prayed, "Father, I don't have any more faith. I've exhausted mine, but I know in Your Word You speak of another faith." (He was referring to the gift of faith found in 1 Corinthians 12:9.)

He said he felt something like a hand on the top of his head. Once he did, he sensed a very strong force and authority rise up from within his spirit, and he shouted at his son, "You will live and not die in the name of Jesus!"

All of a sudden the EKG machine started beeping, with pulse motions appearing on the screen. The paramedics jumped with excitement. By the time they got my friend's son down the stairs and into the ambulance, he had gone from blue to pink, his eyes were fully restored, and his body was now warm.

My friend was so excited. His son was now alive and well. He also had a great miracle story for all his friends of what God had done. What he didn't realize was the fight for his son's life had only begun. The doctors reported his son was in a coma. After examination, they found kidney tissue coming out of the catheter, which meant, in layman terms, that his body had a meltdown. They told him that if his son lived he would be a vegetable; and later on reported his socially functional age to be that of a three-month-old baby; with an IQ of 0.01.

To make a very long story short, after seven months of praying and refusing to give up, suddenly the boy came out of the coma. His father was by his bedside when this occurred and started firing questions to his son, to which he received immediate answers. My friend's son went on to graduate from high school, UCLA, and Bible school, all with honors. He was even the senior class president of his high school. He is happily married today with two children.

"DAD, I'VE BEEN WITH JESUS"

Three days after he was out of the hospital, my pastor friend noticed his son's face was glowing. He asked, "What's going on?"

His son replied, "Dad, I've been with Jesus. When the TV hit the bathtub, I didn't feel a thing. A huge angel grabbed my right arm and took me right out of my body. We flew through a tunnel at an amazing rate of acceleration. We hit the speed of light before landing on one of the streets of heaven."

He went on to tell his father that the streets were not golden, but made of pure gold; he could see through them. On earth, gold cannot be refined to the purity it is in heaven; however, on earth many times gold is used in windows to give them a gold color (such as the shield of the older face masks of astronauts, some cockpit windows of jets, buildings, etc.). So gold in its purest state is transparent.

The boy shared that the first people to greet him on the street were relatives who had died, and he named each of them, some of whom he had never met nor even knew their names; however, his mom and dad knew them. There was also in this welcoming group a lady named Phyllis. She was a neighbor whom the boy's mother had prayed with to receive Jesus a month before he was electrocuted. She had died two weeks after her conversion.

They were all conversing when suddenly he heard rustling, and the group around him split apart. There stood Jesus. The Lord took the boy on a tour of heaven. There were many streets and buildings; it was definitely a large city. The flowers, grass, and even rocks were all alive and singing in harmony. He said it seemed as if they were praising God. If he stepped on grass or a flower, it wouldn't crush but immediately rebounded to its previous position. He noticed the colors were vibrant and bright, much more so than he'd seen on earth. There were even colors he'd never seen before. He also got the privilege of seeing his mother's, father's and two siblings' mansions.

Then came the shock; Jesus told the boy he had to go back. He didn't want to leave heaven, but then Jesus brought him to a place where He pulled open a veil, and my friend's son could see his father calling him back. Jesus then said, "He is your father and has the authority to call you back."

Since that time, the boy has told his father to never call him back if he happens to die again—I found that part amusing when his father shared this with me. But heaven is so much better than earth; I've found those who experience it always have a very difficult time returning. Paul also fought this as he said to the Philippian church, "My yearning desire is to depart (to be free of this world, to set forth) and be with Christ, for that is far, far better" (Phil. 1:23, AMP). Not just better, or far better; but far, far better! He had experienced the city and wanted to return, but he chose to stay for the good of the kingdom.

The boy later shared with his father that he wasn't ten years old when he was in heaven. He had the body of a grown man. Many, including my friend's son, believe we will all be thirty-three years old when we are in our glorified bodies, Jesus' age when He was crucified, for Scripture says, "Yes, dear friends, we are already God's children, and we can't even imagine what we will be like when Christ returns. But we do know that when he comes we will be like him" (1 John 3:2, NLT).

This is just one of many real stories I could share. However, it along with Scripture shows the reality of heaven. Those who are faithful servants of Jesus shall enter this city upon leaving this earth.

SALVATION OF SPIRIT, SOUL, AND BODY

As already stated, a person's spirit becomes a brand new creation the moment they receive Jesus as their Lord. They are instantaneously in the likeness of Jesus. This is affirmed by John the Apostle's statement, "because as He is, so are we *in this world*" (1 John 4:17, emphasis mine). As you can see, John distinctly addresses those believers who are here on earth rather than those who have already gone on to their reward. A person who is truly born again by the Spirit of God is made perfect in spirit, here and now.

Once our spirit is saved, then starts the process of the saving of our soul, which, as indicated earlier, is comprised of our mind, will, and emotions. Our soul is saved or transformed by the Word of God and our obedience to it. The Apostle James confirms this by stating, "So then, *my beloved brethren* . . . lay aside all filthiness and overflow of wickedness, and receive with meekness the *implanted word*, which is able to *save your souls*. But be *doers* of the word, and not hearers only, deceiving yourselves" (James 1:19, 21-22, emphasis mine). It is important to note James is speaking to *brethren* in regard to their souls' salvation, not unbelievers. He emphasizes both hearing and obedience to the Word of God.

The soul is the only part of man in which we help determine the rate of salvation. We cooperate by hearing and obeying, which in turn speeds up the process, or, conversely, slows it. The transformation of our soul is crucial to our finishing well as believers.

Finally, there is one last part of us that must be saved: our bodies. Read carefully what Paul writes on this matter.

For we know that when this earthly tent we live in is taken down—when we die and leave these bodies—we will have a home in heaven, an *eternal body* made for us by God himself and not by human hands. We grow weary in our present bodies, and we long for the day when we will put on our *heavenly bodies* like new clothing. *For we will not be spirits without bodies*, but we will put on new heavenly bodies. Our dying bodies make us groan and sigh, but it's not that we want to die and have no bodies at all. We want to slip into our *new bodies* so that these dying bodies will be swallowed up by *everlasting life*. God himself has prepared us for this, and as a guarantee he has given us his Holy Spirit. So we are always confident, even though we know that as long as we live in these bodies we are not at home with the Lord. That is why we live by believing and not by seeing. Yes, we are fully confident, and we would rather be away from these bodies, for then we will be at home with the Lord.

2 CORINTHIANS 5:1-8, NLT (EMPHASIS MINE)

Reading these words gives us great hope and even purifies our souls. Notice he doesn't just mention but dwells on the fact that we will have eternal bodies. In another place he states, "For the perishable must clothe itself with the imperishable, and the mortal with immortality" (1 Cor. 15:53, NIV). Our bodies will be no different than Jesus', for Scripture states, "We also shall be in the likeness of His resurrection" (Rom. 6:5); and, "Beloved, now we are children of God; and it has not yet been revealed what we shall be, but we know that when He is revealed, we shall be like Him" (1 John 3:2).

Let's ponder Jesus' body after His resurrection; any trait His physical body possessed, we'll have once we experience the salvation of our bodies. Let's begin with what happened right at the tomb the morning He arose. Mary Magdalene first discovered the empty tomb and wept, thinking the Lord's body had been stolen.

She turned around and saw Jesus standing there, and *did not know that it was Jesus*. Jesus said to her, "Woman, why are you weeping? Whom are you seeking?" She, *supposing Him to be the gardener*, said to Him, "Sir, if You have carried Him away, tell me where You have laid Him, and I will take Him away."

JOHN 20:14–15 (EMPHASIS MINE)

Jesus wasn't different than a normal man; He didn't look like an alien from a sci-fi movie. She mistook him for the gardener; He therefore had a body that is very similar to what we possess. She didn't recognize Him for she couldn't dare believe He was alive. She saw Him brutally murdered, carried away, and buried. It wasn't until He spoke to her personally that she could believe it was really Him.

His body didn't appear different than a normal man, but we must ask, Was she seeing a vision of His spirit, or did he actually have flesh? This question is answered clearly when he later appeared to his disciples. He said, "Why are you troubled? And why do doubts arise in your hearts? Behold My hands and My feet, that it is I Myself. Handle Me and see, for a spirit does not have *flesh* and *bones* as you see I have" (Luke 24:38–39, emphasis mine). He has flesh and bones! But notice He says nothing about blood. That's because His blood was sprinkled on the Mercy Seat of God. Now what flows through His veins is, I believe, the glory of the God. So we too will have flesh and bone.

Jesus also was able to eat physical food: "But while they still did not believe for joy, and marveled, He said to them, 'Have you any food here?' So they gave Him a piece of a broiled fish and some honeycomb. And He took it and ate in their presence" (Luke 24:41–43).

Eating in His disciples' presence didn't happen just that one time; there were two other recorded incidents. Once in the home of certain men He met on the road to Emmaus, and the other when He cooked breakfast for His eleven by the sea. Therefore, we will be able to eat in our eternal bodies.

Jesus could speak, sing, walk, hold objects, and so forth as a normal man in His glorified body, but He could also walk through walls and disappear in a flash! You may question, "But He had flesh and bone and could walk through walls? And disappear?" Oh yes, see what John recorded. "That evening, on the first day of the week, the disciples were meeting behind locked doors because they were afraid of the Jewish leaders. Suddenly, Jesus was standing there among them!" (John 20:19, NLT).

In this encounter with His own, He asked Thomas to put his fingers in His hands and hand in His side. So again we definitely see He had flesh and bone. How was it that Jesus was just suddenly standing among them when the doors were locked? He came through the wall and just appeared, as He could just as easily disappear, which is recorded as well. After breaking bread for the men He met on the road to Emmaus, "then their eyes were opened and they knew Him; and He vanished from their sight" (Luke 24:31).

We too will have the capability to vanish in our resurrected bodies and reappear in a different location. This explains how we'll be able to travel far distances in the new heaven and earth. We'll have to do this because the city of God is 1,400 miles long and wide, saying nothing of the distance involved in travel to other galaxies. We'll also be able to drift in the air; recall Jesus floated up to heaven after forty days of interacting with His disciples. One of the things the boy from our earlier story reported to his father, as well as others I know who've been to heaven, is that you can walk, float, or immediately translate somewhere. There were parts of the tour where he walked and other parts he hovered and floated to locations.

THE MILLENNIAL REIGN OF CHRIST

We need to turn our attention to the relocation of the city of God, but first let's discuss the events that will transpire beforehand. At the conclusion of the Church Age, there will be a seven-year tribulation. The man of lawlessness, the antichrist, will be revealed and deceive many. He will oppose and exalt himself above God. He will persecute the saints and lead many nations into great darkness in rebellion against God.

In this time period, the Lord will come for His saints. Some believe it will happen before the seven years begin, others midway, and still others at the end. This is a matter that I will not discuss in this work. However, what's important is whether we are ready. Paul discusses this catching away of the church a few times in the New Testament. One such passage reads,

> For the Lord Himself will descend from heaven with a shout, with the voice of an archangel, and with the trumpet of God. And the dead in Christ will rise first. Then we who are alive and remain shall be caught up together with them in the clouds to meet the Lord in the air. And thus we shall always be with the Lord.
>
> I THESSALONIANS 4:16-18

This is not the Second Coming of Christ, because He will not come to the earth, but will meet His faithful in the clouds. The Second Coming occurs at the conclusion of the seven-year tribulation, with Jesus returning on a white horse, leading the armies of heaven; there will be a multitude of His saints in this number (Jude 14).

The antichrist, false prophet, world leaders, and armies of nations shall gather together to fight against the Lord and His army. Jesus shall smite them with His sword in a single day of battle, and the birds of the air will consume their flesh. This is commonly referred to as Armageddon because it will occur at a place in the valley of Megiddo, which extends from Mount Carmel southeast to Jerusalem (Rev. 16:16; Rev. 19:11–21).

There will be multitudes of peoples throughout the world who didn't rebel against the Lord in this battle, nor did they give their allegiance to the antichrist. Many theologians believe these will survive and go on living into the next age, commonly referred to as the millennial reign of Christ. They will remain in their nations and will be subject to Christ's global rule. They'll have natural bodies and continue to populate the earth.

So, in essence, there will be two types of people who will inhabit the earth, those who survived the battle of Armageddon and the saints who return with Jesus. The saints will have their glorified bodies in the likeness of King Jesus. They will be the ones who rule with Him on the earth. It is not difficult to understand how the two groups will relate; it will be no different than Jesus' interaction with his followers after His resurrection. The glorified saints will be able to talk, walk, eat, and socialize with those in natural bodies.

Scripture shows there will be global peace, in fact universal peace, as Satan and his cohorts will be bound for a thousand years. There will be no wars, prejudices, hatred, shame, crime, sickness, and so forth, because of the great turning to God by all the nations. The prophet Micah states:

In the last days, the Temple of the Lord in Jerusalem will become the most important place on earth. People from all over the world will go there to worship. Many nations will come and say, "Come, let us go up to the mountain of the Lord, to the Temple of the God of Israel. There he will teach us his ways, so that we may obey him." For in those days the Lord's teaching and his word will go out from Jerusalem. The Lord will settle international disputes. All the nations will beat their swords into plowshares and their spears into pruning hooks. All wars will stop, and military training will come to an end. Everyone will live quietly in their own homes in peace and prosperity, for there will be nothing to fear. The Lord Almighty has promised this!

MICAH 4:1-4, NLT

There will be global prosperity and a secure financial system, as the nations will abide by the laws of God. It will be an amazing time!

THE GREAT WHITE THRONE JUDGMENT

After the thousand years expire, Satan will be released from his prison for a short while. He will be given permission to go out and deceive the nations. This will not include the saints in their glorified bodies, but those in natural bodies who lived through Armageddon and or those born during the Millennium who populate the nations.

Rebels will assemble together and surround the city of Jerusalem to make war, and then the fire of God will proceed from heaven and devour them. The devil will be cast into the "lake of fire and brimstone" and tormented day and night, forever and ever. He will never be released again (see Rev. 20:7-10).

The Great White Throne Judgment will immediately follow. Hades will surrender the dead of every generation, spanning from Adam to this final battle. All humanity who did not enter into Jehovah's covenant in Old Testament times or submit to the lordship of Jesus thereafter will stand before the King and give an account, just as we saw in the judgment of Independent, Deceived, Faint Heart, and Double Life in our allegory. Anyone whose name is not written in the Book of Life will be cast into the Lake of Fire with Satan and his cohorts forever and ever.

THE NEW HEAVEN AND EARTH

Once the existing heavens and earth are purged by fire (see 2 Pet. 3:10-13), the New Heaven and New Earth will emerge. The Apostle John writes,"I saw a new heaven and a new earth, for the first heaven and the first earth had passed away" (Rev. 21:1).

The Apostle John then described the New Jerusalem's descent from above to be eternally located on earth. It's referred to as the Lamb's wife, or bride, because it will be home to all the ransomed of the Lord, stretching from Adam to those received into glory at His Second Coming. John gives an overall description of this New Jerusalem:

> So he took me in spirit to a great, high mountain, and he showed me the holy city, Jerusalem, descending out of heaven from God. It was filled with the glory of God and sparkled like a precious gem, crystal clear like jasper. Its walls were broad and high, with twelve gates guarded by twelve angels. . . . There were three gates on each side—east, north, south, and west. . . .
>
> The angel who talked to me held in his hand a gold measuring stick to measure the city, its gates, and its wall. When he measured it, he found it was a square, as wide as it was long. In fact, it was in the form of a cube, for its length and width and height were each 1,400 miles. Then he measured the walls and found them to be 216 feet thick (the angel used a standard human measure).
>
> The wall was made of jasper, and the city was pure gold, as clear as glass. The wall of the city was built on foundation stones inlaid with twelve gems. . . . The twelve gates were made of pearls—each gate from a single pearl! And the main street was pure gold, as clear as glass.
>
> REVELATION 21:10-21, NLT

The city is breathtaking. A wonder like no earthly city we have ever seen. It will emanate opulence, radiance, and splendor. There will be no corruption whatsoever because it is utterly pure.

John continues his description:

And the angel showed me a pure river with the water of life, clear as crystal, flowing from the throne of God and of the Lamb, coursing down the center of the main street. On each side of the river grew a tree of life, bearing twelve crops of fruit, with a fresh crop each month. The leaves were used for medicine to *heal the nations.*

No longer will anything be cursed. For the throne of God and of the Lamb will be there, and his servants will worship him. And *they will see his face,* and his name will be written on their foreheads. And there will be no night there—no need for lamps or sun—for the Lord God will shine on them. And they will *reign* forever and ever.

REVELATION 22:1-5, NLT (EMPHASIS MINE)

Notice Scripture clearly reveals we will see His face. What Moses longed for and was denied we will behold. How awesome and exciting!

Also notice that the leaves of the tree of life will bring healing to *the nations.* This raises some interesting questions. Who will comprise these nations since the saints will dwell in the city? Who will the saints reign over forever and ever? Will there be natural-born people alive in this time as well? Isaiah answers this.

Look! I am creating *new heavens* and a *new earth*—so wonderful that no one will even think about the old ones anymore. Be glad; rejoice forever in my creation! And look! I will create Jerusalem as a place of happiness. Her people [*the redeemed saints*] will be a source of joy. I will rejoice in Jerusalem and delight in my people. And the sound of weeping and crying will be heard no more.

[Now Isaiah turns to people outside the New Jerusalem] No longer will babies die when only a few days old. No longer will adults die before they have lived a full life. No longer will people be considered old at one hundred! Only sinners will die that young! In those days, people will live in the houses they build and eat the fruit of their own vineyards. It will not be like the past, when invaders took the houses and confiscated the vineyards. For my people will live as long as trees and will have time to enjoy their hard-won gains. They will not work in vain, and their children will not be doomed to misfortune. For they are people blessed by the Lord, and their children, too, will be blessed. I will answer them before they even call to me. While they are still talking to me about their needs, I will go ahead and answer their prayers! The wolf and lamb will feed together. The lion will eat straw like the ox. Poisonous snakes will strike no more. In those days, no one will be hurt or destroyed on my holy mountain. I, the Lord, have spoken!

ISAIAH 65:17-25, NLT (EMPHASIS MINE)

Many incorrectly apply this Scripture to the millennial reign of Christ; however, it clearly speaks of the age when the *New Heaven* and New Earth are in place. By examining the writings of both the Apostle John and Isaiah, we learn that there are people who live outside the city. They build their own homes in an everlasting time of universal peace and prosperity. This couldn't be the saints residing in the holy city, for they will have already had mansions prepared for them by Jesus Himself (John 14:2-4).

Notice also that there will be children. This also couldn't refer to the glorified saints because Jesus made it clear that those with glorified bodies would not give birth to babies, for they'll not marry. Jesus said, "For in the resurrection they neither marry nor are given in marriage, but are like angels of God in heaven" (Matt. 22:30). This was another fact the electrocuted boy confirmed in his tour of heaven.

These nations will inhabit the new earth, enriching it with planting, harvesting, and building. They will multiply and replenish the Earth unhindered; just as Adam and his seed would have if he had not fallen.

How can this logically be explained? One possibility, which can be argued, is that Scripture shows us that once the Millennium begins, natural human life will be extended because our final enemy, death, will be put under and destroyed (see 1 Cor 15:26). Jesus will have destroyed the curse of death, both spiritual and physical. Therefore, mankind could potentially endure the thousand-year period. At the end of the Millennium, they may be granted this gift forever if they don't rebel against God when Satan is briefly loosed. The psalmist writes, "Therefore the nations will praise you forever and ever" (Ps. 45:17). One way to bring understanding to this possibility is to view these people as Adam and Eve before the fall. Adam was not created for death, but to live forever. This gift was lost through his disobedience; he brought the curse of death and decay onto his race.

Only the redeemed of Christ, with glorified bodies, will reside in the New Jerusalem; however, it appears from Scripture that those in natural bodies will be able to traffic through and partake of the fruit and worship the Lord. This is seen in John's writings,

> The nations of the earth will walk in its [The New Jerusalem's] light, and the rulers of the world will come and bring their glory to it. Its gates never close at the end of day because there is no night. And all the nations will bring their glory and honor into the city.
>
> REVELATION 21:24–26, NLT

In the beginning, man fell to the temptation of sin. The penalty was death, both physical and spiritual, resulting in eternal death. However, the Fall didn't deter God from His original *eternal plan* for man on earth. Can God suffer in the end a failure to His design because of man's disobedience? No. God instead reversed man's defeat into a blessing by gathering out of fallen mankind a *glorified heavenly people* through Christ's redemption who would eventually *reign* over humanity in the new earth. This helps in understanding Jesus' words to the faithful steward, "Well done, good servant; because you were faithful in a very little, *have authority over ten cities*" (Luke 19:17, emphasis mine). Could these be cities in the Millennium and eternal era of the new earth?

If the Fall hadn't occurred, God wouldn't have had a glorified class of people to help Him administrate and rule over the affairs of earth and the universe forever and ever. He foresaw this in His eternal wisdom; for this reason Jesus is referred to as the "Lamb slain from the foundation of the world" (Rev. 13:8).

Once the Millennium begins and on into the eternal era of the new earth, God's original purpose—populating of this earth by natural man who will live forever—will be fulfilled. Jesus' words will be completely fulfilled: "Your kingdom come. Your will be done on earth as it is in heaven" (Matt. 6:10). It will be on earth just as my pastor friend's son witnessed in heaven. Beautiful new colors, living plants and rocks that sing praises to God, perfect architecture, living water, etc. A truly perfect world!

Isaiah concludes his prophetic book saying this of the new earth age:

"As surely as my new heavens and earth will remain, so will you always be my people, with a name that will never disappear," says the Lord. "All humanity will come to worship me from week to week and from month to month. And as they go out, they will see the dead bodies of those who have rebelled against me. For the worms that devour them will never die, and the fire that burns

them will never go out. All who pass by will view them
with utter horror."

ISAIAH 66:22-24, NLT

It is rather sobering, but throughout all eternity we will be
able to go to a certain place outside the city and view the horri-
ble fate of Satan, his angels, and mankind who rebelled against
the Lord. Perhaps this is the wisdom of God to always keep before every creature the terrible consequence of sin and rebellion.
Think of it: Satan fell into rebellion without a tempter, and if
God keeps this before His entire creation throughout eternity, it
will be a strong deterrent from falling into the terrible sin that
Lucifer and his angels fell into.

UPCOMING

As already stated, the glorified saints will live in the city of God,
the New Jerusalem. They'll receive their rewards and eternal positions of service to the Eternal King prior to the Millennium at
the Judgment Seat of Christ, which we will explore in depth in
the next chapter.

Chapter 10

THE JUDGMENT SEAT
OF CHRIST

—◆—

But why do you judge your brother? Or why do you show contempt
for your brother? For we shall all stand before the judgment seat of
Christ. . . . So then each of us shall give account of himself to God.
ROMANS 14:10, 12

W e all will stand before the judgment seat of Christ." Who
is Paul referring to, believers or unbelievers? In examining
these Scriptures in context, there's no misunderstanding: it is believers. He addresses the seriousness of a Christian judging or
showing contempt for a fellow brother, and those who do such
will have to give an account. Therefore, not only will unbelievers stand before God in judgment, as seen in earlier chapters, but
all Christians will also stand before the throne of God to give an
account of their lives here on earth. This is further emphasized in
his letter to Corinth, which we examined the previous chapter:

> We would rather be away from these bodies, for then we
> will be at home with the Lord. So our aim is to please
> him always, whether we are here in this body or away

from this body. For we must all stand before Christ to be judged. We will each receive whatever we deserve for the *good* or *evil* we have done in our bodies. It is because we know this solemn fear of the Lord that we work so hard to persuade others.

2 CORINTHIANS 5:8-11, NLT (EMPHASIS MINE)

Again, it is evident Paul is not talking about the judgment of sinners, but of Christians. His statement "We would rather be away from these bodies, for then we will be at home with the Lord" gives no room for doubt to whom he's addressing. No unbeliever will be at home with the Lord once he leaves his body; his eternal home is the Lake of Fire.

As stated earlier, the ungodly will stand before the judgment that has come to be known as the Great White Throne Judgment, and occurs long after the believer's judgment referred to in the above Scripture. Let's quickly review what we observed in the previous chapter. Jesus will return to this earth with the armies of heaven, conquer the antichrist, throw Satan into prison, and then set up His rule in Jerusalem for a thousand years. Afterward, Satan will be released from the bottomless pit and will be permitted to deceive the nations globally for a short time. Fire from heaven will consume the rebels, and the devil will be hurled into the Lake of Fire for all eternity. Then all the ungodly and unbelievers will be raised up from Hades to stand before the Great White Throne. Jesus refers to this as the resurrection of condemnation (John 5:29). All those whose names are not written in the Book of Life will be cast into the Lake of Fire.

On the other hand, the believer's judgment occurs long before the Great White Throne Judgment. The timing of this is not made clear in Scripture; however, we do know it will take place sometime after the church is caught away in the clouds and before the thousand-year reign of Christ commences. So there is roughly a thousand years separating the two major judgments. This is one of the points not reflected in our allegory of Affabel.

"For we must all appear before the *judgment seat* of Christ" (2 Cor. 5:10). The English words *judgment seat* in both Romans and Corinthians are from the single Greek word *bema. Strong's Concordance* defines this word as "*a step, foot-breath, a rostrum* (an elevated platform), *i.e. a tribunal* (a court of justice)."[1] The UBS Commentary states, "The *judgment seat was the judicial bench of a city court in the Roman Empire. Paul uses this imagery to refer to the judging activity of Christ.*"[2] Based on this, we will refer to the believer's judgment as the *Judgment Seat of Christ.*

The Judgment Seat of Christ is literally the divine tribunal of God. Scripture declares that the Father has committed all judgment to the Son (John 5:22). Jesus Christ is not only our Savior, but He is our Judge and will soon judge His own household. The simplest way to define the original word for judgment is to say it is a decision resulting from an investigation, *for* or *against*.

There are numerous individuals in church unaware that they will give an account of what they've done in their short stay on earth. Many have the erroneous idea that all future judgment is eradicated by their salvation. Indeed, Jesus' blood cleanses us from the sins that would have kept us from the kingdom; however, it does not exempt us from the judgment of how we conducted ourselves as believers, whether good or bad.

ETERNAL DECISIONS

The judgments or decisions rendered over us at His seat will be *eternal*; they will last forever; never altered or changed. Pause a moment and reflect back to our discussions in the first chapter, when we tried to mentally grasp eternity. James states our temporary life on earth is a passing vapor (James 4:14). This is his figurative way of comparing a lifetime of eighty to one hundred years with eternity. If he possessed the mathematical knowledge we have today, he could have been more exact in his portrayal. As a student of mathematics in college, I learned early in my education that anything divided by infinity is zero.

$$80 \text{ years} \div \text{infinity (eternity)} = 0$$

or

$$100 \text{ years} \div \text{infinity (eternity)} = 0$$

Any finite number divided by, or compared to, infinity is zero. It doesn't matter how long you live on earth. Even if you were to make it 150 years before dying; our life on earth is zero compared to eternity. That means, as believers in Jesus Christ, everything we do here in this zero window of time will determine *how* we spend eternity. Remember, *where* we spend eternity is determined by what we do with the cross of Jesus and His saving grace, but *how* we will live for eternity in His kingdom is determined by the way we lived here as believers.

Do you recall in our allegory how Selfish and the others he met in the back parts of the Great Hall regretted how they wasted their short time in Endel? A good part of their five years in Endel was spent for their own desires and benefits, rather than giving themselves entirely to the will of Jalyn. They faced the rest of their lives living far below their potential, for each had the opportunity to work and live closely to Jalyn, even to reign beside him in the city. They may, or even may not, have enjoyed the brief time following their graduation from the school; either way, their future was now set. For the next 130 years, their lifestyle would be a direct result of how they lived those five short years. Think of it: 130 years compared with 5 years. That is a very long time. Few people even come close to living this long on earth. If they only would have considered this before their time expired in Endel, they most likely would have lived differently.

As sobering as the lesson from this allegory is, it doesn't come close to comparing with what we are discussing. So let's try another scenario. Try imagining this: You are given one day, and how you spend that single twenty-four hour period will determine how you spend the next thousand years. Try to imagine a thousand years. That would date back before the birth of the

United States of America, before Christopher Columbus set sail to discover the new world, even before the Norman Conquest of England. A thousand years is a very long time. The rewards, the position you will hold, where you live, and everything else for a thousand years will all be determined by how you spent that one single day. Do you think you would give it your best? How would you live? Would you live differently than you're living now? Would obeying the Master take absolute precedence? Would you seek to influence people's lives for the kingdom? Would you treat people differently? The list is endless. Yet that is nothing in comparison to what we are discussing here, for one day divided by 365,000 days (the equivalent of one thousand years) is still not zero.

Let's go further. Let's say the way you spend that single day will determine how you spend the next one million years! Try to imagine this amount of time. Man has only been on earth approximately six thousand years. So this would be over 150 times longer than man has been on earth. That in itself is almost unfathomable. Yet this also is nothing in comparison to what we are discussing, for one day divided by 365,000,000 days (the equivalent of one million years) is still not zero. So it makes no difference if I was to say a billion or trillion years, you still would have a finite number when comparing it to one day.

So no matter how long we live on this earth, our time here compared to eternity is exactly zero. Could this be why the Apostle Paul tells us with urgency to live in such a way to receive our maximum reward? In his letter to the Corinthians he tells us that anyone who competes in athletics does so to win and then says to all of us:

> You also *must run in such a way that you will win*. All athletes practice strict self-control. They do it to win a prize that will fade away, but we do it for an *eternal prize*. So I run straight to the goal with purpose in every step. I am

not like a boxer who misses his punches. I discipline my body like an athlete, training it to do what it should.

1 Corinthians 9:24–27, NLT (emphasis mine)

We are to run in this life to win. In order to win, we must develop discipline and self-control and live with purpose. We are not competing against others, only ourselves, and our goal is to be well-pleasing to Jesus in everything we do (2 Cor 5:9). Read the Scriptures carefully; find out what our Lord desires in the way we treat people, what we pursue, what we give our time to, how we affect souls for eternity, how we give to His kingdom and to others, do we forgive others, etc. We will discuss this in more depth later. Bottom line: Live to win!

WIDE RANGE OF REWARDS

Scripture shows the eternal rewards and positions given to believers will not only differ but will span a wide range. They will vary from seeing everything lost and burned up all the way to reigning beside Christ for all eternity (1 Cor. 3:15; Rev. 3:21).

Many flinch when they hear the terms *lost* and *burned up* in regard to their lives; they find it hard to believe this could ever happen in heaven. However, it is made crystal clear to us in Scripture. Before I share the verses, let me preface by explaining that many times in Scripture the metaphor of a building is used to represent an individual life, and other times Scripture speaks of the church as a single building or temple. In these metaphors, we are depicted as the builders in regard to how we affect our own lives, others' lives, or the overall church. In fact, I'll reference this metaphor frequently throughout the rest of this book. Paul clearly states:

You are also God's building. . . . *But each one must be careful how he builds.* For God has already placed Jesus Christ as the one and only foundation, and no other foundation can be laid. Some will use gold or silver or precious stones in building on the foundation; others will use wood or grass or straw. And the quality of each person's work will be seen when the Day of Christ exposes it. For on that Day fire will reveal everyone's work; the fire will test it and show its real quality. If what was built on the foundation survives the fire, the builder will receive a reward. But if anyone's work is burnt up, then he will lose it; but *he himself will be saved, as if he had escaped through the fire.*

1 CORINTHIANS 3:9–15, TEV (EMPHASIS MINE)

We determine how we will build, and we have two major choices in our construction every moment of our life. One is to gravitate toward the temporal, that which appeases the flesh (wood, grass, or straw). The other is to live in line with our born-again spirit's desire, the eternal Word of God (gold, silver, and precious stones). How we build, or how we live our lives, will determine how we fair when the fire of His presence examines our work.

Not only will our works be examined, but our thoughts, motives, and intentions as well. This is why it is so crucial for believers to carefully listen to, heed, and hide in our hearts the Word of God, for it is continually "exposing and sifting and analyzing and judging the very thoughts and purposes of the heart" (Heb. 4:12, AMP). Nothing else can get to the depths of our heart as His Word.

If we *listen* to human reason, logic, or wisdom, we will gravitate in our thoughts and heart motives toward the temporal, and we will most often be completely unaware, just as Selfish was before he came into the Judgment Hall. For this reason Jesus warns,

Whatever is hidden away will be brought out into the open, and whatever is covered up will be found and brought to light. *Be careful, then, how you listen,* because whoever has something will be given more, but whoever has nothing will have taken away from him even the little he thinks he has.

LUKE 8:17-18, TEV (EMPHASIS MINE)

Jesus tells us it is what we *listen to* or *heed* that sinks into our heart and shapes our inner thoughts and purposes, which in turn determines how we build our lives. We must carefully heed the Word of God because it is a light to our path. Without it we will certainly stray, just as anyone would stray from a path in a dark night. You may stay on course for a short while per chance, but eventually you will wander off course. Once we stray, our construction can easily become motivated by the temporal and will not be exposed until the light of God's word shines on it. Paul amplifies this by saying, "But when anything is exposed and reproved by the light, it is made visible and clear" (Eph 5:13, AMP).

If we stray, two things can happen. First, which is the better of the two, as we hear the Word of God either as it is preached, read, or spoken by a friend, it convicts us in our conscience. This is why it is so crucial for us to maintain a steady diet of the Word of God. If we are wise, we will be quick to repent and ask forgiveness for our thoughts, motives, or intents. However, if our conscience is dull from our repetitive erring, it is harder to hear, and if our conscience is seared, it becomes practically impossible. For this reason, Scripture speaks of the importance of keeping our conscience pure (Prov. 4:23; 2 Tim. 1:3). If we protect and keep our conscience clear, we can easily sense the dealings of the Living Word in our hearts.

The second, which is not preferable, is to have our motives exposed at the Judgment Seat. If this happens, we lose our potential reward. So you must ask, is it worth resisting the conviction of the Word of God? For each time you do, your heart becomes harder and in a state of greater deception. We will not realize our own condition and will have it exposed by the light of His glory at the Seat of Judgment.

PREPARING FOR OUR ETERNAL FUTURE

The judgment of our lives will leave nothing undone; everything will be made visible and clear. This is why Paul refers to the Judgment Seat as the *"solemn fear of the Lord."* It will be a thorough investigation of our motives, intentions, thoughts, words, actions, etc. Paul's words as stated in *The Message Bible*, 1 Corinthians 3: 9, 12-15, are so powerful in regard to building and judgment:

> Or, to put it another way, you are God's house. . . . Take particular care in picking out your building materials. Eventually there is going to be an inspection. If you use cheap or inferior materials, you'll be found out. The inspection will be thorough and rigorous. You won't get by with a thing. If your work passes inspection, fine; if it doesn't, your part of the building will be torn out and started over. But *you* won't be torn out; you'll survive— but just barely.

I don't know about you, but I don't want to just barely survive the Judgment Seat of Christ. We're speaking about our eternal destiny here. Can you imagine how shocked many are going to be? In our allegory every character was caught completely off guard by what they faced except for the one who was prepared, Charity. They didn't take seriously the elementary doctrine that they should have been aware of from the beginning.

I constantly see wise people of this world preparing for their future. It starts out with working hard in school to open the door for a good career. Once in their career, they strive to purchase a house in order to build equity. They also develop some sort of savings. Some will take their excess money and invest, so it will work for them. All this is done to prepare for their future; they don't want to be found lacking, especially when they hit their retirement years. If these we speak of prepared for their retirement years like many are preparing for eternity, they would not only be headed for huge trouble, but they, unlike many in the church, would be very concerned and frightened.

Those who are wise in the kingdom realize we are not working to provide a future in "retirement years." I sometimes struggle with this—where is retirement in the believer's life? Don't get me wrong, I'm not talking about wise financial planning for later years; that is scriptural. But honestly, we should plan financially to free us up to serve in the kingdom. I've met several men and women who've retired from their careers and now are thrilled to be able give their lives completely in service to their churches or have gone to the mission fields.

To get back to the point, the wise I speak of are those who are planning their eternal future; they live with purpose and know their eternal destiny is being written by how they live on earth. This will provide for them a grand entrance into the Kingdom of God, rather than them slipping in with all they've done burned up and destroyed. See what Peter says in regard to this:

> Therefore, my brothers, be all the more eager to make
> your calling and election sure. For if you do these things,
> you will never fall, and you will receive a *rich welcome* into
> the eternal kingdom of our Lord and Savior Jesus Christ.
>
> 2 PETER 1:10-11, NIV (EMPHASIS MINE)

A *rich welcome* is to hear the Master say to us, "Well done, good and faithful servant; you were faithful over a few things, I will make you ruler over many things. Enter into the joy of your lord" (Matt. 25:21).

A few months back, the Lord gave me a vision. I saw the champions of the kingdom come marching in to the city of God. They were parading through the streets of gold with multitudes of men and women cheering on the sidewalks. King Jesus was high up on a platform, visible to the entire city. The faithful soldiers marched up the steps carrying to Jesus His spoils while the crowds rejoiced. In the vision it was as if the Lord was saying to those warriors, "Well done."

Then the Lord spoke to my heart. "Do you want to be one of these soldiers who bring the fruit they've harvested for Me, or do you want to be one of these on the sidewalks cheering?" I determined more than ever before to make my calling and election sure. I was resolute in that I wanted to see a smile of pleasure on my Lord's face when He reviewed my life, not one of sadness, knowing the potential He had given to me was lost. I'm determined also to make this known to all who love Him in my generation in order that they will walk with me into His great presence with His well-deserved spoils and see that longed-for smile of pleasure. We determine whether or not we will have a rich welcome through our service here. That is the main reason for the upcoming chapters.

UPCOMING CHAPTERS

The upcoming chapters will contain discussions of the major areas we'll be judged and rewarded for. Though room will not permit all to be covered extensively, we will address some of the more important issues. A good foundation will be laid, upon which you can further build in making your life count for eternity.

In closing, read slowly and allow the words of Peter to speak to you in regard to all you've read this chapter. You'll see key words and phrases that will make what we've said more alive. His words will also prepare us for what we'll soon discuss in the upcoming chapters:

Everything that goes into a life of *pleasing God* has been miraculously given to us by getting to know, personally and intimately, the One who invited us to God. . . . So don't lose a minute in *building* on what you've been given, complementing your basic faith with good character, spiritual understanding, alert discipline, passionate patience, reverent wonder, warm friendliness, and generous love, *each dimension fitting into and developing the others.* With these qualities active and growing in your lives, no grass will grow under your feet, no day will pass without its *reward* as you mature in your experience of our Master Jesus. . . . So, friends, *confirm* God's invitation to you, his choice of you. *Don't put it off; do it now.* Do this, and you'll have your life on a firm footing, the streets paved and the *way wide open into the eternal kingdom* of our Master and Savior, Jesus Christ. Because *the stakes are so high,* even though you're up-to-date on all this truth and practice it *inside* and *out,* I'm not going to let up for a minute in calling you to attention before it. This is the post to which I've been assigned—keeping you alert with frequent reminders—and I'm sticking to it as long as I live.

2 PETER 1: 3, 5-8, 10-13, MES (EMPHASIS MINE)

Chapter 11

GOD'S CUSTOM HOUSE

—

For God's gifts and his call can never be withdrawn.
ROMANS 11:29, NLT

We'll divide the believer's judgment into two major categories. First, our involvement in building the Kingdom of God in accordance with our callings and gifts. Second, how we built individual lives, which certainly would include our own. In regard to building others, our influence upon them; in regard to our individual life, how we cooperated with God's grace in developing Christlike character. This certainly would be a by-product of how we responded to His Word, what we believed, and our obedience to it. Our actions and works, words, thoughts, and motives will all be examined in all cases. We'll first examine the judgment of our role in building His kingdom, then later we'll discuss our personal lives.

"WHAT CAN YOU DO FOR ME?"

Our ability to build the kingdom is entirely based upon our obedience to the Holy Spirit because we can do nothing of eternal value unless it is by the grace of Jesus Christ. We are told, "Unless the Lord builds the house, they labor in vain who build it" (Ps. 127:1). We can build apart from the Spirit of God, yet our labor is worthless in the light of eternity; it will be burned up at the Judgment Seat. It is crucial we understand this.

God tells a group of people in the Old Testament who were busy serving Him,

> Heaven is my throne, and the earth is my footstool. What kind of house, then, could you build for me, what kind of place for me to live in? I myself created the whole universe! I am pleased with those who are humble and repentant, who fear me and obey me.
>
> ISAIAH 66:1-2, TEV

Simply put, the Lord is saying, "I'm God. Are you fully aware of Who I really am? So what is it you think you can do for Me?" It could be compared to a bunch of ants saying to a human being, "We are going to build a house for you." How ridiculous! We can do nothing in our own strength to serve and please our majestic, unfathomable, and awesome God. He really doesn't need us.

On the other hand, God then states who can please and benefit Him; those who are humble, repentant, and who fear and obey God. They are the ones who can build His house. How can they benefit such an awesome God? " 'Not by might nor by power, but by My Spirit,' Says the Lord of hosts" (Zech. 4:6). It is man cooperating in obedience to the Holy Spirit that brings results. It is only then that the laborers' work is not in vain.

COLABORERS

Here is the staggering fact; as majestic and awesome as the Lord God is, He, by His own choice, restricted Himself in what He does in the earth when He gave man the authority in the beginning. This results in the fact that God can be limited. That may shock you, but there are examples of this throughout Scripture. The descendents of Abraham "limited the Holy One of Israel" (Ps. 78:41). And again, Jesus said to the spiritual leaders of His nation, "Thus you are nullifying and making void and of no effect [the authority of] the Word of God through your tradition" (Mark 7:13, AMP). We are responsible to cooperate with Him to fulfill His desired goal, which is chiefly to have a people in Jesus' image and likeness whom He can inhabit for all eternity. For this reason we are called colaborers.

> For we are fellow workmen (joint promoters, laborers together) with and for God; you are God's garden and vineyard and field under cultivation, [you are] God's building.
>
> 1 CORINTHIANS 3:9, AMP

Almost every time in the New Testament you hear a reference to eternal labor in the kingdom, you will see it likened to working in a field or on a building. Why a field? Because the earth is the field where the growth of the Kingdom of God presently occurs. All of heaven cheers watching the saints build the kingdom on earth.

Why a building? Because God is looking for a permanent habitation, and we are the living stones that comprise His place of residence. Peter writes, "Now God is building you, as living stones, into his spiritual temple" (1 Pet. 2:5, NLT). So in essence our reason for being here on the earth is to build up His glorious temple or *house*, whether it's getting others saved, teaching, serving, ministering to them, etc. We have a role to be a pure living stone, as well as a builder of others, causing the living stones to be fit and joined together for a glorious house for God. Hence the personal and the kingdom responsibility we will all give an account for.

THE CUSTOM HOUSE

If I'm a custom home builder, I will design and plan the construction of the house before any work begins. Drawings will be prepared detailing how to assemble the house and the materials needed. But that's not all; every home builder knows that one of the most crucial parts of his job is scheduling the subcontractors at the proper times. These are the framers, concrete men, plumbers, tile layers, electricians, and the list goes on extensively. They are the ones who actually do the labor of putting up the building. If they are not scheduled properly, chaos is inevitable.

If a subcontractor does a bad job or misses his assigned time, then the builder will call on someone else who can do the job. The newly appointed worker will have to come in on short notice and possibly have to rip out the bad job done by the previous sub. Even though a subcontractor might miss his assigned job, the builder will make sure the work is finished.

I've also observed when the builder is working on *his own house*, he is quite particular to find the choice subcontractors. He makes sure they have the finest materials and anything else they require to get the job done right. He will oversee the work with great care.

God is the Custom Builder of *His own house*, but His house is a city, made up of people! He calls it Zion. We read, "For the Lord has chosen Zion; He has desired it for His habitation: 'This is My resting place forever; Here I will dwell, for I have desired it' " (Ps. 132:13-14). If you've had the privilege of designing your dream house, you know the excitement and anticipation of finishing it. You desire to rest there, for it will be where you will find joy and peace. Zion is just that for the Father, and He's anticipating it. In other references we are told, "For the Lord shall build up Zion" (Ps. 102:16), and "the Lord, who dwells in Zion" (Ps. 9:11), and "Out of Zion, the perfection of beauty, God will shine forth" (Ps. 50:2).

He's been working on His house for a few thousand years.

He laid out the plan before man was placed on earth. He knew in His omniscience that man would fall, even though that wasn't His design or doing. So out of His foreknowledge, He planned to build Zion out of redeemed mankind.

He had to start out with the foundation and chief cornerstone, who is none other than the Redeemer Himself; Jesus. "See, I lay a stone in *Zion*, a tested stone, a precious cornerstone for a sure foundation" (Isa. 28:16, NIV, emphasis mine). Because the Father designed and planned His house before creation, Jesus is called "the Lamb slain from the foundations of the world" (Rev 13:8), and Peter states, "He indeed was foreordained before the foundation of the world" (1 Pet. 1:20).

Not only is Jesus the foundation and chief cornerstone, but He is the Chief Subcontractor. Jesus didn't miss His assignment; He fulfilled it perfectly. In prayer He spoke these words to the Father just before His crucifixion: " 'I have finished the work which You have given Me to do' " (John 17:4).

God the Father began the whole design by scheduling Jesus at the appointed time (Gal. 4:4); then He scheduled all the subcontractors. However, they would not only be subcontractors, but also the materials of His House. These subcontractors are you and me. "He chose us in Him *before the foundation of the world*, that we should be holy and without blame before Him in love" (Eph. 1:4, emphasis mine). This speaks of our being the material of the house; we are the living stones.

But He also chose us as subcontractors, for again we read, "For we are God's workmanship, created in Christ Jesus *to do good works, which God prepared in advance for us to do*" (Eph. 2:10, NIV, emphasis mine). Notice He prepared our assigned tasks in advance. It doesn't say anywhere in Scripture that our assignments were given from the foundation of the world, although that is certainly possible, but we do know that "the works were finished from the foundation of the world" (Heb. 4:3). However, in regard to our personal assignments as subcontractors, the only thing we find written is that they were given before we were born. David says,

"You saw me before I was born. Every day of my life was recorded in your book. Every moment was laid out before a single day had passed."

PSALMS 139:16, NLT

Our life's work was foreordained before we were formed in our mother's womb. This truth is captured in God's word to Jeremiah. He said, "I knew you before I formed you in your mother's womb. *Before you were born I set you apart and appointed you as my spokesman to the world*" (Jer. 1:5, NLT, emphasis mine). The Apostle Paul also writes, "But when it pleased God, who separated me from my mother's womb and called me through His grace" (Gal. 1:15-16). Jeremiah's and Paul's testimony only confirm David's words that all of us were set apart to do a specific work for God before we were born. Each day was ordained; every moment was laid out, before a single day passed! The question is, Will we fulfill what was planned for us? Solomon states,

I know that whatever God does, It shall be forever. Nothing can be added to it, and nothing taken from it. God does it, that men should fear before Him. That which is has already been, and what is to be has already been; and God requires an account of what is past.

ECCLESIASTES 3:14-15

There is so much in these Scriptures. First of all, God has a plan. Nothing can take away from it being accomplished, and mankind cannot add anything to it. That plan, in a nutshell, is His completed custom house. He then goes on to say that those things that are presently being accomplished have been in the mind of God beforehand. What is to be accomplished in the future also has been in the plan of God beforehand. However, for that which has been done already, we will have to give an account! Did we walk in what He ordained for us to fulfill? Or did we mess it up or miss our assignment altogether. Did He have to assign another to do what we were called to do in the master plan?

So at this juncture I need to make this most important statement. Everyone has a divine calling on his or her life. Each of us has an important part of the master plan of God's house. So it is good that we know this truth:

> In regard to your calling;
> you'll not be judged according to *what you did*,
> but rather according to *what you were called to do*!

Let me give you an example. At the Judgment Seat, Jesus may say something like this, "Evangelist Anderson, please step forward and give an account of all the souls I called you to lead to Me."

That man may come before Jesus a bit confused and trembling, saying, "Sir, You mean accountant Anderson; right? I was an accountant with my own firm. This was my occupation. I set up many church and non-profit organizations. Those ministries influenced many souls into Your Kingdom. Do you have me mistaken for someone else?"

The Master may reply, "No, I called you before you were born to win multitudes in Asia to Me; give an account of where they are. If you had obeyed Me, you would have been rewarded greatly for all the fruit you harvested for My kingdom. Now as a result, your works will be burned up, as they were not in obedience to Me."

Then we may see this scenario. Jesus may then say, "Accountant Jones, please step forward and give an account of what I called you to do."

That man may step forward also very confused and trembling saying, "Sir, You mean Pastor Jones; right? I was a pastor of a church and had 250 members. I built that church from ground up."

To which the Master may reply, "No, I called you to work in the marketplace as an accountant and build a strong firm that would help many of My churches and ministries effectively fulfill what I ordained them to accomplish. If you would have sought Me earnestly, I would have shown you this. Then all the multitudes of people those ministries eternally changed would have been credited to you; you would have been rewarded for each soul. But now you will receive nothing for what you did, as it was not in obedience to Me. I also ordained you to be the head usher in a church across town from where you started your church. Had you obeyed, all seven thousand souls that this church eternally touched also would have been credited directly to you because you would have been a vital part of this body I called you to. Since you were not there, you will receive no reward for those seven thousand souls."

Allow me to give an example. I have a board member who is a dear friend and pastors a thriving church in the southeastern part of the United States. He started the church in 1991 with twenty-two people and is now pushing four thousand members. It is one of the easiest churches to preach in because of the hunger of the people. Multitudes have been saved and discipled in this church.

The church grew rapidly through much prayer, strong preaching, and hard labor, and they built a beautiful building to accommodate the large numbers of people. After several years, my friend observed a distinguished white-haired gentleman, always well dressed, attending the services. He also noticed that this man would sit in service after service and watch with tears running down his face. However, the pastor felt these weren't tears of joy.

Finally, this gentleman approached one of the associate pastors and shared that in 1981 the Lord spoke clearly to him that he was to start a church in this city. A few days later he had a dream of the building this church would meet in that he was to pastor. The dream was so vivid that he got a professional to draw a rendition of the building he saw in his dream. He then said that he ran into some resistance and backed off from starting the church. After a while, he traveled and ministered in other cities for a short time and eventually ended up back in the business world.

He then opened up a carefully folded paper and told the associate that it was the artist's rendition of the building he had drawn up in 1981. When the associate looked at the drawing, he almost went into shock. It was the exact building my friend had built years later in which they were now meeting. My friend has since ministered comfort to this man, but the gentleman has shared the difficulty he's had in getting over it. God does not intend for him to live in condemnation but to learn, grow, and find out how he can effectively serve the Lord the rest of his life.

I've heard many examples of people missing their destinies such as this. I've seen examples of it as well. In over twenty years of traveling to churches worldwide, I have seen senior pastors whom I knew in my heart were called to be associates, businessmen whom I knew were suppose to be in full-time ministry, and even pastors I knew whose calling was in the marketplace. I've seen people out of place in the corporate or business world; they worked for someone else because of fear of failing on their own. And then I've seen those who were not faithful to another because they just wanted to be their own boss. I've seen people marry out of the will of God and their calls have been thwarted, and others who have been entangled with certain friends who kept them from their calling. I've seen those entangled in a recreation, sports, lust for money or power, or other various scenarios—the situations are endless, but all kept these believers from fulfilling their role in the master plan of building God's house.

FIRST: HAVE YOU SOUGHT GOD EARNESTLY?

Bottom line: Are you fulfilling your destiny? You may think, *But I don't know what I'm called to do!* There could be a couple reasons for this. First, have you sought God earnestly? We are told that God rewards those who diligently seek Him in faith, not casually seek Him in wonder or doubt (see Heb. 11:6). If anyone earnestly seeks God, fully expecting an answer, he will be shown what he's been put on the earth to do.

I recall when I was saved in my college fraternity at Purdue University. I immediately started seeking God's desire for my life. I was a student of engineering and worked every other semester at IBM. One of the reasons that motivated me to know my calling, other than just desiring to obey God, was that just a few months after being saved I was in an office with a group of eight to ten engineers celebrating a man's thirty-eighth year of service. We were casually chatting and this man said to all of us, "I've hated coming into this job every day for thirty-eight years." Every one else in the room either agreed or snickered, except me; I was in shock.

As a rookie among these seasoned professionals, I wondered why no one else commented differently, so I blurted out, "Why have you done this for thirty-eight years if you've hated it?"

He looked back at me and said, "It's a job."

I, too, had found myself having an aversion to coming in. My dad was an engineer, and he said it was a good profession that was secure and paid well. But this encounter caused me to change my outlook. I thought, *No money, security, or anything else is going to keep me from my reason for being placed on earth.* I made up my mind right there that I would find out what I was called to do and what the next step was that I needed to take to move toward it.

I've learned that God will give you the overall picture of your life's calling if you seek Him early in your walk with Him. In other words, He'll show you the end from the beginning. Joseph was shown as a young boy that he would be a great leader; even his father, mother, and brothers would serve under him. It wasn't until years later this was fulfilled. Moses knew he would lead Israel at least forty years before his time had come. David was shown he was to be king while he was still a young boy watching sheep. It was years afterward that he became ruler of Israel. And the list continues.

My plans were to finish my engineering degree at Purdue, pursue an MBA at Harvard, and move up into high-level management in corporate America. I would marry and take several vacations a year and give a tenth of all I made to God. That was my personal idea of serving Him.

The more I sought God, the more I felt drawn to ministry. I didn't like the sounds of that either, but I was smart enough to know that in obeying God I would find fulfillment and satisfaction. Once I made the commitment to Him that I would obey no matter what, He began to show me an overall picture of what He had called me to do on this earth. In the early 1980s God had already shown me I would one day influence many nations with the Word of God as long as I stayed in obedience to Him. Needless to say, it blew my mind and I saw no way it could ever be accomplished because I was a small-town boy who didn't know anyone in ministry on a national or international level.

In the same manner as Joseph, Moses, or David's example, God will show us the final picture, but not all the steps to accomplish it. This keeps us in faith rather than reasoning. We need to seek and obey what He tells us, and then we move toward that goal. Frequently, however, our next step may not look as if we are headed toward the goal, rather the opposite direction. Being sold as a slave for ten years after your dream of leadership isn't exactly the logical step. This is why we are told to "trust in the Lord with all your heart; do not depend on your own understanding. Seek his will in all you do, and he will direct your paths" (Prov. 3:5-6, NLT).

A few months later, during my senior year of college, I stayed at the school in my fraternity house while every student went home for a four-day Thanksgiving break. I fasted and prayed those days, seeking God's direction and will for my life. A couple months later I received the direction for the next step, and it seemed totally opposite the natural direction to take for ministry. It seemed only logical for me to go to Bible school, but the Lord showed me I was to interview for a position of engineer. This is why God tells us to not lean to our own understanding.

I met with many companies on our campus and knew almost immediately I was to work for the Rockwell Corporation in Dallas, Texas. It didn't make sense at all because there were no Bible schools in Dallas that I was aware of, and I had thirteen job offers in various other cities, some that had Bible schools, and every one offered more money than Rockwell. However, I just obeyed. Once I arrived in Dallas, I walked into a church and the Lord showed me I was to plant myself there. It was in this church that I was raised up through serving, which led to the path that brought me to where I am right now.

SECOND: HAVE YOU PLANTED YOURSELF?

This brings us to the second reason why many don't find the will of God for their lives. They don't plant themselves in the local church. God's Word tells us, "Those who are planted in the house of the Lord shall flourish in *the courts of our God*" (Ps. 92:13, emphasis mine).

Those who plant themselves in the house of God, which in this life would be the local church, shall flourish in the *courts of our God*. An aspect of *the courts of our God* is the Judgment Seat of Christ. So we will flourish both now and at the judgment if we've been firmly planted in a local church. This is God's design.

It is the Lord who ordained the church, not men. Jesus says, "I will *build* My church, and the gates of Hades shall not prevail against it" (Matt. 16:18). Notice the word *build*. How can He build His church without physically being here? The answer is through His body, which is us. Again, this is why we are called colaborers. The grace, ability, and gifts are given by Him, and He is the One who supplies the supernatural power, but He must have yielded and obedient vessels to fulfill His work. The question is, are we erecting His church in cooperation with Him, or are we motivated by our own agenda; even if it is ministry masked?

Jesus has an overall church subdivided into local churches. One of the numerous examples of this would be His words to each of the seven local churches in Revelation: Ephesus, Smyrna, Pergamos, Thyatira, Sardis, Philadelphia, and Laodicea.

The church is also referred to as the body of Christ. Paul says, "He is the head of the body, the church" (Col. 1:18). Just as the overall church is subdivided into local churches, so the overall body of Christ is subdivided into local bodies as well.

The Lord is the One who places His people: "But now God has set the members, each one of them, in the body just as He pleased" (1 Cor. 12:18). This may be a shocking statement to you: *We are not the ones who choose where we go to church. He does!* Stop and ponder that for a moment. How many pick churches like they select clothes or restaurants rather than seeking God's desire in prayer in regard to where He wants them? How can you fulfill your destiny if you aren't even in the right location of His body? We shouldn't go to a city or a church unless we have sought to know God's agenda in the matter.

Every one of us has a role in the local church. We read: "Now you are the body of Christ, and members individually. And God has appointed these in the church: first . . ." (1 Cor 12:27-28).

Paul then gives a list of some of the major positions within the local church. Even though he doesn't give an exhaustive list, we know from other New Testament references that every believer is a part of the body of Christ and each of us plays a vital role, no different than each of the members of our physical body. If we are not functioning in our assigned body, then the local church is crippled, just as if one or more of your physical members, such as a leg, eye, or kidney, wasn't working or was working independently.

The sad fact is that much of the ministry of Jesus Christ is not being accomplished in our communities because of severely disabled local churches. Why are they crippled? It's usually not ineffective leaders, but professing believers who are living independently. Can you imagine if my eyes decided they were going to do whatever they wanted, or my legs or feet or any other part of my body? I'm amazed at what God has been able to do in America with the state of our church.

Why did the early church explode in growth so quickly? Let's examine and see,

> They joined with the other believers and devoted themselves to the apostles' teaching and fellowship, sharing in the Lord's Supper and in prayer. . . . And all the believers met together constantly and shared everything they had. They sold their possessions and shared the proceeds with those in need. They worshiped *together* at the Temple *each day*, met in homes for the Lord's Supper, and shared their meals with great joy and generosity—all the while praising God and enjoying the goodwill of all the people. And each day the Lord added to their group those who were being saved.
>
> ACTS 2:42, 44-47, NLT (EMPHASIS MINE)

Do you see that the believers were planted in the local body? They worshipped together while submitted to the leaders, shared the excess they had with those who were without, and this resulted in healthy church growth. People served the Lord through their local church, which included their home life as well. Being a part of the local church was their life. In fact, later a problem arose where some widows were neglected in being served food. The apostles summoned the local body of believers and told them it wasn't good for them to leave the ministry of the Word of God to serve tables. "Look around among yourselves, brothers, and select seven men who are well respected and are full of the Holy Spirit and wisdom. We will put them in charge of this business" (Acts 6:3, NLT).

Notice it wasn't, "We need some volunteers. Would anyone

mind giving their time to serve these ladies?" No, all the believers were committed to serve because they were planted in the local church. I personally believe each member was hoping he would be selected to serve. Seven men were chosen and then:

> Whom they set before the apostles; and when they had prayed, they laid hands on them. Then *the word of God spread*, and the number of the disciples *multiplied greatly* in Jerusalem, and a great many of the priests were obedient to the faith.
>
> ACTS 6:6-7 (EMPHASIS MINE)

They laid hands on these seven men. Wow, it wasn't to minister from the pulpit, teach a home group, lead praise and worship, go out on a ministry trip, but to serve food to widows at the church.

However, notice that once they took their working place in the body, as insignificant as it seemed, then the *word of God spread* and the number of the disciples *multiplied* greatly in Jerusalem. Here we find an amazing fact. In Acts 1-5, the word *added* is used several times in describing the growth of the church in Jerusalem. Here are some occurrences (emphasis mine throughout):

"And that day about three thousand souls were *added* to them" (Acts 2:41).

"And the Lord *added* to the church daily those who were being saved" (Acts 2:47).

"And believers were increasingly *added* to the Lord, multitudes of both men and women" (Acts 5:14).

Up to this point only the apostles were doing the work of the ministry in the local church, and Peter was the only one recorded preaching. However, at some point the believers realized everyone had two major responsibilities. First, to preach the gospel to other individuals, and, second, they had a role to play in the local church. The discovery that all believers were to tell the amazing story of Jesus' resurrection is found in Acts 5:42-6:1: "And daily in the temple, and in every house, they did not cease teaching and preaching Jesus as the Christ. Now in those days, when the number of the disciples was multiplying. . . ." There is no possible way for Peter to preach in every house because there were no radios, televisions, or Internet. All the believers were now preaching the gospel of Jesus Christ to their neighbors. Notice now the church was not growing by addition, but by multiplication. This is the first time in the Book of Acts you will find multiplied growth.

However, it doesn't stop there, for once believers took their places in serving in the church—the example given was the men serving widows in need—we then read that the number of the disciples wasn't just multiplying, but *greatly* multiplying. Greatly multiplying is *exponential growth!* Let me share with you the difference between addition and great multiplication (or exponential growth).

Let's consider a pastor who wins 10,000 people to the Lord every month. Would you consider this a fairly effective ministry? Do you know how long it would take him to reach the world? The answer is a staggering 60,000 years! However, that is provided nobody was born or nobody died in that 60,000 years! That is over ten times the span of years man has been on earth. Impossible!

Now let me give you an example of great multiplication. Let's say you win 2 people to the Lord and get them plugged into your local church. Then the next month each of those 2 lead 2 others to the Lord and get them plugged into the church. The next month each of those 4 do the same, and the following month each of those 8 lead 2 each to the Lord and get them plugged in. If this trend continues, do you know how long it would take to reach the entire earth's population with the gospel? The answer is a staggering 33 months. Yes that's right—less than 3 years! This is great multiplication.

Now do you understand how we can read this in the Bible? "This continued for two years, so that *all* the inhabitants of [the province of] Asia, Jews as well as Greeks, heard the Word of the Lord" (Acts 19:10, AMP, emphasis mine).

All the inhabitants. If the Scripture says *all*, it means *every* person. We are not talking about a city, but an entire region. They didn't have satellites, televisions, radios, cars, or even bicycles. This is exponential growth.

It takes a healthy body of believers to experience great multiplication. A healthy body is made up of believers planted into a local church, which includes serving in that local church (such as waiting on widows' tables; or ushering, working the parking lot, greeting, prison outreach, children's ministry—the list is huge). They are also reaching people where they work or live and getting them plugged into their local church. Remember, Jesus tells us to make disciples of all nations, not just converts. We must get those we reach plugged into our church for them to be taught all of the things Jesus commanded us (see Matt. 28: 20). It takes the entire local body, all the gifts within it, to get people mature in Christ.

The key is being planted in the local church. Here we will flourish. If you notice, Philip was one of the seven who were chosen to wait on widows' tables. However, later in the Book of Acts he is called Philip the evangelist. His work of ministry was now expanded to include many cities. "On the next day we who were Paul's companions departed and came to Caesarea, and entered the house of Philip the evangelist, *who was one of the seven*, and stayed with him" (Acts 21:8).

Even though he was now a great evangelist and had been moved by the Lord to a different city, he was still recognized as one of the seven. Serving in the local church was a crucial role to getting him into his life's calling. I tell people this, "You may have a life calling to do something great, but it will not mature properly if it's not first birthed from being *planted* in a local church."

Let me restate the Psalmist's words, "Those who are *planted* in the house of the Lord, shall flourish in the courts of our God" (Ps. 92:13, emphasis mine). Think of the word *planted*. To understand the operation of the kingdom, you must consider the law of seedtime and harvest. Jesus told His disciples that if you don't understand the principle of the seed, ground, and harvesting, you cannot understand all the parables (Mark 4:13). Simply put, the entire kingdom of God is:

> . . . as if a man should scatter seed on the ground, and should sleep by night and rise by day, and the *seed* should *sprout and grow, he himself does not know how.* For the earth yields crops by itself: first the blade, then the head, after that the full grain in the head. But when the grain ripens, immediately he puts in the sickle, because the harvest has come.
>
> MARK 4:26-29 (EMPHASIS MINE)

Let's say I have a handful of various seeds, all of which are fruit trees, but I'm not familiar with them. The only way I'll be able to discover their kind is if I plant them. Once planted, as time progresses, I'll discover the nature of each different seed. God places in each of us a predetermined calling. He then gives us gifts to accomplish it: "For the gifts and the calling of God are irrevocable" (Rom. 11:29). According to Jesus, my calling and gifts are in seed form. If I plant myself in the church, I will reach my God-given destiny. If not, I may use the gifts in my life for a different purpose than my Creator intended. So don't be deceived by success by the world's standards. You may be very successful in your gifts, but they may not be in obedience to the Master's plan. Allow me to give examples.

You'll see many in the world who have great voices and can move people to tears. Their gift was given to glorify God and stir people to pursue His heart and desires. They never fulfilled their destiny because they didn't get saved or were not planted in a church. This is one example of many I could give of those who never came to Jesus in their lifetime.

However, there are also people who have given their hearts to Jesus but attend church irregularly. They are not fulfilling their highest kingdom calling either because they've not been planted.

They may have been called to influence lives outside the church and they may be doing it to a degree, but their true destiny would have been different had they planted themselves in the church. A person can perceive certain gifts and use them in the way deemed best, but just as you will never know the exact type of a tree—its form, shape, strength, etc.—even so you will never know your true God-given destiny unless you've been planted in the church. This is God's design, not man's.

Another problem occurs with believers transferring churches when problems arise. Today, men and women leave churches readily if they see something wrong, especially in its leadership. Perhaps it is the way the leadership and staff run the church. Maybe it is the way the offerings are taken or the money spent. If they don't like what the pastor preaches, they leave. He is not approachable, or he is too familiar. Or it could be the lack of attention given by fellow congregation members. This list goes on and on.

Rather than face the difficulties and maintain hope, they run to where there appears to be no conflict. Let's face it: Jesus is the only perfect pastor or member of the church. But why do we run from difficulties in our Western society instead of facing them and working through them? Sometimes we say our ministry just was not received. We then go from church to church looking for a place with flawless leadership or members.

I have only been a member of three churches in the last twenty years, one in Dallas, another in Orlando, and my current church in Colorado Springs. Early on, I had numerous opportunities to become offended with the leadership over me (most of which, I might add, ended up due to my own fault or immaturity). I had the chance to become critical and judgmental with the leadership; however, I knew in my heart leaving was not the answer. In the midst of a very trying circumstance one day, the Lord spoke to me and told me, "This is the way I want you to leave a church: 'For you shall go out with joy, and be led out with peace' (Isa. 55:12)."

Most do not leave this way. They think churches are like vacation destinations. They can pick and choose what they like. They feel the freedom to stay as long as they are happy and trouble free. Remember, the place where God places us is the place the devil wants to offend us and get us out. He wants to uproot men and women from where God plants them. If he can get you out, he has been successful. If you will not budge, even in the midst of great conflict, you will spoil his plans and fulfill God's.

Again, "Those who are *planted* in the house of the Lord shall flourish in the courts of our God." What happens to a plant if you transplant it every three weeks? Its root system will begin to diminish and it will not blossom or prosper. If you keep transplanting it, it will die of shock. Many go from church to church trying to develop their calling. If they are not recognized in the place where God sets them, an offense is easily perceived. If something is done in a manner in which they do not agree, they are offended and gone. They leave blaming the leadership. They are blind to any of their own character flaws, and they do not realize God was refining them with the pressure they were under. This is not just limited to ministry, but to marriages, employment, and other such relationships.

Let's learn from the examples God gives with plants and trees. When a fruit tree is put in the ground, it has to face rainstorms, hot sun, and wind. If a young tree could talk, it might say, "Please, get me out of here! Put me in a place where there is no sweltering heat and no windy storms!" If the gardener listened to the tree, he would actually do the plant harm. Trees endure the hot sun and windy rainstorms by sending their roots down deeper. The adversity they face is eventually the source of great stability. The harshness of the elements surrounding them causes them to seek deeper for their source of life. They will one day come to the place that even the greatest of windy storms cannot affect their ability to produce fruit.

We used to live in Florida, a citrus capital. Most Floridians know that the colder the winter for the trees, the sweeter the oranges. If we would not run so fast from resistance, our root systems would have a chance to become stronger and reach deeper, and our fruit would wax plentiful and sweeter in the eyes of God and more palatable to His people. We would be mature trees that the Lord delights in rather than those uprooted for their lack of fruit (see Luke 13:6-9). We should not resist the very thing God allows us to live through in order to strengthen us in our calling.

THIRD: ARE YOU ENTANGLED?

The final reason we'll discuss why people don't find and fulfill their calling is entanglement. Weights hold them back from running and completing their race. Paul says of himself,

> "But I reckon my own life to be worth nothing to me; I only want to complete my mission and finish the work that the Lord Jesus gave me to do."
>
> ACTS 20:24, TEV

He was keenly aware of his life's mission. He had a job to finish, and he was also aware the job wasn't yet complete. How did he know? Just as Jesus knew, Peter knew (2 Peter 1:14), and others know who seek God, plant themselves in the church, and endure. The Lord reveals this to anyone who does not count his life more valuable than the will of God. In this lies the final key.

When we wholly lay down our lives to fulfill God's desired plan for us, then we will not only discover our calling, but fulfill it as well. An example is seen in the Gospels. On a certain day Jesus was traveling from one town to another and we read, "Now it happened as they journeyed on the road, that someone said to Him, 'Lord, I will follow You wherever You go' " (Luke 9:57). This man is excited, passionate, and sincere. He wants to follow Jesus all the way.

However, Jesus has a way of seeing right through enthusiasm

and going right to the true motive or snares of the heart. He saw an entanglement that would hinder this man in fulfilling his destiny, so Jesus addressed it by saying: "Foxes have holes and birds of the air have nests, but the Son of Man has nowhere to lay His head" (Luke 9:58).

This man most likely took comfort in earthly securities that he had in place. He probably had a good job, sizable equity in his home, and a retirement program set up for his latter years. Jesus hit this desire for earthly security head on by saying He had no secure place to lay His head.

I can just see this man, as well as many others in the crowd, beginning to back up slowly to the rear and eventually slip away. He's most likely saying, "Jesus, I'll usher for your meetings, play in the orchestra, or even park cars for the elderly who attend your convention in my town." The glamour of following Him just lost its luster, the good intentions of serving Him quickly faded, so he and many others drift off with the intentions of still supporting Him but not committing all.

Then Jesus looked at another who was still eager and said, " 'Follow Me.' But he said, 'Lord, let me *first* go and bury my father.' Jesus said to him, 'Let the dead bury their own dead, but you go and preach the kingdom of God' " (Luke 9:59-60, emphasis mine).

Wow, what a strong reply. Some may think Jesus was being insensitive and a bit harsh. However, we must understand the culture of that day. Scholars tell me tradition was when a father died and the firstborn fulfilled his obligation to bury him, then he would receive a double portion of the inheritance with the other sons receiving a single portion. However, if he didn't fulfill his duty to bury the father, the double portion would then go to the second-born son. This man had money on his mind. He most likely had a love for being well off, which would eventually have hindered him from following Jesus. He would have been distracted or made decisions based on finances rather than the plan of God.

With this instruction from the Master, I'm almost certain this man began to back up along with a slew of others. His reply was something to this order, "Jesus, I serve in your conferences you hold in my city, I'll sing in the choir or play the drums. I can do that. I'd love to do this and won't charge you a thing for my services." The excitement of following Him lost its appeal to this man and a good number of others.

Notice also this man didn't say he would not follow Jesus. He said he would follow, but the key to his loss is found in his words "let me *first.*" He wanted to make sure what he desired was accomplished. Nothing can come before the will of God if we are going to discover and fulfill His plan for our lives. I've seen countless believers who drew back from obedience because of the intent of attending to their priorities first. How sad that they missed their calling; someone else had to come in and fulfill their role. How will they fair at the Judgment Seat?

The crowd was getting smaller, and another eager volunteer stepped up. "And another also said, 'Lord, I will follow You, but let me *first* go and bid them farewell who are at my house.' But Jesus said to him, 'No one, having put his hand to the plow, and looking back, is fit for the kingdom of God' " (Luke 9:61-62, emphasis mine).

Again notice the word *first.* This man obviously was very close to his family, or had friends or a girlfriend back home and just wanted to run his decision to follow the Man from Galilee by them. His tight-knit relationships would have been the final determining factor in how he served Jesus. So the Lord directly confronted this by saying he would not be suited for kingdom service.

I can just see this man now backing up with still another large group of others. I can almost hear him saying, "Jesus, I'm good with public relations and human resources. I can be a consultant for your ministry and get you hooked up with some really good employees. I can also help secure the local conference center for your next meeting in our city. And when You come I'll be in charge of all the greeters and ushers who work your meetings. Shoot, I'll even just usher for You if you need me. I'm there for You!"

More than likely at this point Jesus had witnessed the large crowd of enthusiastic followers whittled down to just around seventy. There were probably thousands to start with, but He had directly dealt with three major areas of entanglement that hinder folks from fulfilling their destiny: security, money, and relationships. There are other areas, such as pleasures or the desire for other things outside the purposes of God, and so forth, but in my years of experience these are the majors.

Most, when reading the Gospels, miss Luke's next crucial statement because of the transition into a new chapter. However, let me remind you that this is one long letter, and the church later added the chapters and verses for easy reference. See what Luke says next,

> *After these things* the Lord *appointed* seventy others also, and sent them two by two before His face into every city and place where He Himself was about to go. Then He said to them, "The harvest truly is great, but the laborers are few."
>
> LUKE 10:1-2 (EMPHASIS MINE)

There is so much in these verses. First of all look at the words, "*After these things.*" We must ask, "after what things?" The answer is after Jesus witnessed the crowd whittled down to a remnant of people who were still standing there saying to themselves, "I don't care what it costs to follow Him, I'm willing and will do it!" They heard His response to security, money, and relationship issues, and they were determined not to allow anything to keep them from fulfilling their destiny in God.

Then Jesus *appointed* seventy new team members, who were most likely the only ones remaining. The words *appointed* and *chosen* are used synonymously in the New Testament. A person who is appointed is one who has been chosen, and one chosen is one who's been appointed. Jesus makes this statement in the Gospel of Matthew in two different places. If He makes an exact statement in two places in the same Gospel, then we need to pay close attention. Here it is:

> For many are called, but few chosen.
>
> MATTHEW 20:16; 22:14

Many are called. How many? Everyone to be exact. All believers have a call upon their life and gifts to accomplish it. However, and this may shock you, only few are chosen or appointed to fulfill that call. Why are only a few appointed? Because only a few will forsake all their own desires, securities, lust for money, hindering relationships, and so on to fulfill the call upon their lives. Notice Jesus said, "The harvest truly is plentiful, but the laborers are few" (Matt. 9:37). It is not God's fault our generation is not being reached, for God, "desires all men to be saved and to come to the knowledge of the truth" (1 Tim. 2:4). We are the ones who will have to stand before His Judgment Seat and give an account of why our generation wasn't reached. If we fulfilled our call, then we will not be judged; however, if we allowed entanglements to hinder us, then it will be sobering at the judgment.

You may say, "I'm only one of many." What if your liver said, "I'm an insignificant member of the body and nobody notices me or my work, so I'm going to do my own thing, rather than what I'm created to do"? As you know, without a liver, a body is in serious trouble. What if the lungs said this, or a leg, or foot, or any other part of our body? Just as every member of the body is significant, so every member of the church is significant.

Here is the sobering fact. Jesus tells us that only a few will fulfill their destiny as subcontractors in the house of God. Every believer will have a call to build, but only few will fulfill it. This means that the majority who stand before the believer's Judgment

Seat will suffer loss and not gain glorious rewards. I know this is not happy news; however, here is the good news: You can start now. You can get on your knees and pray and ask God to forgive you for all that you have allowed to keep you from obeying His will for your life, then move forward step by step. Smith Wigglesworth, a great evangelist of the twentieth century, didn't start his ministry until he was in his fifties. It is not too late for you.

Remember: The keys are first to seek God in faith; second, get planted in the local church God shows you, and by doing this stay submitted and obedient to the leadership or appointed leadership of that local body; and, third, forsake the entanglements of your life. As God shows you the weights, ask for His sword to sever the ties they have in your soul or flesh. His grace is sufficient to free you. Toward the end of your life, you want to be able to say with the Apostle Paul:

> As for me, my life has already been poured out as an offering to God. The time of my death is near. I have fought a good fight, I have finished the race, and I have remained faithful. And now the prize awaits me—the crown of righteousness that the Lord, the righteous Judge, will give me on that great day of his return. And the prize is not just for me but for all who eagerly look forward to his glorious return.
>
> 2 TIMOTHY 4:6-8, NLT

There is a crown waiting for those who finish faithful to the plan God laid out for their lives. They are the ones who will eagerly look forward to His return. The key word here is *eagerly*. Those who have placed other things before the will of God look forward to meeting Him, but not with such eagerness. I believe this is one of the main purposes of this book. To get you on track so you will be one of the warriors of this generation who eagerly looks forward to meeting your Commander and hearing Him say, "Well done, you good and faithful servant."

Chapter 12

MULTIPLICATION

—

The harvesters are paid good wages, and the fruit they harvest is
people brought to eternal life. What joy awaits both the planter and
the harvester alike! You know the saying, "One person plants and
someone else harvests." And it's true.
JOHN 4:36-37, NLT

The one who plants and the one who waters work as a team
with the same purpose. Yet they will be rewarded
individually, according to their own hard work.
1 CORINTHIANS 3:8, NLT

Those who serve faithfully in the kingdom receive handsome
eternal wages, and we will be rewarded individually, according to our own labor. Each of us has different responsibilities, but
all our different callings produce one result: lives being impacted
for eternity.

Many believe only the ministers who've touched millions of
lives publicly will stand in the front lines of heaven, receiving the
greatest rewards. However, this is not true. God does not reward

as man does, but according to righteous works of obedience. If He did reward according to human standards, entrepreneurial accomplishments would be the focus of ministry. As we saw in the last chapter, this is absolutely not the case. God judges and rewards according to what we've been called to do, what He's empowered us to accomplish.

EMPOWERED BY GRACE

In A.D. 56, roughly ten years before he finished his course, Paul wrote that he was the "least of the apostles" (1 Cor. 15:9). That would seem odd to those who've studied church history. He had impacted the entire known world and accomplished more than anyone else in his day. There was no doubt he was the greatest. So how could he make such a statement? The answer is found in what he continued to write: "But *by the grace of God I am what I am*, and His grace toward me was not in vain; but *I labored more abundantly than they all, yet not I, but the grace of God which was with me*" (1 Cor. 15:10, emphasis mine).

Interestingly enough, Paul acknowledged his accomplishments were more than any other apostle's, yet he still considered himself the least. The explanation of this oxymoron is found in his words "by the grace of God I am what I am." He was able to separate himself from all God did through him. Paul was completely aware he could not add to God's calling on his life, nor accomplish anything beyond the ability given him, and it is all summed up in one word, *grace*. This applies to all believers in regard to their calling.

Let me comment on my own experience in ministry. The books I've written are now in over thirty languages worldwide. They number in the millions, and the testimonies of changed lives are countless. Often people approach me asking for the secret to how I write. I laugh inside and think how terrible an English student and writer I was before God's grace manifested upon my life. It would take hours to write a two-page English paper and it seemed I would go through half a notepad before coming up with the first paragraph. Now when I write, the words fly out of me. I'm aware more than anyone else Who it is that writes these books. I'm really just the first guy to get to read them.

I was interviewed on a national television talk show, and the focus was to be the messages of the books I've written. However, as it progressed, the interviewer became more focused on me and my accomplishments rather than the message. I became very uncomfortable and looked within to seek the Holy Spirit's counsel for how to change the focus.

Within moments, there was a break in our discussion, and it was a perfect time to interject the comment the Holy Spirit gave me. So I quoted Solomon's words, "I know that whatever God does, it shall be forever. Nothing can be added to it, and nothing taken from it. God does it, that men should fear before Him. That which is has already been, and what is to be has already been; and God requires an account of what is past" (Eccles. 3:14-15).

I then said, "There are untold multitudes of pastors and ministers out there doing what God has called them to do. Some are overseeing churches of three hundred members in rural areas. Others are ministering to the lost and hurting in developing nations; they've sown their lives into the mission fields. Others are working in the inner city, placing their lives on the line daily to help those whom many consider worthless. And the list is endless. You will most likely never have any of these people on this program, but many will stand on the front lines of heaven because they've been obedient to what they've been called to do and they've done it out of pure motives."

I proceeded to say, "In regard to me, God has called me to do a specific work for Him, and its scope has touched many lives; this is why you've asked me on this program. However, I cannot add one thing to what He's called me to do. I can't enlarge, enhance, or make it go further in my own ability. The only thing I can do is mess it up, and that causes me to fear!"

The atmosphere of that interview immediately became solemn. The man who interviewed me, who also has an international ministry, registered the realization of what I said and changed the whole focus of the remainder of the interview back to ministering to the people.

This is true for anyone. If you've been called to be a wife, a mother of children, to serve in the nursery at your local church, and to intercede in the prayer closet, and you've done this faithfully to the end, then you will be rewarded greatly for your obedience. If you've been called to serve in prison ministry in your church, touch lives in the marketplace, and give largely to the work of the ministry, and you've done this from your heart as unto the Lord faithfully to the end, you'll be rewarded the same as an evangelist who faithfully won multitudes. The list is endless. I personally believe we will see far more mothers, businesspeople, secular leaders, etc. than we anticipated in the front lines receiving the greatest rewards from the Master.

GOD'S ARMY ON EARTH

The Church of Jesus Christ is God's army on earth. We all have positions of rank and gifts to accomplish our missions. Years ago, my wife was awakened by the Lord and shown in the Spirit this great army. She immediately woke me up at 4 in the morning reporting what she had just seen in the vision.

"John, it was a military in which everyone knew their rank, position, and responsibilities. They marched in perfect order, and there were open positions throughout the ranks, which I saw people slipping into. I saw you and me move into our two places of service. No one had to look at another to see where to march; they were all in perfect unison because their eyes were on the Master."

Then she made the comment that particularly caught my attention. "No one coveted another's position. Everyone was content to serve in the place the Lord created for them."

Keeping this in mind, let's revert to the custom home example. Recall, "Through wisdom a house is built" (Prov. 24:3). There are two types of wisdom through which we can build, one which is from above and the other is not.

> Who is wise and understanding among you? Let him show it by his good life, by deeds done in the humility that comes from *wisdom*. But if you harbor bitter *envy* and *selfish ambition* in your hearts, do not boast about it or deny the truth. Such "*wisdom*" does not come down from heaven but is earthly, unspiritual, of the devil. For where you have envy and selfish ambition, there you find disorder and every evil practice.
>
> JAMES 3:13–16, NIV (EMPHASIS MINE)

No matter what we do or how good it appears, if it is fueled by the motive of envy or selfish ambition, we are building with fleshly, unscriptural, and demonic motives that will certainly not be rewarded.

Webster's defines *envy* as "a feeling of discontent or covetousness with regard to another's advantages, success, possessions, etc."[1] If we view the call of God through the eyes of the world, then envy is unavoidable. There were preachers who envied Paul's life assignment. He wrote, "It is true that some preach Christ out of *envy* and rivalry, but others out of goodwill. The latter do so in love, knowing that I am put here for the defense of the gospel. The former preach Christ out of *selfish ambition*" (Phil. 1:15–17, NIV, emphasis mine).

These ministers were not content in the callings God had placed on their lives, and they desired Paul's success. This *envy* was fueled by their *selfish ambition. Ambition* is an eager and strong desire to accomplish something. When it is selfish, the focus is on ourselves rather than on the good of others. This motive will only produce disorder and strife, and will open the door to every evil thing.

Godly wisdom, on the other hand, will fuel *kingdom passion*, not *selfish ambition*. It will build according to the Master Planner's wishes, with His heart's desires motivating the labor. We read of this wisdom:

> But the wisdom that comes from heaven is first of all pure; then peace-loving, considerate, submissive, full of mercy and good fruit, impartial and sincere.
>
> JAMES 3:17, NIV

The wisdom of God is first pure; in other words, it is not two faced, having an outward appearance of godliness mixed with an envious or selfish motive. Its motives are to be faithful to the Master, accepting His assignments with joy. Its goal is not to be the greatest, but to be obedient to the call. It will rejoice at the advancement of the kingdom, whether it occurs through us or another.

Godly wisdom always focuses on the good of others, not itself. It's peaceable, not quarrelsome, overbearing, critical, or dominating. Its root motive is to see others walking in godliness and to fulfill their destiny. There are those who love the ministry and endure people; and there are those who love people and view their ministry as a vehicle to serve them. The latter do so motivated by godly wisdom.

Another trait of godly wisdom as seen in the above verse is *submission*. When we are content in our calling, we will be submissive to God's direct and delegated authority. We see the big picture of God's house being built, and there is only one Architect, Designer and Builder in charge. He's delegated His authority, abilities, and assignments to various individuals in His church. Those who will be rewarded greatly at the Judgment Seat are those who've stayed submitted to those in positions over them. Associate pastors who've split churches, wives who've resisted their husband's domestic authority in order to achieve their own ministries, employees who've built their own business while being paid by their employers, etc.—all will suffer tremendous loss at the judgment, even if they did produce great results in their rebellion.

Don't allow results to deceive you. We can have great results and still be in rebellion to God's authority. Consider Moses. The Lord told him to speak to the rock, and water would miraculously come out. He didn't obey, but rather out of anger struck the rock. Water still came out, enough to give three million people a drink in the desert. The people were probably saying to each other as they drank, "Wow, God sure listens to Moses. What power!"

Yet after they all drank, God called Moses aside and told him he would not enter the Promised Land because he didn't obey. Moses had results, in fact, miraculous results. But results are not the indication of success—obedience is. Godly wisdom is rooted in the fear of the Lord, which is to place God's will above anything or anyone else. Those who fear God are completely submitted to His authority.

Let's return to my wife's vision. She reported to me early that morning, "John, all the warriors had the exact same faces." In other words, it was a faceless army. This shows God doesn't have superstar positions. Understanding this will keep us from coveting another's place in the church or rebelling against authority in order to gain greater positions. Our promotion will come from above only if we stay planted.

DIFFERENT LEVELS

In the Gospels, we find two similar parables; however, each illustrates a different truth relating to the Judgment Seat. The first parable of the talents emphasizes that not all believers are given the same level of callings and gifts. Jesus says,

> For the kingdom of heaven is like a man traveling to a far country, who called his own servants and delivered his goods to them. And to one he gave five talents, to another

two, and to another one, to each according to his own ability; and immediately he went on a journey.

MATTHEW 25:14-15

The man who travels to the far country is Jesus, and the servants represent us. A talent is a measure of money; however, this being a parable the talent likely represents something else. One possibility, which I personally believe true, is the level of our call and gifts. There are certain individuals who have levels of ministry that reach nations, others that reach cities, and still others who reach home groups within the church. Another example could be some writers who reach millions, others who reach thousands, and still others who reach hundreds. Still another could be a person possessing an administrative gift that could bring a ministry to a megachurch level, while others could only handle churches of intermediate or smaller sizes.

Notice two important points in this parable. First, all the servants are given something, which tells us that there isn't one person in the church without a call on his or her life accompanied by gifts. Second, the different levels of calls and gifts given to each servant were according to his own ability. However, we must remember God gives us our abilities. We have nothing of value that wasn't given to us, for Scripture states, "For who makes you differ from another? And what do you have that you did not receive?" (1 Cor. 4:7).

In this parable, the man with the level five calling and gifts doubled his invested effort. The man with two did the same. I personally believe this shows that even if God gives us gifts, we must cooperate in our labor in order to hit the desired return of the Master.

However, the man with the level one calling and gifts most likely felt his were insignificant. He viewed his master as unfair, unreasonable, and austere. Why was he given less than the others? Why did they get national or citywide influence? Why did they get the ability to preach, sing, or write and not me? And so forth.

So he hid his talent. He didn't fulfill his calling; he used his gifts for himself or in arenas that did not profit the kingdom.

After a long time, the lord of the servants came and settled with them. The two individuals who doubled what they were entrusted with were rewarded with the same praise, "Well done, good and faithful servant; you were faithful over a few things, I will make you ruler over many things. Enter into the joy or your lord" (Matt. 25:21). The level five individual was not praised any more than the level two servant because they were both faithful and diligent. This again affirms God only requires us to be faithful to what He's given us.

The man with the single talent was sternly rebuked, and his lord commanded that what he was entrusted with be taken and given to one of the other men. He suffered great loss, while the man who was faithful gained even more.

In hearing this, I reflect on 1992 when God instructed me to write. I almost laughed in unbelief to what I'd heard in my heart in prayer. I hated English! If anyone had said I would write a book, I would have laughed him out of the room. However, ten months later two women came to me within two weeks of each other and gave me the same prophetic word: "John, if you don't write what God has given you to write, He'll give the message to someone else and you will be judged." I trembled and stepped out in faith, and the rest is history. If I had not obeyed, someone else would have written the messages and I would have lost the talent entrusted to me.

MULTIPLYING WHAT WE'VE BEEN GIVEN

We've extensively discussed that you can't add to your calling or gifts. Now let's turn our attention to *multiplying* what every believer has. The other parable similar to that of the talents, but different in a huge way, shows this truth. Jesus says,

A certain nobleman went into a far country to receive for himself a kingdom and to return. So he called ten of his servants, delivered to them ten minas, and said to them, "Do business till I come."

LUKE 19:12-13

A mina, as with a talent, is also a measure of money. However, in this parable each man is given the same amount, a mina each. Therefore, the mina doesn't represent the level of our calling or gifts, as with the talents. Rather, it represents the truths of God's Word, our foundational faith, the love of God shed abroad in our hearts and covenant blessings that are given to each believer. Each individual has the same; no one is given extra to start.

This parable speaks of what every one of us as believers possesses in Christ. Scripture states, "Therefore let no one glory in men. For all things are yours" (1 Cor. 3:21); and again, "Blessed be the God and Father of our Lord Jesus Christ, who has blessed us with every spiritual blessing in the heavenly places in Christ" (Eph. 1:3). These blessings are ours in Christ, but it is our faith that appropriates and manifests them here on the earth and it's our obedience and giving which causes them to multiply. This is why the nobleman, who represents Jesus, says to his servants, us, "Do business till I come." We are to take what we've been given and *multiply* it to the glory of God.

Examine the results of these servants:

And so it was that when he returned, having received the kingdom, he then commanded these servants, to whom he had given the money, to be called to him, that he might know how much every man had gained by trading. Then came the first, saying, "Master, your mina has earned ten minas." And he said to him, "Well done, good servant; because you were faithful in a very little, have *authority over ten cities*—" And the second came, saying, "Master, your mina has earned five minas." Likewise he said to him, "You also be *over five cities*—" And another came, saying, "Master, here is your mina, which I have kept put away in a handkerchief."

LUKE 19:15-20 (EMPHASIS MINE)

231

The nobleman sternly rebuked the final man, and the mina he had was taken away and given to the man who multiplied his mina to ten. The Master said, " 'For I say to you, that to everyone who has will be given; and from him who does not have, *even what he has will be taken away from him*' " (v. 26, emphasis mine).

In this parable, Jesus only addresses three of the ten servants. Again, the important difference of this parable is that each individual started with exactly the same amount; however, one man increased it tenfold, another fivefold, and the third did not multiply his at all. We also see the rewards differ according to how effectively they did business; their success directly determined how many cities they ruled over. The manner we multiply what is entrusted to us will directly determine how much authority is entrusted to us in the Millennium and in the New Heaven and New Earth. The faithful will rule with Christ, but not all will have the same authority. Our diligence here will determine the scope of our rule with Him throughout eternity. Notice that this is based on all of us starting at an equal place: a mina each. So the faithful wife and mother who serves diligently in the church has the same opportunity as the evangelist who wins hundreds of thousands.

This parable shows that each man had the potential of multiplying his mina many times over. In regard to our personal life, we can affect and build the Kingdom of God as much or little as we desire; the choice is ours. In fact, in certain ways we are unlimited. You may hedge at this comment, but allow me to expound through examples. There are many I can give, but just a few will open the door in your heart of this spiritual law. Let's first look at the Apostle Peter's words:

Grace and peace be *multiplied* to you in the knowledge of God and of Jesus our Lord, as His divine power has given to us all things that pertain to life and godliness, through the knowledge of Him who called us by glory and virtue, by which have been given to us exceedingly great and precious promises, that through these you may be partak-

ers of the divine nature, having escaped the corruption
that is in the world through lust.

2 PETER 1:2-4

Grace can be *multiplied* in our life. James says, "But He gives
us more and more grace" (James 4:6, AMP). It's by grace we can
do anything of worth in the kingdom. This ability is multiplied
in knowing God intimately. This is why every believer should
spend quality time with God. We should pray, read the Scripture,
read inspired books, listen to anointed messages, all the while
looking and listening to the Holy Spirit for His revelation. As we
do this, grace is multiplied in our lives, which gives us the ability
to do more.

I've discovered that the more intimately I come to know
Him and His ways, the more effective I become. If I possess an
ax that has a very dull blade, chopping a tree down may take all
day. However, if I sharpen it, I can chop five trees down in one
day using the same energy. This is what happens when grace is
multiplied in our lives. We labor with greater efficiency.

I recall street witnessing at a homosexual parade in Dallas,
Texas, years ago. For two hours I told these lost souls about Jesus,
and they just looked at me as if I were from another world. Some
fired Scriptures back to me as fast as I was speaking them. I sensed
somehow I was beating my head against a wall. It was like casting seeds on concrete. Then the Lord whispered to me, "Look to
Me, and I will show you what to do." In the thirty minutes following, He led me to people and gave me the words to speak.
The words were now sinking in, and three men gave their lives
to Jesus Christ. Looking to the Holy Spirit and listening to His
spoken word in my heart multiplied my efforts.

I've seen this in all areas of life. As I've grown in the Word of
God, I've had the ability to do more in less time. I've discovered
paths of truth that saved me hours, days, and even months of
time. Prayers become more powerful, God's presence stronger,
the impact on lives more efficient. Scripture promises this: "Fear

of the Lord is the beginning of wisdom. Knowledge of the Holy One results in understanding. Wisdom will multiply your days and add years to your life" (Prov. 9:10-11, NLT).

Two things are promised: more years, which means a longer life, and multiplied days are promised as well. This doesn't mean more years, as that would be redundant, but the ability to accomplish more in the same amount of time. It is described in another place as length of days. "For length of days and long life and peace they will add to you" (Prov. 3:2). The writer speaks of adhering to the Word of God, as Peter discussed above. Notice not only long life is given, but length of days. It multiplies our time.

MULTIPLY THROUGH GIVING

Anyone who comes to know God intimately becomes a joyful and generous giver because God Himself is an extravagant giver. He gave the greatest gift of all, His only Son. Nothing was of more value to Him than Jesus. The Lord never gives a halfhearted insignificant gift. He gave Jesus looking for a multiplied harvest, which was many sons and daughters coming into His family, and the harvest is still coming in.

Giving in faith is another sure way to multiply what we have; it can multiply what we possess to eternally affect lives, just as the Father did with Jesus. Jesus pointedly tells us, "I tell you, use worldly wealth to gain friends for yourselves, so that when it is gone, you will be welcomed into eternal dwellings" (Luke 16:9, NIV). Our money, used properly, can affect our quality of life in heaven and the New Jerusalem, long after the money is gone. "As it is written, He [the benevolent person] scatters abroad; He gives to the poor; His deeds of justice and goodness and kindness and benevolence will go on and endure forever!" (2 Cor. 9:9, AMP).

The poor are not only the financially poor, but also those who are poor in spirit. A person can have millions of dollars and still be poor in spirit. King David called himself a poor and needy man (Ps. 86:1) yet had stockpiles of gold and silver. In describing His mission, Jesus said, "The Spirit of the Lord is upon Me, because He has anointed Me to preach the gospel to the *poor*" (Luke 4:18, emphasis mine). There were many financially wealthy people Jesus ministered to, but they needed the Word of God. Ministries are raised up to do the work of Jesus, to proclaim and teach the Word of God to the poor. In giving financially to the work of God, we sow into the poor and our deeds endure forever.

It makes no difference how much or little you have financially. As long as you have a seed, which God says He will give you, you can multiply your efforts in building the kingdom. How does it multiply? Consider an apple seed. If you plant it, you'll eventually receive a crop of apples; but even more important is that within all those apples will be many more seeds. If all of those seeds are planted, they will yield many times more, and the cycle continues. It is exactly the same with our finances. See what Paul says to the Corinthians in regard to their giving:

> Remember this: Whoever sows sparingly will also reap sparingly, and whoever sows generously will also reap generously. Each man should give what he has decided in his heart to give, not reluctantly or under compulsion, for God loves a cheerful giver.
>
> 2 CORINTHIANS 9:6-7, NIV

Our multiplied harvest is in direct proportion to how much we sow. Notice it's not as God decides, but according to what we decide to give. If we purpose in faith and love to be generous, then our giving is greatly multiplied, "Now he who supplies seed to the sower and bread for food will also *supply* and *increase* your *store of seed* and will enlarge the *harvest of your righteousness*" (2 Cor. 9:10, NIV, emphasis mine).

The Lord will increase our store of seed, similar to the example of the apple seed just given. If we sow it, we will get many more seeds, and the process continues until we find in our possession a storehouse of seeds, giving us greater ability to bless others.

Through our giving, God will also enlarge the *harvest of our righteousness.* This is where it gets very exciting. This speaks of increasing our harvest of eternal rewards from the lives we've touched through our giving. So, in essence, we are multiplying our minas as the men in the above parable.

PARTNERING WITH OTHERS

Our giving to others, especially those in need who can't repay us, brings rewards both now in this life and at the judgment. In regard to multiplying our efforts to build the kingdom, we can do this through *partnership* in the gospel. See what Paul says to the believers in Philippi, who supported his ministry financially:

> But it was right and commendable and noble of you to contribute for my needs and to share my difficulties with me. And you Philippians yourselves well know that in the early days of the Gospel ministry, when I left Macedonia, no church (assembly) entered into *partnership* with me and opened up [a debit and credit] account in giving and receiving except you only. For even in Thessalonica you sent [me contributions] for my needs, not only once but a second time.
>
> PHILIPPIANS 4:14-16, AMP (EMPHASIS MINE)

Notice Paul speaks of the Philippian believers' *partnership* with his ministry. A *partnership* is defined as *a relationship between individuals or groups that is characterized by mutual cooperation and responsibility, as for the achievement of a specified goal*[2]. Healthy God-given partnership always gives the individuals involved the ability to do more than they could ever dream of doing on their own.

As I've repeatedly stated, Jesus commissioned us to go into the entire world and make *disciples* of all nations, not just converts. This assignment encompasses every believer. However, if all believers were in the field accomplishing this mission on a full-time basis, how will the gospel be funded? (This again is why God gives different callings and gifts to individuals.) The Lord never intended ministries to receive their necessary finances by the distribution of angels or by money falling from the sky. Rather, He entrusted His body with the privilege of giving, which creates a partnership.

God has called and ordained ministry gifts to reach the masses. As already stated, He gives special gifting, abilities, and anointing to accomplish this purpose. He didn't give this task to all, but to some in the church (see Eph. 4:11). The rest He commissioned and entrusted with another integral part. This includes working, making money or receiving wages, and reaching those within their circle of influence with the gospel. However, if you work full time, how can you reach the masses? The answer is found by way of partnership.

If you had a life-changing product but you were only able to produce two per month, it would be impossible to distribute this item to your city, country, or the world. However, if there were a company with both the ability and special equipment necessary to produce and distribute thousands of these same products per month, you would partner with them in order to get the job done. In doing this, you would not only be reaching your two people a month (personal evangelism), but also the additional thousands the company reached. You would have effectively multiplied your talents and efforts through simple partnership. This very same principle applies to Paul's comments to the Philippians. He continues:

> "Not that I seek or am eager for [your] gift, but I do seek and am eager for the *fruit which increases to your credit* [the harvest of blessing that is accumulating to your account]."
> PHILIPPIANS 4:17, AMP (EMPHASIS MINE)

Notice the phrase "*fruit which increases to your credit*." These Philippian believers multiplied their efforts in reaching and teaching souls by sowing finances into Paul's life and ministry through partnership. They gave that which is temporal, thereby converting it to the eternal, and in the process it is multiplied as well.

When you enter this type of partnership, Paul says you will have a "harvest of blessing that is accumulating to your account." This is your heavenly account. When you stand before the Judgment Seat of Christ, you will not only be rewarded for the lives you personally affected in your work place, neighborhood, school, etc., but also there will be the thousands or millions of others you reached and trained through partnering with God-ordained ministries. For this reason the Scripture tells us, "Give generously, for your gifts will return to you later. Divide your gifts among many" (Eccles. 11:1-2, NLT). It is important to note that this does not include your tithe (10 percent of your income). That should be given to your local church; your offerings of partnership are above your first 10 percent.

As you consistently give to God ordained ministries, you join with them as they touch others through their outreach. You have a part in all this because you partner with them. Here is the exciting news: The more you invest, the greater your reward. Know that God does not judge the gift so much by the amount but by your faithfulness to sow. God the Father is looking for quality gifts of the heart. He loves and blesses this, not just the amount. For example, someone could be faithful to give a gift to a ministry of thirty dollars each month and, by doing this, there may be some personal cost to him or her. God would see this gift as more than merely financial, for it is given from the life. Then there could be another who gave one thousand dollars each month, but this gift is extended out of their abundance. There is no personal cost or sacrifice involved. Both are beautiful and valuable to God, but the one who gave more through God's view is the one who gave the thirty dollars. This dynamic is illustrated with the widow giving her two mites (see Mark 12:41-44).

We must also keep in mind that God multiplies our gift in

this earthly life as well. This flow gives you a greater ability to give more. Scripture states, "There are those who [generously] scatter abroad, and yet increase more" (Prov. 11:24, AMP). Think of it; your investment not only grows eternally, but it also expands in the natural world, and this gives you the ability to reach more. It is a cycle that continually renews itself and increases.

Twelve years ago, a group of businessmen I know got together and committed to designate a certain portion of their business profits to the furtherance of the gospel. It started small, but with each passing year it grew. They remained consistent in their giving and partnership. Now their giving has expanded to the point where they have given over $120 million to the gospel. They have taken their mina and multiplied it for kingdom purposes; their reward shall be great.

There are a large number of men and women in the church whose businesses are very successful; however, many give to the kingdom a fraction of what they've earned. Even though they are hugely successful in society's eyes, what will be the Master's view of what they've held on to? Even if they made millions, will they be judged as the one who hid his mina? They didn't multiply what was given them for the sake of the kingdom. These who live in this manner are not *driven by eternity*.

On the flip side, my wife and I know a man who was planted in our home church and was very active in it, serving wherever he was needed. He knew he was not called to minister full time but to work in the marketplace. He set a goal to live off of 10 percent of his income and give 90 percent. He hit that goal. Yet with that 10 percent he drove a very nice car and lived in a beautiful home. His kingdom partnership caused his businesses to blossom and his 10 percent to expand. He applied the principles of Jesus: Those who are faithful in little will be faithful with much.

Another reason for partnering is that it is our chance to give back to the ministries that have touched us. Paul states, "If we have sown [the seed of] spiritual good among you, [is it too] much if we reap from your material benefits? If others share in this rightful claim upon you, do not we [have a still better and greater claim]?" (1 Cor. 9:11-12, AMP). This translates in the natural world as well. If you were given a gift from one friend, you would not write a thank-you note to another. You would thank the one who blessed you, and in doing this you would be establishing a relationship. God designed it this way on purpose, for the more people a ministry reaches and touches, the greater the financial needs become for them to operate. So if all who are being touched by the ministry give finances back (even if it is the two mites of the widow), then the expenses to continue at that level of ministry, as well as to expand, are covered.

Paul concludes his statement to the Philippians by saying:

> But I have [your full payment] and more; I have everything I need and am amply supplied, now that I have received from Epaphroditus the gifts you sent me. [They are the] fragrant odor of an offering and sacrifice which God welcomes and in which He delights. And my God will liberally supply (fill to the full) your every need according to His riches in glory in Christ Jesus.
>
> PHILIPPIANS 4:18-19, AMP

The promise of God supplying every need according to His riches is made to the ones who partner with ministries. If you tithe and partner with ministries, then you stand strong on this promise of God. You will never lack.

MULTIPLICATION THROUGH PRAYER

Another way we can multiply is through prayer. Just as through giving our finances to ministries, we can eternally touch lives we'll not meet until heaven by praying for individuals, families, churches, cities, and nations. We can also touch lives by praying for ministries. In our ministry, we have both financial partners and prayer partners. A prayer partner is someone who commits to pray for Messenger International on a daily basis.

People come to me often and say, "I'm praying for you every day." I can always tell if they sincerely do or if they are just saying it. To the ones who sincerely intercede for us, I say, "That is the greatest thing you can do to help us." It's true! If people pray, more lives get touched and with a greater impact. Prayer will also cause God to move on hearts to give toward His work, so if I had to choose between a prayer and a financial partner, I'd take the prayer partner first. However, both are very necessary.

MULTIPLICATION THROUGH
SERVING MINISTRIES

Another way we multiply is by serving ministries. There are many helpers and staff members in our organization whom Lisa and I constantly remind they'll receive credit at the Judgment Seat for every life our ministry touches. I know this from David's statement to all his men when returning from battle.

In 1 Samuel 30, we find the account of David pursuing the Amalekites and recovering what had been captured and stolen from the camp. When David and his men returned to the camp, some of the men who had gone with David didn't want to share the rewards with those who stayed behind to guard the equipment. But listen to David's response: "We share and share alike— those who go to battle and those who guard the equipment." From then on David made this a law for all of Israel, and it is still followed" (1 Sam. 30:24-25, NLT).

David is a type of Christ. So the statement, "From then on David made this a law for all of Israel, and it is still followed," tells me that it still applies today with Jesus and His church. All a ministry touches just isn't credited to the leader at the Judgment Seat, but all those who faithfully served, gave, and prayed, even if they were not on the scene of the battlefield.

ATTITUDE IS IMPORTANT

An integral part of receiving rewards for your service is your attitude, as we have discussed previously. It is not just our works that count, but the motives that fuel our works, and our attitude will affect our motives. God says, "If you are willing and obedient, you shall eat the good of the land" (Isa. 1:19).

I recall a time when I was very dry in my walk with God. I seemed to get nothing from our church services and especially my pastor's preaching. I certainly was not flourishing. I worked on the staff of this eight-thousand-member church reporting directly to the pastor, but I had become critical of him. In prayer one morning God spoke to me and said, "The problem is not your pastor, the problem is with you."

I was stunned. "What's my problem?"

The Lord then asked me what Isaiah 1:19 stated. I quoted the above verse as I had memorized it. He then said, "There is your problem. You keep saying you are not being fed, and this is correct, for you are not eating the good of the land."

I immediately countered with, "I am obedient; I do everything my pastor requests of me!"

Then the Lord responded, "I didn't say, 'If you were obedient you would eat the good of the land.' I said, 'If you are *willing* and obedient. . . .'"

He then said, "Obedience deals with your actions, and *willing* deals with your attitude; and your attitude stinks!"

The Lord went on to reveal how I did obey and even looked submitted, but my attitude was one that was critical, complaining, and judgmental, thus affecting my motives for serving.

I immediately repented, and the next service the heavens opened; I received from heaven once again. I shed tears while my pastor preached, thinking of all I had missed for months because of my attitude. Shortly afterward, these words of Paul inspired by the Holy Spirit became very clear to me: "For this was my purpose in writing you, to test your attitude and see if you would stand the test, whether you are obedient and altogether agreeable [to following my orders] in everything" (2 Cor. 2:9, AMP).

I realized that God will test our attitude of submission toward His will for us. I'm not discussing tolerating what the devil tries to throw on us, which Jesus paid the price to set us free from. We are to resist the enemy steadfastly through faith, prayer, and speaking God's Word. Rather, I'm speaking of our attitude toward the path God has chosen for us to walk. Paul says, "Your attitude should be the same that Christ Jesus had" (Phil 2:5, NLT). He not only drank from the cup the Father prepared for Him, but He did it willingly. For this reason Paul tell us to "be constantly renewed in the spirit of your mind [having a fresh mental and spiritual attitude]" (Eph. 4:23, AMP).

Why? Because our attitude will affect our motives, and at the Judgment Seat we will be rewarded not only for our works, but our motives that fueled them. Again, let's look at Paul's words.

> For we must all appear and be *revealed* as we are before the judgment seat of Christ, so that each one may receive [his pay] according to what he has done in the body, whether good or evil [considering what *his purpose* and *motive* have been, and what he has achieved, been busy with, and given himself and his attention to accomplishing].
>
> 2 CORINTHIANS 5:10, AMP (EMPHASIS MINE)

I've grieved in seeing how some have become bitter serving God. They've lost sight of the eternal perspective and they continue to work, but their attitude grew jaded and their motives became envious and self-seeking. This, more than anything else I can think of, has caused more people who started passionate to not finish well. This is why we are warned, "Looking diligently lest anyone fall short of the grace of God; lest any root of bitterness springing up cause trouble, and by this *many* become defiled" (Heb. 12:15, emphasis mine).

Notice it says "many." I have witnessed this repeatedly in over twenty years of full-time ministry, and it is heartbreaking. In the *Amplified Bible* this verse encourages us to, "Exercise foresight and be on the watch to look [after one another]." We should speak words to one another that will prevent this bitterness from setting in because we don't want to see our loved ones fall or fail to receive their full reward due to a root attitude that was not confronted.

My wife and I have especially looked out for our children and staff. Because we are called to travel full time, our children have grace on their lives for it; however, we don't want them to fall short of that grace. We have spoken words to them to encourage, guard their attitudes, and keep them strong.

I recall one day sitting down with our four sons and saying, "Boys, you are well aware that I travel many days a month, and your mother is out a few days a month as well. We do this because it is the call of God on our lives. This is how He has ordained us to touch people's lives for His glory and build His kingdom. You can view the call of God on our lives one of two ways. You can see it as your parents are being taken from you, and you are being ripped off of normal family life. Or you can see it as *your* ministry, not just your parents'. The way it becomes your ministry is that you are sowing your parents—sending them into the lives of multiplied thousands for God's purposes. If your attitude is this, then every soul we touch you will be rewarded for at the Judgment Seat. If you see us as being taken, then you will not receive one reward for the lives we touch. So boys, it all comes down to one word: *attitude*."

They grabbed what was said to them, and as a result they have never complained about us going. In fact, many times when Lisa and I have hedged over accepting an invitation they've encouraged us to do so. We have a fabulous relationship with them, and they all love God. Thanks be to God for His amazing grace. Now as a result they are multiplying their minas at a very young age.

I've done the same with our staff. I've told them, "You can

see working here as a job, and you will eventually get tired and bitter and not receive a reward at the Judgment Seat. Or you can see it as your privilege to touch millions of lives. With every book you mail out, every email you help us answer, every meeting you arrange, etc., you are a vital part of what God is doing to touch the lives He's ordained this ministry to touch. You are like David's men guarding the equipment." They grabbed it and have a great attitude. It's my job as a leader to speak words of life that will help protect that attitude, although the ultimate responsibility is theirs.

Keeping a great attitude helps us to multiply our minas and finish well. God is building His custom home, and what a privilege we have of being colaborers with Him. So no matter how insignificant your part seems, remember that every part is vital; and you can be as effective or ineffective as you choose. My hope for you is the same as John the Apostle's: "Look to yourselves, that we do not lose those things we worked for, but that we may receive a full reward" (2 John 8).

Chapter 13

PERSONAL INFLUENCE

—

But you know . . . how I live, and what my purpose in life is.
You know my faith and how long I have suffered.
You know my love and my patient endurance.
2 TIMOTHY 3:10, NLT

We'll be rewarded or suffer loss in regard to our influence in other's lives. This will not only result from our ministries, but also, and just as important, from our personal walk, the manner in which we lived and treated others.

How we view others motivates our treatment of them, either in an edifying or destructive way. If we see people as below us, we'll treat them as such; we'll take their needs lightly and speak down to them. If we value individuals, we'll seek to build and strengthen their lives out of a heart of compassion and love.

If we see people as sources, then we will use them, especially when our wishes, needs, or desires are placed above their value. If we view people as ones who are created in the image of God and are extremely precious and valuable, then our motive will be to bless others, even when it appears to be at our own expense. This is Christlike behavior.

SELFISH STRONGHOLDS

I was a very self-focused person before coming to know Jesus. After my conversion in 1979, the Holy Spirit had to attack selfish strongholds in my behavioral patterns. Needless to say, my first decade in Christ was a period of strong confrontation. One of the strongholds in my life was sexual lust. If tempted with pornography, I found it very difficult to resist. After struggling for six years, I was delivered on the fourth day of a fast in 1985. Once free, the process of being renewed in the spirit of my mind began.

Over the next few years I discovered the root of lust. The love of God continued to grow in my heart, and the value of people steadily increased. I realized the extreme selfishness of this addiction. To look upon a woman in a pornographic or lustful way was to reduce her to a piece of meat, and that fact grew to be revolting to my heart.

The revelation of a woman being created in the image of God, crowned with glory and honor, steadily grew stronger in me. I knew it long before, but it was only mental knowledge rather than being a part of my being. Over a period of time, I discovered the reality of God's transforming process. When pornographic images were flashed before me on a billboard, magazine cover, or television, I would feel assaulted and find myself very upset that this person whom Jesus shed His blood for was being reduced to a piece of meat. How I responded to women changed significantly as the revelation grew.

I'm shocked how women are treated by some, even in the church. They are looked down upon, viewed as if they are less valuable, and even scorned. This is absurd. Men and women are equal heirs of the Kingdom of God, and men, as the stronger vessels (which means stronger physical bodies, not stronger souls or hearts), should honor women above themselves. Men should respect, value, esteem, protect, and always seek to build up women. Husbands, you are the head of the union, but headship in the kingdom means you lay your life down for your family through serving, not lord it over your wife and children. If you see your headship role as putting you above your wife, then you will treat her in such a way that will wound and tear down rather than build up. You will give an account at the judgment.

WANTING ACCEPTANCE

There was another area of selfishness God exposed which was even more deceptive to me. In the mid-1980s I served on a church staff of roughly four hundred employees. Our church had over eight thousand members and an outreach to thousands of churches nationwide. I hated confrontation at the time, so I would avoid it at any cost. I was extremely kind and polite to people. At every opportunity I spoke nice things to people, even if what I said wasn't true. I built a reputation of being one of the nicest guys on staff. These reports were leaking back to me, and I reveled in them.

Then one day in prayer God asked me, "Where did I say in 1 Corinthians 13 that 'love is nice'?"

I was a bit taken back and responded, "Nowhere."

Then He said, "Son, do you know the reason you tell others only nice things, even if they are not true?"

I answered, "Why, no, I've not thought about it."

He quickly responded, "You fear their rejection. So who is the focus of your love, you or them? If you really love people, you would tell them the truth, whether they like it or not. You would be more concerned for their welfare to help them, even if it meant their rejection of you."

I clearly saw my selfishness masked by politeness; the painful truth was made clear. I used people for my need of acceptance. I wanted affirmation to appease my insecurities and didn't place as a priority helping others. I just wanted their acceptance.

This is why there are countless ministers who will only preach the positive side of the Word of God. They will refrain from warning, correction, or rebuke. They are more concerned about not offending their members and not seeing the size of the church dwindle than genuinely loving them. Who is the focus of your love, you or the people? If you saw someone headed for a cliff blindfolded, would you not cry out to them in order to turn their direction from harm's way? I've heard some of these "loving ministers" speak in private, and the way they talk about people is alarming. They treat waiters, bellmen, and other service people like they were lower-class citizens. How are they impacting people outside their public life? They will give an account how they influenced each individual they came in contact with.

FROM NICE TO HARSH

Once this revelation came in my life, the pendulum swung to the complete other side. I then became a harsh preacher. I still did not have God's love for people burning in my heart. I was more focused on being right than I was of the eternal well-being of individuals. I would sometimes come in and fry congregations. The focus was still me, but my selfishness was manifesting in a different way. My behavior was a classic example of this verse of Scripture: "You think that everyone should agree with your perfect knowledge. While knowledge may make us feel important, it is love that really builds up the church" (1 Cor. 8:1-2, NLT).

I look back now on the earlier days of our traveling ministry and feel so bad for some of the pastors who had to clean up after my departure. If I were a pastor back then, I certainly wouldn't have invited John Bevere to come and minister in my church. I'm so grateful to these leaders who saw in me the sincere desire to serve God and His people even though I still needed a lot of growth.

I wasn't flattering any longer to gain acceptance and avoid rejection, now I was speaking truth and confronting, but with the same selfish motives hidden away that God was purging in me. After a few years, a well-known pastor criticized me to some very influential leaders; I heard his comments from three different continents. I was very angry and devastated at first, but I knew offense would only cause me to drift from God. Eventually this man's attack against me caused me to cry out to God like never before for more of the love of God. I passionately petitioned God for a greater measure of compassion in my life. Without my realizing it, over time God matured His love in my heart for His precious people.

During this process, the Lord gave me a revelation that changed my ministry. You may think you're going to hear something very deep and profound, but it's really quite simple. You may even think it sounds silly until you ponder it. The revelation was, "A spoonful of sugar helps the medicine go down." I realized medicine's potency is not diminished if it is given with something sweet. It just makes it easier to take, and most times even makes it delightful. Now numerous leaders have said to me, "John, I'm amazed how you had us all laughing as we were being filleted by the Word of God. You made such a serious subject lifegiving." I realized I was being matured by God's grace. I'm so grateful to Him!

Even though the pastor who criticized me to the other leaders most likely didn't intend to bless me, he actually was one of the greatest blessings to my life. You have to remember sometimes God will use people's ill intent to get you into His will for your life. He used Judas's betrayal to orchestrate Jesus' destiny, the Cross. He used Joseph's brothers' evil intents to bring about Joseph's God-given dream. The list continues.

THE GOAL IS THE LOVE OF GOD

It all comes down to the way we view people. If we allow the love and compassion of God to grow in our lives, we will not look down upon others. Seeing people as below us fuels critical treatment, judgmental attitudes, harshness in our behavior, etc. See what Paul says to the Roman believers,

Why do you criticize and pass judgment on your brother? Or you, why do you look down upon or despise your brother? For we shall all stand before the judgment seat of God. . . . And so each of us shall give an account of himself [give an answer in reference to judgment] to God.

ROMANS 14:10, 12, AMP

If believers lose sight of the second greatest commandment, to love one another, we will inevitably fall into the trap Paul discusses above, looking down upon others. This mentality is especially found when one possesses biblical knowledge apart from the foundation of the fruit of the spirit.

Scripture tells us that *God is love*. Nowhere do we read *God has love*. He has power; He has gifts; He has authority; and the list continues. But Jesus is the very essence of love. Since this is so, then we should be no different, for we are reborn in His nature. This is why Paul says,

If I could speak in any language in heaven or on earth but didn't love others, I would only be making meaningless noise like a loud gong or a clanging cymbal. If I had the gift of prophecy, and if I knew all the mysteries of the future and knew everything about everything, but didn't love others, what good would I be? And if I had the gift of faith so that I could speak to a mountain and make it move, without love I would be no good to anybody. If I gave everything I have to the poor and even sacrificed my body, I could boast about it; but if I didn't love others, I would be of no value whatsoever.

I CORINTHIANS 13:1-3, NLT

Love doesn't originate in our words because we can say we care for someone, but our actions would deny it. It doesn't begin with our actions either. For Paul says in the above verse that we can perform the deeds that have the appearance of the highest love—giving everything to the poor and sacrificing our bodies—but it can be done apart from love. This tells us that true love originates from the heart.

When we love, we will be patient and kind with others. We'll not envy others' success because it will be our passion to see them win. We'll never boast of ourselves and refrain from all haughtiness and pride. We'll not demand our own way. We will not be irritable because of our impatient attitude. We'll keep no record of when we've been wronged but choose to forgive and release any debts. We'll never smile upon injustice, but our passion will be for mercy and truth. We'll never give up on people or lose faith, and we will always hope and believe the best. We'll always see others innocent unless proven guilty, and even then we will remain hopeful for repentance and restoration. We will be full of hope and endure any hardship for the benefit of the kingdom or another's well-being. Bottom line: We will live for the godly edification of others, which is only found in their conformity to Christ and fulfilling His will in their lives.

A LEADER WHO PERSONALLY TOUCHED MANY

Recently I attended a very close friend's funeral. His name is Jack Wallace. He founded Detroit World Outreach, in Detroit, Michigan. It is a multiracial church that grew to four thousand members in just ten years. On the way to Zimbabwe to preach a crusade, he collapsed with a heart attack just after getting off the plane.

Thousands of people attended his funeral—leaders of ministries from all over the United States, community leaders, and vice presidents of major corporations along with what society calls blue-collar workers, street people, and moms on food stamps. This is the demographic of his church. Many who didn't know Jesus as Lord attended the funeral as well, such as hotel and restaurant personnel along with others in the community whom he greatly impacted by his personal encounters.

The attendance of the citizens outside his church didn't surprise me because Jack and I spent considerable time together outside his church, and I was so blessed by how he behaved toward everyone he met. He treated each individual as valuable and precious. He tipped the waitresses and valets handsomely. I sometimes hedged a bit, thinking it may be a tad excessive, but this stupid mindset was corrected one day when he told me how valuable and precious all these people were to God. Jack didn't just make you feel as if you were the most important person when you were with him. You really were the most important person to Jack when he was with you.

The funeral service was four and a half hours long. Many of the leaders who were close to him were asked to get up and share a few minutes. After hearing from four or five of us, of our closeness to him and what he meant to us, finally one very well-known leader got up and said, "I thought I was his best friend!" Everyone laughed.

We all knew that Jack viewed us as and treated each of us as his closest friends. Not only did this great leader impact nations through his crusades and television broadcasts, but he also impacted all those he came in contact with on an individual basis. It didn't matter if you were a CEO of a major corporation or someone on welfare, Jack knew how to communicate with you and love you as a human being. Jack was not only faithful to his calling and gifts, but he caused his minas to multiply in every area of life.

A JANITOR WHO HAS TOUCHED MULTITUDES

Some of the individuals who've had the most profound impact on my life you will never see behind pulpits. One of them was a financial worker at Rockwell International. His name is Mike, and I came to know him only two years after I became a Christian. He was seated close to me, and we used to talk of the things of God during breaks and at lunchtime. Later, we connected for hours in each other's homes and at church. It was Mike's integrity and practical wisdom from the Scriptures that impacted me the most. I was also affected by the way he honored, loved, and respected his wife, children, and any individual who came across his path.

I eventually left Rockwell and went into the ministry. A short while later he also left and started his own accounting firm, which is still in existence today. His business became very successful. He's helped over twelve thousand clients with their tax returns and books, and five thousand come to him on a regular basis. They've been with him for years because of his honesty and integrity.

I asked him recently how many of his clients he had ministered the Word of God to. He said, "John, a conservative estimate would be 90 percent." So that would be over ten thousand people.

I was floored. I then asked how many he had led to salvation. His reply was, "Hundreds." He said, "Just last week I led a Cuban man to the Lord and prayed with him to be healed of cancer."

He has also helped many ministries set up their books. Ours was one of them when we were in our infant stage. He saw the call on my life and for years did my tax returns for no charge. Mike's life has impacted people in so many ways.

I remember in our long conversations Mike talking about the janitor who influenced his life more than anyone else had. So I called him recently to again ask about this man. He began to weep on the phone.

He said, "John, six of my nine aunts and uncles ended up in an insane asylum. My own mother ended up in one as well. Both of my grandfathers were shot by other men. My family was very messed up, and I was headed for this destiny.

"However, due to financial stress, my mother sent me to another family for them to care for me. I lived with them for seven years. The man of the house was a janitor of a local paper mill. His name was Charlie. His integrity, commitment to Jesus, and love for people broke the curse off my life. Every week he took me to church and taught me the ways of God. His influence on my life helped form who I am today. My daughter once wrote a paper and entitled it, 'The Greatest Man I Never Knew.' It was Charlie."

You'll most likely never hear about Charlie on earth. However, his influence has touched the thousands Mike has ministered to. Also, his influence has touched me through Mike. So the millions I've had the privilege to minister too have all been touched indirectly through Charlie as well. Do you see how one janitor multiplied his minas and will one day be rewarded greatly?

INFLUENCE TO LEGACY

This reminds me of a true account that one of my employees read to me recently. It is about an atheist named Max Jukes and a godly man named Jonathan Edwards. Here's the story:

Max Jukes, the atheist, lived a godless life. He married an ungodly girl, and from the union there were 310 who died as paupers, 150 were criminals, 7 were murderers, 100 were drunkards, and more than half of the women were prostitutes. His 540 descendants cost the State one and a quarter million dollars.

But, praise the Lord it works both ways! There is a record of a great American man of God, Jonathan Edwards. He lived at the same time as Max Jukes, but he married a godly girl. An investigation was made of 1,394 known descendants of Jonathan Edwards of which 13 became college presidents, 65 college professors, 3 United States senators, 30 judges, 100 lawyers, 60 physicians, 75 army and navy officers, 100 preachers and missionaries, 60 authors of prominence, one a vice-president of the United States, 80 became public officials in other capacities, 295 college graduates, among whom were governors of states and ministers to foreign countries. His descendants did not cost the state a single penny.[1]

That is yet another case of multiplying minas. These men—Charlie, Mike, and Jonathan Edwards—have affected so great a number of lives. Their influence led to great legacies. Yet it wasn't their public ministry that impacted these multitudes we speak of, but their personal lives. This is the privilege God gives everyone of us.

How you respond to a police officer, the way you speak of your pastor, the manner in which you conduct your financial affairs, the words you use to speak to individuals, and the list continues, these all affect the lives of others around you. Will you be a builder or a stumbling block?

> Yes, each of us will have to give a personal account to God. So don't condemn each other anymore. Decide instead to live in such a way that you will not put an obstacle in another Christian's path. . . . Let us aim for harmony in the church and try to build each other up.
>
> ROMANS 14:12, 19, NLT

Paul speaks this in direct relationship to the Judgment Seat of God. Every influence we've had on individuals will come into clear examination. It is most important we keep this before us at all times. It will motivate us to win rather than to look out for ourselves.

Rebecca Ruter Springer lived in the nineteenth century and was given an extended visit of heaven before her final departure to her reward. Upon returning, she wrote her classic novel entitled *Intra Muros*. She quotes a relative who spent much time with her in heaven. She reported this relative, her husband's brother, was close to the Master. His words to her were:

> "If only we could realize while we are yet mortals, that day by day we are building for eternity, how different our lives in many ways would be! Every gentle word, every generous thought, every unselfish deed, will become a pillar of eternal beauty in the life to come."[2]

LEADING OTHERS TO JESUS

The greatest influence we can have on an individual is to lead that person to Christ. When you understand eternal judgments, you will be motivated to tell those you know the plan of salvation. We read: "He who is wise captures human lives [for God, as a fisher of men—he gathers and receives them for *eternity*]" (Prov. 11:30, AMP, emphasis mine).

As a young believer, I used to feel the pressure of preaching the gospel to every individual I came in contact with. However, later I learned to look to the Holy Spirit for guidance of when and what to speak. I realized that even Jesus stated that He only did what He saw His Father doing. There is a flow when we walk with God, not a compulsion that leads to frustration and turns others away.

However, the urge to lead others to eternal life will be ever present until we are taken home. The love of God fuels this desire. To lead someone to Christ causes all the angels, as well as God Himself, to rejoice with unspeakable joy. It carries a certain reward. Jesus says, "The harvesters are paid good wages, and the fruit they harvest is people brought to eternal life" (John 4:36, NLT).

I had the privilege of leading my wife to the Lord on our first date. Shortly after coming to Jesus I made a commitment to not date another girl until God brought my wife to me. I figured God brought Eve to Adam; He could do the same for me. I had dated many girls before becoming a Christian, then afterward I dated a few Christian girls and found out it was interfering with my walk with God. There were rips and tears in our souls when we broke the relationships. It didn't take long to discover it wasn't healthy. So I made the commitment to pray before going out with a girl.

My wife was a party girl. Another guy on campus said she was the wildest girl on campus. I don't know if that was entirely true, but it was close to accurate. I hadn't been out with a girl on a date for a year and a half because every time I'd ask the Lord would tell me not to go. However, I felt compelled by the Holy Spirit to ask her to our Bible study picnic. She accepted.

Afterward, we walked on the campus and I shared with her the gospel from midnight till 1:30 in the morning. She interrupted me and requested to get saved immediately. Shortly afterward both of us knew it was God's will for us to marry. I can honestly say I got the better end of the deal. I wouldn't be the man I am today had it not been for her.

Lisa has touched hundreds of thousands of women's lives. She is asked to speak at women's conferences all over the world. Myriads of women have been liberated, young girls have pledged themselves to purity, and countless numbers have been healed and saved through the ministry God has given her. What if I wouldn't have taken the chance to reach out to her? What if my fear of her making fun of me would have kept me from telling her about Jesus? I believe God would have sent someone else, and I would have lost out on God's best choice for my wife and would not have a part of all the people she has eternally ministered to. Thank God for His gifts!

Remember, a seed will multiply; but a seed looks insignificant. Don't ever take the leading of the Holy Spirit for granted, and especially don't ignore Him. The most insignificant things He's led me to do have turned out to be the most significant multiplication factors of my life. God wants you to multiply. God also wants to reward you for your multiplication.

A FINAL EXHORTATION

So much is at stake. We can't take lightly our entrusted time here on earth. People's eternal destinies are dependent upon our obedience to the plan of God. It's His will that all be saved and conformed into the image of Jesus. He doesn't want any left behind.

An entire generation was lost in the wilderness after coming out of Egypt. They had one of the greatest leaders of all time, but still they failed. We can have magnificent leaders, but it is up to all of us as a generation to fulfill the plan of the Master Builder. He has decreed, "This gospel of the kingdom will be preached in all the world as a witness to all the nations, and then the end will come" (Matt. 24:14). Let's not miss our assignment! It's time, the season is upon us, and He's at the door! If we don't fulfill our destiny, then God will have to raise up another generation like He did with Joshua's to complete His house, for he has already decreed that His house will be full.

All it takes is us doing our part and multiplying what He's entrusted to us. Don't be discouraged. Don't see your part as insignificant. Don't lose your passion. Don't lose sight of the heavenly vision made clear in the New Testament, which has been outlined in this book. Not only are others in your generation counting on you—some are in desperate need for you to reveal to them Jesus, others are in need for you to extend His encouragement and strength—but your eternal destiny awaits you. You can succeed by utterly depending on His grace. He is faithful!

I appeal to you as a fellow citizen of the kingdom. Fulfill your calling and make your election sure; run your race fully to the end. You'll look back ten million years from this moment and rejoice that you did. You cannot be too committed to the will of God. So run your race to win! As final words of encouragement, I leave you with one of Paul's earnest prayers for all the saints:

May the Lord make your love for one another and for all people grow more and more and become as great as our love for you. In this way he will strengthen you, and you will be perfect and holy in the presence of our God and Father when our Lord Jesus comes with all who belong to him.

1 THESSALONIANS 3:12–13, TEV

Appendix A

SCRIPTURE RELATING TO ETERNAL REWARDS

—

But all will be well for those who are godly. Tell them, "You will receive a wonderful reward!" But say to the wicked, "Your destruction is sure. You, too, will get what you deserve. Your well-earned punishment is on the way."

ISAIAH 3:10-11, NLT

In this appendix we'll explore Scriptures that reveal the major areas of examination at the Judgment Seat. From the Divine assessment we'll either receive eternal rewards or losses. Meditate on these Scriptures and allow the Holy Spirit to hide them in your heart that you may please God. Your eternal reward will be rich and full. Recall, Paul writes that since we will all face the judgment seat of Christ, "We make it our goal to please him" (2 Cor. 5:9, NIV).

Our Work for Him

For God is not unfair. How can he forget your hard work for him, or forget the way you used to show your love for him—and still do—by helping his children? And we are anxious that you keep right on loving others as long as life lasts, so that you will get your full reward.

HEBREWS 6:10-11, TLB

For the Son of Man will come in the glory of His Father with His angels, and then He will reward each according to his works.

MATTHEW 16:27

Each one will receive his own reward according to his own labor.

1 CORINTHIANS 3:8

And remember that the heavenly Father to whom you pray has no favorites when he judges. He will judge or reward you according to what you do. So you must live in reverent fear of him during your time as foreigners here on earth.

1 PETER 1:17, NLT

Our Actions

Behold, I am coming soon, and I shall bring My wages and rewards with Me, to repay and render to each one just what his own actions and his own work merit.

REVELATION 22:12, AMP

Yes, says the Spirit, they are blessed indeed, for now they shall rest from all their toils and trials; for their good deeds follow them to heaven!

REVELATION 14:13, TLB

You [God] are very aware of the conduct of all people, and you reward them according to their deeds.

JEREMIAH 32:19, NLT

Righteous people will be rewarded for their own goodness, and wicked people will be punished for their own wickedness.

EZEKIEL 18:20, NLT

Our Godliness
The Lord has dealt with me according to my righteousness; according to the cleanness of my hands he has rewarded me.

PSALM 18:20, NIV

Great [are You] in counsel and mighty in deeds, Whose eyes are open to all the ways of the sons of men, to reward or repay each one according to his ways and according to the fruit of his doings.

JEREMIAH 32:19, AMP

Judgment will come again for the righteous, and those who are upright will have a reward.

PSALM 94:15, NLT

Our Motives
I, the LORD, search all hearts and examine secret motives. I give all people their due rewards, according to what their actions deserve.

JEREMIAH 17:10, NLT

You may say that it is none of your business, but God knows and judges your motives. He keeps watch on you; he knows. And he will reward you according to what you do.

PROVERBS 24:12, TEV

But [as for me personally] it matters very little to me that I should be put on trial by you [on this point], and that you or any other human tribunal should investigate and question and cross-question me. I do not even put myself on trial and judge myself. I am not conscious of anything against myself, and I feel blameless; but I am not vindicated and acquitted before God on that account. It is the Lord [Himself] Who examines and judges me. So do not make any hasty or premature judgments before the time when the Lord comes [again], for He will both bring to light the secret things that are [now hidden] in darkness and disclose and expose the [secret] aims (motives and purposes) of hearts. Then every man will receive his [due] commendation from God.

1 CORINTHIANS 4:3-5, AMP

And all the assemblies (churches) shall recognize and understand that I am He Who searches minds (the thoughts, feelings, and purposes) and the [inmost] hearts, and I will give to each of you [the reward for what you have done] as your work deserves.

REVELATION 2:23, AMP

Our Attitude

For if I do this work of my own free will, then I have my pay (my reward); but if it is not of my own will, but is done reluctantly and under compulsion, I am [still] entrusted with a [sacred] trusteeship and commission.

1 CORINTHIANS 9:17, AMP

If you serve Christ with this attitude, you will please God.

ROMANS 14:18, NLT

I warn you, you yourselves are in danger of punishment for your attitude. Then you will know that there is judgment.

JOB 19:29, NLT

For this was my purpose in writing you, to test your attitude and see if you would stand the test.

2 Corinthians 2:9, AMP

Our Integrity

The Lord rewarded me according to my righteousness (my conscious integrity and sincerity with Him); according to the cleanness of my hands has He recompensed me.

Psalm 18:20, AMP

Judge me, O Lord, according to my righteousness, and according to my integrity within me.

Psalm 7:8

Our Faithfulness

The trustworthy will get a rich reward.

Proverbs 28:20, NLT

The Lord rewards every man for his righteousness and faithfulness.

1 Samuel 26:23, NIV

Our Humility

For everyone who exalts himself will be humbled (ranked below others who are honored or rewarded), and he who humbles himself (keeps a modest opinion of himself and behaves accordingly) will be exalted (elevated in rank).

Luke 14:11, AMP

"Once there were two men who went up to the Temple to pray: one was a Pharisee, the other a tax collector. The Pharisee stood apart by himself and prayed, 'I thank you, God, that I am not greedy, dishonest, or an adulterer, like everybody else. I thank you that I am not like that tax collector over there. I fast two days a week, and I give you one tenth of all my income.' But the tax collector stood at a distance and would not even raise his face to heaven, but beat on his breast and said, 'God, have pity on me, a sinner!' I tell you," said Jesus, "the tax collector, and not the Pharisee, was in the right with God when he went home. For everyone who makes himself great will be humbled, and everyone who humbles himself will be made great."

LUKE 18:10-14, TEV

Our Words

Good people will be rewarded for what they say.

PROVERBS 13:2, TEV

Your reward depends on what you say and what you do; you will get what you deserve.

PROVERBS 12:14, TEV

You can be sure that on the Judgment Day everyone will have to give account of every useless word he has ever spoken. Your words will be used to judge you—to declare you either innocent or guilty.

MATTHEW 12:36-37, TEV

How We've Influenced Peoples Lives

After all, what gives us hope and joy, and what is our proud reward and crown? It is you! Yes, you will bring us much joy as we stand together before our Lord Jesus when he comes back again.

1 THESSALONIANS 2:19-20, NLT

Dear brothers and sisters, I love you and long to see you, for you are my joy and the reward for my work.

PHILIPPIANS 4:1, NLT

A curse on those who lead astray the godly. But men who encourage the upright to do good shall be given a worthwhile reward.

PROVERBS 28:10, TLB

Being Persecuted for Righteousness's Sake

But even if you suffer for doing what is right, God will reward you for it.

I PETER 3:14, NLT

Blessed (happy—with life-joy and satisfaction in God's favor and salvation, apart from your outward condition— and to be envied) are you when people despise (hate) you, and when they exclude and excommunicate you [as disreputable] and revile and denounce you and defame and cast out and spurn your name as evil (wicked) on account of the Son of Man. Rejoice and be glad at such a time and exult and leap for joy, for behold, your reward is rich and great and strong and intense and abundant in heaven.

LUKE 6:22-23, AMP

For I, the Lord, love justice. I hate robbery and wrongdoing. I will faithfully reward my people for their suffering and make an everlasting covenant with them.

ISAIAH 61:8-9, NLT

Loving Those Who Don't Love You

Love your enemies! Do good to them! Lend to them! And don't be concerned that they might not repay. Then your reward from heaven will be very great.

LUKE 6:35, NLT

If your enemies are hungry, give them food to eat. If they are thirsty, give them water to drink. You will heap burning coals on their heads, and the Lord will reward you.

PROVERBS 25:21-22, NLT

Blessing Those Who Cannot Repay Us

Then at the resurrection of the godly, God will reward you for inviting those who could not repay you.

LUKE 14:14, NLT

But when you do a charitable deed, do not let your left hand know what your right hand is doing, that your charitable deed may be in secret; and your Father who sees in secret will Himself reward you openly.

MATTHEW 6:3-4

Honoring, Receiving, Welcoming, or Caring for God's Servants

Anyone who welcomes you is welcoming me, and anyone who welcomes me is welcoming the Father who sent me. If you welcome a prophet as one who speaks for God, you will receive the same reward a prophet gets. And if you welcome good and godly people because of their godliness, you will be given a reward like theirs. And if you give even a cup of cold water to one of the least of my followers, you will surely be rewarded.

MATTHEW 10:40-42, NLT

May the Lord show special kindness to Onesiphorus and all his family because he often visited and encouraged me. He was never ashamed of me because I was in prison. When he came to Rome, he searched everywhere until he found me. May the Lord show him special kindness on the day of Christ's return. And you know how much he helped me at Ephesus.

2 TIMOTHY 1:16-18, NLT

For God is not unfair. He will not forget how hard you have worked for him and how you have shown your love to him by caring for other Christians, as you still do.

HEBREWS 6:10, NLT

Prayer

But when you pray, go away by yourself, shut the door behind you, and pray to your Father secretly. Then your Father, who knows all secrets, will reward you.

MATTHEW 6:6, NLT

How We Labored In Our Jobs

In the same way, workers who protect their employer's interests will be rewarded.

PROVERBS 27:18, NLT

Work hard and cheerfully at whatever you do, as though you were working for the Lord rather than for people. Remember that the Lord will give you an inheritance as your reward, and the Master you are serving is Christ. But if you do what is wrong, you will be paid back for the wrong you have done.

COLOSSIANS 3:23-25, NLT

Work hard, but not just to please your masters when they are watching. As slaves of Christ, do the will of God with all your heart. Work with enthusiasm, as though you were working for the Lord rather than for people. Remember that the Lord will reward each one of us for the good we do.

EPHESIANS 6:6-8, NLT

Our Giving

I tell you, use your worldly resources to benefit others and make friends. In this way, your generosity stores up a reward for you in heaven.

LUKE 16:9, NLT

Not that I seek or am eager for [your] gift, but I do seek and am eager for the fruit which increases to your credit [the harvest of blessing that is accumulating to your account].

PHILIPPIANS 4:17, AMP

They give generously to those in need. Their good deeds will never be forgotten. They will have influence and honor.

PSALM 112:9, NLT

There are certainly more areas that are not covered, but from my overall study of Scripture, these seem to me to be the foremost. If we stick close to the Word of life, not allowing ourselves to drift off course, we will make our calling and election sure throughout eternity.

Rewards

Those who live in accordance with the Master's desires will receive wonderful rewards, and "the good man's reward lasts forever" (Ps. 57:2, AMP). These who are faithful to the end will be called *overcomers*, and Jesus promises them many things; here are just a few:

"To eat from the tree of life, which is in the midst of the Paradise of God" (Rev. 2:7).

To "not be hurt by the second death" (Rev. 2:11).

"Power over the nations" (Rev. 2:26).

To be "clothed in white garments" (Rev. 3:5).

Jesus will "confess his name before My Father and before His angels" (Rev. 3:5).

To be made "a pillar in the temple of My God" (Rev. 3:12).

"I will write on him the name of My God and the name of the city of My God, the New Jerusalem, which comes down out of heaven from My God" (Rev. 3:12).

"I will write on him My new name" (Rev. 3:12).

"I will grant to sit with Me on My throne, as I also overcame and sat down with My Father on His throne" (Rev. 3:21).

"Shall inherit all things, and I will be his God and he shall be My son" (Rev. 21:7).

Crowns are promised to His faithful servants. These crowns are imperishable (1 Cor. 9:25); they'll never taint, decay, or grow old. Some of the crowns listed in Scripture are:

The crown of righteousness (2 Tim. 4:8)

The crown of rejoicing (1 Thess. 2:19)

The crown of life (James 1:12; Rev. 2:10)

The crown of glory (1 Pet. 5:4)

The overcomers will cast these crowns at the feet of the King in adoration and praise (see Rev. 4:10-11). It is important to the Lord that we not lose the promised crowns, for hear His words to us: "Behold, I am coming quickly! Hold fast what you have, that no one may take your crown" (Rev. 3:11-12).

SALVATION, AVAILABLE TO ALL

There are two standards for living, one set by society and one set by God. Our culture may deem you "good" according to its parameters, but what does God think? Scripture tells us that every human has fallen short of God's standard of right. As the Scriptures say: "There is no one who always does what is right, not even one" (Rom. 3:10, NCV). And again, "For all have sinned; all fall short of God's glorious standard" (Rom. 3:23, NLT).

To sin means to miss the mark of God's standard. Man was not created to be a sinner; rather, Adam chose this course of his own free will. God placed the first man, Adam, in a beautiful world without sickness, disease, poverty, or natural disasters. There was no fear, hatred, strife, jealousy, and so forth. God called this place Eden, the very garden of God.

Adam chose to disobey God's command and experienced an immediate spiritual death, even though he did not die physically until hundreds of years later. Darkness entered his heart. This spiritual death differs from physical death because in physical death the body ceases to exist; however, spiritual death is best described as separation from God, the very Giver and Source of all life.

Sin had entered Adam's makeup and he fathered children after this nature. "And Adam lived one hundred and thirty years, and begot a son in his own likeness, after his image" (Gen. 5:3). As a father, Adam's offspring were born after his nature. From this point forward, all humans were born into the image of his sin through their parents. Adam gave himself and his descendants over to a new lord, Satan, and with this captivity the natural world followed suit. A cruel lord now had legal claim to God's beloved creation. This is made clear in the following verses:

> Then the devil, taking Him [Jesus] up on a high mountain, showed Him all the kingdoms of the world in a moment of time. And the devil said to Him, "All this authority I will give You, and their glory; for this *has been delivered to me*, and I give it to whomever I wish."
>
> LUKE 4:5-6

Notice it was delivered to Satan. When? The answer is in the Garden, for God originally gave the dominion of earth to man (see Gen 1:26-28). Adam lost it all: This included himself and his seed for all generations. Again we read, "The whole world lies under the sway of the wicked one" (1 John 5:19).

Before God sent Adam from the Garden, He made a promise. A deliverer would arise and destroy the bondage and captivity to which mankind had been subjected. This deliverer was born four thousand years later to a virgin named Mary. She had to be a virgin, as the father of Jesus was the Holy Spirit who impregnated her. If Jesus had been born to natural parents, He would have been born into the captivity of Adam.

He was fathered by God, and His mother was human. This made Him completely God and completely man. It had to be a son of man who would purchase our freedom. For this reason,

Jesus constantly referred to Himself as the Son of Man. Though He was with the Father from the beginning, He stripped Himself of His divine privileges and became a man in order to give Himself as an offering for sin.

When He went to the Cross, He took the judgment of our sin on Himself to free us from our bondage. Scripture declares, "He personally carried away our sins in his own body on the cross so we can be dead to sin and live for what is right" (1 Pet. 2:24, NLT).

It's amazing! Man sinned against God, and yet God (manifest in the flesh) paid the price for man's grave err. We read again, "For God made Christ, who never sinned, to be the offering for our sin, so that we could be made right with God through Christ" (2 Cor. 5:21, NLT).

Notice it says that we could be made right. We do not receive the freedom that He paid so great a price for until we believe in our hearts that He died for us and was raised from the dead and then receive Him as our Lord—that is when He becomes our personal Savior. As Scripture states, "But to all who believed him and accepted him, he gave the right to become children of God. They are reborn! This is not a physical birth resulting from human passion or plan—this rebirth comes from God" (John 1:12-13, NLT).

When we receive Jesus Christ as our personal Lord and Savior, we die and are spiritually reborn. We die as slaves in the kingdom of Satan and are born as brand new children of God in His kingdom. How does this happen? When we believe this in our hearts, all we have to do is confess with our mouths Jesus as our Lord and we are born again. Scripture affirms this:

For if you confess with your mouth that Jesus is Lord and believe in your heart that God raised him from the dead, you will be saved. For it is by believing in your heart that

you are made right with God, and it is by confessing with
your mouth that you are saved.

ROMANS 10:9–10, NLT

It's that simple! We are not saved by our good deeds. Our
good deeds could never earn us a place in His kingdom. For if
that were true, Christ died in vain. We are saved by His grace. It
is a free gift that we cannot earn. All we have to do to receive it
is to renounce living for ourselves and commit our life to Him
as Lord, which means Supreme Master. "He died for all, that
those who live should live no longer for themselves, but for Him
who died for them and rose again" (2 Cor. 5:15).

So if you believe Christ died for you and you are willing to
give Him your life and no longer live for yourself, then we can
pray this prayer together and you will become a child of God:

God in Heaven, I acknowledge that I am a sinner and
have fallen short of Your righteous standard. I deserve to
be judged for eternity for my sin. Thank You for not leaving me in this state, for I believe You sent Jesus Christ,
Your only begotten Son, who was born of the virgin
Mary, to die for me and carry my judgment on the Cross.
I believe He was raised again on the third day and is now
seated at Your right hand as my Lord and Savior. So on
this day of _____, 20____, I give my life entirely to
the Lordship of Jesus.

Jesus, I confess you as my Lord and Savior. Come into
my life through Your Spirit and change me into a child
of God. I renounce the things of darkness that I once
held on to and from this day forward I will no longer live
for myself, but for You, who gave Yourself for me that I
may live forever.

Thank You, Lord. My life is now completely in Your hand and heart, and according to Your Word I shall never be ashamed.

Now, you are saved. You are a child of God. All heaven is rejoicing with you at this very moment!

Welcome to the family!

NOTES

Chapter 1

1. *Webster's Encyclopedic Unabridged Dictionary of the English Language* (New York: Gramercy, 1993), s.v. "eternity."

2. *The American Heritage Dictionary of the English Language,* 4th ed. (New York: Houghton Mifflin, 2000), s.v. "eternity." Eternity: *the state or quality of being eternal;* eternal: *existing outside of time;* hence: *the state of existing outside of time.*

3. Merrill F. Unger, *The New Unger's Bible Dictionary,* ed. R. K. Harrison (Chicago: Moody, 1988), BibleSoft PCStudyBible Version 4.

4. Robert Young, *Young's Literal Translation of the Holy Bible* (Grand Rapids, Mich.: Baker, 1986).

Chapter 3

1. Luke 16:2
2. Hebrews 4:13, AMP
3. John 8:24
4. Acts 4:12, AMP
5. James 2:10, TLB
6. Ephesians 2:8-9, NLT (the name *God* was changed to *Jalyn* to fit the story)
7. Ecclesiastes 9:5-6, NLT
8. Proverbs 24:20, NLT
9. Proverbs 13:13

10. Matthew 22:13-14

11. Titus 1:16, NLT (the name *God* was changed to *Jalyn* to fit the story)

12. Luke 6:46, TEV

13. Matthew 7:21-23, TLB, (the word *heaven* was changed to *Affabel* to fit the story)

14. James 2:14, 17-20, NLT (the name *God* was changed to *Jalyn* to fit the story)

15. Ezekiel 18:25, 27-28, TLB

16. Psalm 50:16-21, TLB

17. Matthew 22:13

18. Proverbs 30:12

19. Matthew 24:12-13, TEV

20. 2 Peter 2:20-21, TEV (the name *Jesus Christ* was changed to *Jalyn* to fit the story)

21. Ezekiel 18:24-27, NLT

22. Matthew 24:13

23. Revelation 3:5, NASB

24. Matthew 22:13-14 (the pronoun *him* was changed to *her* to fit the story)

25. Hebrews 10:26-27, 30-31, NLT (the name *God* was changed to *Jalyn* to fit the story)

26. James 3:1, NLT (the word *church* was changed to *school* and the name *God* was changed to *Jalyn* to fit the story)

27. Mark 9:42

28. Luke 12:45-48, NLT

29. Jude 13, TEV

30. Matthew 22:13-14

31. Revelation 16:5-7, TEV

Chapter 4

1. *The American Heritage Dictionary*, 3rd ed. (New York: Houghton Mifflin, 1992), s.v. "elementary."

Chapter 5

1. Movie Reviews: *The Matrix*.http://www.pluggedinon-line.com/movies/movies/a0000128.cfm. Accessed September 5, 2005.

2. Roberts, Alexander and Donaldson, James, eds. *The Ante-Nicene Fathers*. "Polycarp: Letter to the Philippians," 10 vols. Grand Rapids: Wm. Eerdmans Publishing Company, 1985. Ch. 1

3. Roberts, Alexander and Donaldson, James, eds. *The Ante-Nicene Fathers*. "Polycarp: Letter to the Philippians," 10 vols. Grand Rapids: Wm. Eerdmans Publishing Company, 1985. Ch. 2

4. Roberts, Alexander and Donaldson, James, eds. *The Ante-Nicene Fathers*. "Clement of Rome Letter to the Corinthians" 10 vols. Grand Rapids: Wm. Eerdmans Publishing Company, 1985. Ch. 32

5. Roberts, Alexander and Donaldson, James, eds. *The Ante-Nicene Fathers*. "Clement of Rome Letter to the Corinthians" 10 vols. Grand Rapids: Wm. Eerdmans Publishing Company, 1985. Ch. 34

6. David W. Bercot, ed. *A Dictionary of Early Christian Beliefs*. Hendrickson Publishers, Inc. 1998, pg. 586

7. ibid

8. Josh McDowell, *Evidence That Demands a Verdict* (San Bernardino, Calif.: Here's Life Publishers, 1972), 50-52.

Chapter 6

1. Kenneth E. Hagin, *I Believe in Visions* (Tulsa, Okla.: Faith Library Publications, 1984, pgs. 68-71 (second edition; tenth printing).

2. From the UBS Handbook Series. Copyright © 1961-1997, by United Bible Societies.

3. David W. Bercot, ed. *A Dictionary of Early Christian Beliefs*. Hendrickson Publishers, Inc. 1998.

4. ibid

5. ibid

6. ibid

7. ibid

8. *The American Heritage Dictionary of the English Language,* 4th ed. Houghton Mifflin Co., 2004 (software edition)

Chapter 8

1. Luke 14:12-14

2. Mark 12:43-44, TEV

3. Colossians 1:28 (the name *Christ* was changed to *Jalyn* to fit the story)

4. Ezekiel 13:10-11, NIV

5. 1 Corinthians 3:12-15, NLT

6. 1 Thessalonians 2:19-20, NLT

7. Matthew 12:36-37, TEV (emphasis mine)

8. Proverbs 12:14, TEV

9. Jeremiah 11:20

10. Jeremiah 17:10, NLT (emphasis mine; the name *the Lord* was changed to *Jalyn* to fit the story)

11. This conversation was adapted from Matthew 25:34-40, TEV (words in italics changed only to make statements singular instead of plural).

12. 2 Corinthians 9:10

13. 2 Corinthians 9:9, AMP

14. Luke 14:11, AMP

15. Luke 19:17, NLT (words in italics added to fit the story)

16. Revelation 2:26-27, NIV (words in italics added to fit the story)

17. Matthew 25:21

Chapter 10

1. James Strong, *Strong's Exhaustive Concordance of the Bible* (Peabody, Mass.: Hendrickson Publishers, 1988).

2. *Biblesoft New Exhaustive Strong's Concordance* (Seattle, Wash: Biblesoft, Inc., ver. 4, 1994).

Chapter 12

1. *Webster's Encyclopedic Unabridged Dictionary of the English Language* (New York: Gramercy, 1993), s.v. "envy."

2. *The American Heritage Dictionary of the English Language*, 4th ed. Houghton Mifflin Co., 2004. (software edition)

Chapter 13

1. Leonard Ravenhill, *Sodom Had No Bible* (Minneapolis, Minn.: Bethany House, 1971), 155.

2. Rebecca Ruter Springer, My Dream of Heaven: A Nineteenth Century Spiritual Classic: Originally Known As Intra Muros (Cincinnati, Ohio: Harrison House), 21.

Please contact us today to receive your free copy of Messenger International's *Messenger* newsletter and our 32 page color catalog of ministry resources!

FREE NEWSLETTER & CATALOG

 MESSENGER INTERNATIONAL

www.messengerintl.org

The vision of MI is to strengthen believers, awaken the lost and captive in the church and proclaim the knowledge of His glory to the nations. John and Lisa are reaching millions of people each year through television and by ministering at churches, bible schools and conferences around the world. We long to see God's Word in the hands of leaders and hungry believers in every part of the earth.

UNITED STATES
PO Box 888
Palmer Lake, CO 80133-0888
800-648-1477 (US & Canada)
Tel: 719-487-3000
Fax: 719-487-3300
E-mail: mail@messengerintl.org

EUROPE
PO Box 622
Newport, NP19 8ZJ
UNITED KINGDOM
Tel: 44 (0) 870-745-5790
Fax: 44 (0) 870-745-5791
E-mail: europe@messengerintl.org

AUSTRALIA
PO Box 6200
Dural, D.C. NSW 2158
Australia
In AUS 1-300-650-577
Tel: +61 2 8850 1725
Fax +61 2 8850 1735
Email: australia@messengerintl.org

The *Messenger* television program broadcasts in 216 countries on GOD TV, the Australian Christian Channel and on the New Life Channel in Russia. Please check your local listings for day and time.